The Meringue Cookbook

Margaret N. Shakespeare

 VAN NOSTRAND REINHOLD COMPANY
NEW YORK CINCINNATI TORONTO LONDON MELBOURNE

to my mother

Printed in the United States of America
Designed by Levavi & Levavi

Published by Van Nostrand Reinhold Company Inc.
135 West 50th Street, New York, NY 10020

Van Nostrand Reinhold Publishers
1410 Birchmount Road
Scarborough, Ontario M1P 2E7, Canada

Van Nostrand Reinhold Australia Pty. Ltd.
480 Latrobe Street
Melbourne, Victoria 3000, Australia

Van Nostrand Reinhold Company Limited
Molly Millars Lane
Wokingham, Berkshire, England RG11 2PY

16 15 14 13 12 11 10 9 8 7 6 5 4 3 2 1

Library of Congress Cataloging in Publication Data

Shakespeare, Margaret N.
  The meringue cookbook.

  Includes index.
  1. Cookery (Meringue) I. Title.
TX745.S49   641.8'6   82-4950
ISBN 0-442-28153-6   AACR2

Acknowledgments

Authors customarily set this page aside to recognize those who contributed toward the completion of their books, and I realize, as I look back over my work, that reciting names here is but a small measure of the gratitude I feel. Warmth, encouragement, and support from friends not only helped me through the tough times but lent an even greater pleasure to a project I have enjoyed enormously. I thank them for sharing: Connie, who requested the peach pie. Professor Victor Fell Yellin and my colleagues in his American music course at New York University, Helen Pellegrini and Bob Sweeney, who were my first taste testers. Marjorie, who on occasions too numerous to count, and in various times of crisis and celebration, graciously lent her kitchen, home, and dinner parties, and then made sure I took time out at least once a week for a healthy salad. Dennis, Michael, Fred, Jerry . . . all those who came by my kitchen door for desserts-to-taste and stayed to visit while I worked. Rosie, who sent nonedible goodies with thought and caring and perfect timing.

Jim and Philip not only sampled the desserts but spent arduous hours helping me photograph them so that Ray could make not only beautiful but accurate drawings.

This book would never have been more than a handwritten collection of recipes were it not for its "grandparents," Sally and Marty. I thank them, too, for sending me to Elise and Arnold who believed in my abilities and who made so many suggestions that shaped this book. It has been a delight to work with my editor, Nancy, who has given generously her patience, thought, enthusiasm, and support.

My mother has been my chief recipe tester and critic. It was in her kitchen years ago that I learned the special joy of preparing beautiful food and sharing it with others. For all that and more I dedicate this book to her.

Contents

Introduction

For centuries meringue has been the confectionary delight crowning dozens of baked and cooked desserts. The ubiquitous pie topping also makes cake textures lighter, icings frothier, cookies crunchier, and soufflés rise. Whether a recipe calls for quick-baked golden peaks or a slow-dried crispy finish, the ingredients are simply egg whites, sugar, and air. Culinary historians have traced this recipe to the Swiss town Mehrinyghen, where it was perfected in the early eighteenth century by the chef Gasparini.

Royalty created and cultivated the art of serving lavishly prepared sweets as part of a meal. Many specialties that dazzle today's dinner guests originated hundreds of years ago in some monarch's kitchen. Meringue delicacies found favor in English and French courts. Elizabeth I christened her favorite meringue pastries "kisses." Petit fours, precious and rich and frosted with meringue, first graced the banquet trays at Versailles during the reign of Louis XIV. Marie-Antoinette enjoyed baking her own pastries and vacherins at the Trianon, no doubt with the same meringue recipe used by King Stanislas of Poland.

By the nineteenth century, with the invention of the forcing (pastry) bag, meringue appeared in intricate, imaginative shapes. American bakers are probably responsible for its popularity as a pie topping.

Types of Meringue

Meringues are classified by how they are prepared and the characteristics of the final product. Today the term *Swiss meringue* refers to the basic recipe of egg whites and sugar beaten together at room temperature until quite thick and firm and then baked in a slow oven to a hard, dry finish. The texture and name of meringue change when these same ingredients are beaten over very gentle heat. After slow baking the outside becomes hard and dry, like a Swiss meringue, but the inside remains tender. It's then called *meringue cuite.* As a rule these methods of preparation are interchangeable, and personal preference for one texture over the other determines the choice. Any classical slow-dried meringue, however, retains its whiteness. Swiss meringue and meringue cuite can be shaped into crusts, shells, baskets, and all kinds of fancy or plain designs.

The same ingredients—egg whites and sugar—whipped only into a soft shape and baked briefly in a hot oven, yield *meringue Chantilly,* the familiar dessert garnish. *Italian meringue* is created by beating a boiled syrup with stiffened egg whites. This confection makes a smooth cake icing and forms the basis of divinity, mousse, and some parfaits.

Proportions of sugar (or other sweetener) to egg whites do vary according to type of meringue, quality necessary for a particular dessert, and, sometimes, just individual taste. In general Italian meringues are the sweetest and Chantillys require the least sugar. But you'll see flexibility as you use this book.

To dispel any myths or mystery enshrouding meringue making, I've put together a few maxims which you should read and take to heart before starting on the recipes.

A Meringue Primer

Try to avoid rainy days and damp atmospheres for baking. Moisture can prevent egg whites from stiffening and also hinder the drying process in the oven. Finished meringues will quickly absorb any moisture in the air and turn soggy.

Start with clean, grease-free utensils. Fats and oils are the greatest deterrents to achieving a full-volumed meringue.

Always let the egg whites stand to room temperature. This maximizes the amount of air they will absorb when they're beaten.

Even the slightest bit of egg yolk will prevent the whites from stiffening. If you accidentally break a yolk, use a paper towel or half an egg shell to remove any speck of it. (See page 11 for how to separate eggs.)

Beat egg whites at a slow steady speed. Add sugar gradually by sprinkling it in one tablespoon at a time, unless a recipe specifies differently. Even after the meringue thickens, add all other ingredients a little at a time, whether they're beaten in or folded.

When making an Italian meringue, beat the whites until they are quite stiff. Then pour the sugar syrup, in a very thin stream, directly into the beaters.

The recipes describe beating whites to any of three stages: a fluid, translucent foam; soft peak, when the meringue is frothy and bends slightly after the beaters are removed; firm peak, when it is thick, glossy, and stands straight after the beaters are removed. Overbeaten meringue looks dull and cannot be folded or shaped, so observe beating times and directions carefully.

Watch oven temperatures cautiously. When a recipe calls for 200°F you may leave the oven door ajar to be sure the meringue doesn't color while it is drying.

Follow drying or baking times attentively. The commonly held notion that meringues drying at a low temperature cannot be overdone is not quite accurate. It is true that the meringue won't burn, but a piece that is too dry certainly will shatter beyond repair.

On the other hand, if a meringue has absorbed moisture or you didn't leave it in the oven long enough to start with, just redry it in the oven at whatever temperature the recipe specified.

Properly dried meringues are fragile and it is not unusual to break them. Simply use a little unbaked meringue to glue the pieces back together. The patching is hardly noticeable.

To avoid disappointment make meringue only in the quantity specified by the recipe. If you want to double the amount, repeat the recipe. Too large a quantity will wilt, especially if you are shaping it from a pastry bag.

Meringue spread onto a hot surface will weep or bead and become sticky. So let pies and cakes cool to lukewarm before you garnish them.

Sugar is a stabilizer for meringue. So are cream of tartar, salt, and vinegar. I prefer cream of tartar in most recipes because I think it works best and interferes least with flavor. It aids in increasing the volume and makes the meringue a little more tender. I discovered one very rainy, humid, hot Fourth of July that I could make the baked Alaska as planned, by adding a little more sugar and tripling the amount of cream of tartar. I recommend this procedure only for emergencies. If you use a copper bowl for meringue making, omit cream of tartar from the recipe.

Essential Tools and Basic Methods

Now you are armed with basic facts about meringue, but it is equally important to take a brief inventory of your kitchen. The proper accoutrements and how you use them can make the difference between dessert and a stunning, smashing culinary treat.

1. *Airtight containers.* I like old-fashioned pie and cookie tins for most hard-baked meringues. Heavy-duty plastic products also work well. As a rule keep them at room temperature.

2. *Parchment paper.* Swiss meringues and meringues cuite are usually baked on a lining of this lanolin-coated paper. It helps diffuse heat and allows the dried meringue pieces to be lifted away easily. Plain brown paper is an acceptable substitute. You can trace outlines (to guide in shaping) directly onto either of these lining papers. Meringue can also be shaped and dried on foil sprinkled with flour or cornstarch with nearly as good results.

3. *Candy thermometers.* These gadgets are fine but not necessary for testing syrups. Here are alternative testing methods: The syrup has reached 234°F (soft-ball stage) when a small amount of it dropped into a bowl of cold water will form a pliable ball between your fingertips. To test for 260°F (hard-ball stage) drizzle a small amount of syrup into a bowl of cold water. If it will form a hard lump between your fingertips, then the syrup is cooking at about 260°F.

4. *Double boilers.* These pans are useful for making custards, melting chocolate, etc., when very low heat is required. As a rule, hot, not boiling, water goes into the bottom pan. You can improvise a double boiler by fitting a metal mixing bowl snugly over a pan of water. Just be sure the bottom of the bowl sits above the water, not in it. Sometimes a double boiler is interchangeable with a heavy saucepan over very low heat.

5. *Egg separators, separation methods, and storing yolks and whites.* I have tried many devices to separate eggs, from simple perforated

metal cups to nicely styled hard plastic sieves with fitted troughs. Some chefs recommend catching yolks in a funnel. But I have found I break fewer yolks using the old-fashioned method below.

Eggs separate best when they are cold and a few days old. It's safest to use three bowls (one for the whites, one for the yolks, and one for the separating process itself). Hold the egg firmly and rotate it slightly as you tap its center against the outside rim of the first bowl. When there is a clean break in the shell hold it over the bowl and, keeping the yolk in one of the shell halves, let as much of the white as possible drip into the bowl. Still holding it over the bowl, transfer the yolk carefully to the other shell half—back and forth several times—until the rest of the white has dripped into the bowl. Drop the yolk into the second bowl; discard the shell. Repeat this process for the remaining eggs, but over the third (empty) bowl, combining the individual whites after each separation.

Some cooks prefer to catch the whole egg in the palm of one hand as they break the shell and then let the white run through their fingers. This method may offer a little more insurance against dribbling unwanted yolk into the whites.

Even with care you will break a yolk sometimes. If only a small amount gets into the white, scoop it out with a shell half, spoon, or corner of a paper towel. If the yolk is broken so that it can't be removed, use the whole egg as a substitute for two yolks in a cake or cookie recipe. Or whip it, pour thin layers into a heated omelet pan, and trim strips of the cooked egg for fried rice.

Don't discard yolks. Unbroken, yolks covered with water to keep them from drying out can be stored in the refrigerator for up to four days. Check the chapter of Recipes for Leftover Yolks. And you can add leftover yolks to omelets or scrambled eggs or poach them in boiling water for salads and casseroles.

Egg whites freeze well in small containers. Plastic ice trays are ideal. Once frozen, run hot water over the bottom of the ice tray and pop the egg whites into a plastic freezer bag. Keep the frozen egg whites for up to three months. They thaw quickly at room temperature or in a warm bowl.

6. *Electric mixers vs. wire whisks.* A wire whisk is the traditional tool for beating egg whites, but I recommend using an electric mixer for meringue making simply because most of us don't have the herculean strength and stamina to whip egg whites evenly to a stiff, full volume. Choose a mixer with at least five speeds. The hand-held kind is all you need. You might want to try using a whisk sometime

to make meringue. You'll notice a subtly softer texture in the final product.

I like whisks or a rotary egg beater to whip heavy cream. Always chill the utensil first.

For most cakes and cookie batters I recommend hand mixing with a large wooden spoon.

7. *Measuring cups.* Use metal cups for dry ingredients (you can level the top with a knife) and lipped glass cups for liquids. I've included a table for metric conversion on page 17.

8. *Mixing bowls.* Must you have a copper bowl for beating egg whites? It is best (the copper hastens stabilization) and it's also traditional, but not necessary. For meringue making, though, I do recommend a metal bowl that is straight-sided. Glass is all right, but do avoid plastic since it absorbs grease that prohibits beating egg whites to a full volume. The size of the bowl you use can determine the quality of your meringue also. Before beating the whites should come up about one-half inch on submerged beaters, allowing for each white to expand to a maximum volume of one and a half cups. Because size, shape, and condition of the bowl are crucial to good meringue making, it would be prudent to set aside at least one mixing bowl in your kitchen just for egg whites.

9. *Oven thermometers.* If you don't trust your oven, or even if you do, I strongly recommend using an oven thermometer. Mercury thermometers are the most accurate.

10. *Pastry bags.* I never travel without mine, as it is a necessity for meringue shaping. The best ones are made of canvas coated with plastic and come in various sizes. For most recipes in this book a 14-inch bag is quite serviceable. The tips are interchangeable and, while I suggest size and type in each recipe, the choice is mostly a matter of personal preference. You should be equipped with at least six tips: one star and one plain in a medium size (about one-half-inch openings), one of each type in a much smaller size, and one of each with a large opening. The plastic couplers available for the smaller tips allow switching them without emptying the bag.

To fill a pastry bag, turn the top about one-third of the way down, forming a sort of cuff. Hold the bag firmly under the cuff with one hand and, with a rubber spatula in the other hand, scoop the meringue (or other filling) into the bag. When the bag is filled almost to the top of the fold, flip the cuff up and twist the bag gently at the top to close it and force out any air pockets. Press the filling out using both hands, one holding the bag closed and pushing the filling down and the other nearer the tip to guide in shaping.

11. *Pie tins.* For meringue crusts use only shiny metal pans. Crumb crusts, dough crusts, etc., that are baked in a hot oven turn out crisper and darker made in black steel pans which absorb more heat.

12. *Tube (angel cake) pans.* Tall cakes with meringue in the batter need the extra support of a center tube when rising in the oven because of the air volume in the batter. I prefer springform pans; their flexibility helps in removing the cake cleanly. (Springform pans are sometimes sold with interchangeable plain bottoms.)

To cool an angel cake, hang the tube pan upside down on the neck of a bottle for up to 45 minutes. Then loosen the cake and remove it from the pan.

13. *Wire racks.* These cooling racks allow air to circulate under and around pies and cakes so that they cool faster and more evenly. Usually cakes should be removed from the baking pan and placed upside down on a rack. Cakes with meringue toppings are cooled in or out of the pan, right side up. And pies, of course, remain in the pan.

I have covered the absolute necessities and interject here a cautionary note: Food processors and blenders are not appropriate tools for meringue making. These otherwise eminently useful kitchen aids don't allow the intake of air required to stiffen egg whites.

A list of kitchenware dealers that carry the equipment mentioned appears in the appendix.

Notes about Ingredients

Remember that freshest is best—from fruit to spices. But, of course fresh is not always possible and if, for example, you must use canned fruit in off season, reduce the amount of sugar. In most recipes I suggest possible substitutions. As a rule, all ingredients should be at room temperature. If something needs to be warmer or colder or softened, etc., I say so in the recipe. Besides the following comments, refer to specific recipes for ingredient information.

1. *Butter.* Most of these recipes call for sweet (unsalted) butter. Margarine is a poor substitute.

2. *Chocolate.* I call for three kinds of chocolate in the book. "Bittersweet" and "semisweet" are interchangeable. "Unsweetened" is not. To melt chocolate put it in a dry double boiler over hot water. The slightest bit of moisture causes chocolate to shrink. Chocolate melts easily but burns quickly, so don't leave it over heat too long. Scrape melted chocolate out of the pan with a rubber spatula. In a few recipes I mention "coating chocolate." It is a commercial chocolate usually available only from wholesalers in ten-pound lots.

3. *Eggs.* Use large or extra-large eggs. Three medium (or small) whites equal two large. Five jumbo whites equal six large whites. Directions for separating eggs can be found on page 11.

4. *Flour.* Use all-purpose flour and always sift before measuring. A few recipes call for cake flour. One cup plus two tablespoons cake flour equals one cup all-purpose flour.

5. *Lemon juice.* The juice of one medium lemon equals about three tablespoons.

6. *Nuts.* Store all nuts in closed containers in the freezer. Use a rotary hand grater to grind nuts. When a recipe calls for ground nuts (usually instead of flour), they must be ground quite fine, not chopped. To blanch almonds, cover them with boiling water in a shallow pan and let them soak until the water is warm. The skins should slide right off when squeezed between your fingertips. Dry the nuts before storing or using them.

7. *Peaches.* To peel, cover them with boiling water for about three minutes. Drain the peaches and the skin should come off easily.

8. *Sugar.* The recipes in this book call for "sugar" (meaning granulated or castor), "confectioners' sugar" (powdered), "brown sugar" (dark brown), "light brown sugar," and "vanilla sugar." Light brown sugar is commercially available but you can also make it by combining one part dark brown sugar with two parts granulated sugar. Vanilla sugar can be made by splitting a vanilla bean and placing it in a tightly closed container of granulated sugar. The vanilla bean will flavor the sugar for a month or two. Then replace the bean. I frequently use vanilla sugar instead of extract in Swiss meringues when

I want them to stay absolutely white. You can substitute extract (about one-quarter teaspoon per one-quarter cup sugar).

9. *Vanilla beans.* The flavor they produce is so much fresher than that of extract. I usually call for vanilla beans in one- or two-inch lengths. Snip off what you need with scissors and split it lengthwise. Store vanilla beans in closed tubes. (They are usually sold that way.)

10. *Whipped cream.* Whip heavy cream in a chilled bowl, using a chilled egg beater, wire whisk, or electric mixer at a very slow speed. I usually prefer not to sweeten cream but, if you do, use no more than two tablespoons sugar per cup cream.

A Few More Notes

Desserts are not low-calorie fare, but many meringue desserts have a relatively low calorie count without sacrificing taste pleasure. Remember that the main ingredient in meringue is air, and an egg white has about six calories. The three tablespoons of sugar in a meringue Chantilly pie topping equal about 150 calories while a comparable garnish of whipped cream contains over 500 calories. Desserts made exclusively of meringue are also low in cholesterol, since the egg yolk has been eliminated.

These recipes are to enjoy—making, serving, and eating. It was a great pleasure to assemble the collection and write about them. Please note that they run the gamut from quick and easy to grandiose and complicated. So for happiest results, read a recipe through before you start any baking preparation; judge your own expertise and allot ample time for whichever recipe you have chosen.

Metric Conversion Table

The metric units here are approximate but workable measurements for the recipes in this book. Use a kitchen scale for dry ingredients and a metric measuring cup for liquids.

U.S. Standard Measure	Approximate Metric Measure
DRY	
Almonds, 1 cup (whole or ground)	170 grams
Butter, 1 cup (8 ounces)	225 grams
Cocoa, 1 cup	120 grams
Coconut, 1 cup (grated or shredded)	90 grams
Confectioners' sugar, 1 cup	130 grams
Flour, 1 cup (sifted)	100 grams
Pecans and Walnuts, 1 cup (halves or pieces)	130 grams
Sugar, light brown sugar and brown sugar, 1 cup	200 grams
Wafer and Cracker Crumbs, 1 cup	120 grams
1 ounce	30 grams (actual 28)
¼ pound	115 grams
½ pound	225 grams
¾ pound	340 grams
1 pound	450 grams (actual 454)
LIQUID	
1 teaspoon	5 milliliters
1 tablespoon	15 milliliters
¼ cup	60 milliliters
⅓ cup	80 milliliters
½ cup	120 milliliters
¾ cup	180 milliliters
1 cup	250 milliliters
1 pint	.5 liter (actual .47)
1 quart	1 liter (actual .95)

Mainly Meringue

The recipes in this chapter use various kinds of meringue as the chief, sometimes only, ingredient.

Meringue Biscuits

These confections are delicate, light, and worth all the care it takes to prepare them. You'll probably want more than one recipe, but for happiest results, make the meringue in the amounts given here and then repeat the recipe.

> 2 egg whites
> 1/4 teaspoon cream of tartar
> 1/4 cup vanilla sugar

Place the oven rack about a third up from the bottom. Preheat the oven to 200°F. Line a large baking sheet with parchment paper. Trace three dozen 1½-inch circles onto the paper.

In a large, grease-free mixing bowl beat the egg whites at a slow steady speed. When they are foamy add the cream of tartar. Gradually add the sugar and, when the meringue will form soft peaks, increase to a moderate beating speed. Beat another 5–8 minutes, until the meringue is thick, glossy, and forms firm peaks when the beaters are lifted.

Glue the parchment paper to the baking sheet with a few pinches of meringue. Use a rubber spatula to scoop about three-quarters of the meringue into a pastry bag fitted with a small (number 0) plain tip. Hold the bag firmly with both hands, keeping it taut and closed with the top hand. Press out a ring of meringue just inside one of the traced circles. Do not break the meringue but continue to fill in the circle evenly. Use the spatula if necessary to make these layers quite smooth and as uniform as possible. Repeat this process to fill in two dozen of the traced circles. With the remaining meringue make one dozen fancy top layers of various designs. I suggest using the same small plain tip for a lattice or two concentric rings. A very small (number 0) star tip will make a rosette or figure eight inside a ring. Play with designs but keep them simple because these tiny meringue pieces are delicate and will shatter easily. Bake them at 200°F for about 15 minutes, until the fancy tops feel dry when touched very lightly. Using a small sharp knife, carefully remove only these top layers from the parchment and set them aside. Return the baking sheet to the 200° oven for another 15–20 minutes, until the solid layers are dry. Use the knife to gently loosen them from the parchment. The meringue pieces are now ready for assembling or can be stored in an airtight container for several weeks.

FILLING I

> *About 2 ounces bittersweet chocolate, melted*
> *About 3 tablespoons apricot, raspberry, or currant jelly,*
> *warmed*

With a small rubber spatula spread the melted chocolate onto the two dozen plain meringue layers. Set them aside to dry. Then spread a thin layer of jelly over the chocolate and stack two plain layers together. Add the fancy layers on top so that each biscuit has three layers. Keep the biscuits in a cool dry place.

FILLING II

> ½ recipe Chocolate Butter Cream (page 207) or Lemon Butter Cream (page 207)
> 1–2 tablespoons confectioners' sugar

Ice the plain layers with the butter cream and stack two together. Add a fancy layer to the top of each biscuit. Lightly coat the sides with butter cream and a dusting of confectioners' sugar. Keep these biscuits in the refrigerator.

Yield: (either filling) 1 dozen biscuits

Quick Almond Biscuits

These are a plain version of Meringue Biscuits; not as fancy looking but they taste just as good. You can also make more of them at once because the meringue does not require a lot of handling.

> 3 egg whites
> ¼ teaspoon cream of tartar
> ⅓ cup sugar
> ½ teaspoon almond extract
> ½ cup ground blanched almonds
> About 4 ounces bittersweet chocolate, melted

Place the oven rack about a third up from the bottom. Preheat the oven to 200°F. Line two large baking sheets with parchment paper.

In a large, grease-free mixing bowl beat the egg whites at a slow steady speed. When they are foamy add the cream of tartar. Gradually beat in the sugar and, when the meringue will from soft peaks, add the almond extract and increase to a moderate beating speed. Beat for another 5–8 minutes, until the meringue is thick, glossy, and forms firm peaks when the beaters are lifted. Use a rubber spatula to fold in the ground almonds, about a heaping tablespoon at a time.

Glue the parchment paper to the baking sheets with a few pinches of meringue. Drop rounded teaspoonfuls of the meringue onto the prepared baking sheets. Bake the meringue at 200°F for 30–45 minutes, until the pieces feel firm and dry. Remove the baking sheets from the oven and loosen the meringue pieces from the parchment with a small sharp knife.

Glue the pieces together, two at a time bottom-to-bottom, with the melted chocolate. Set the biscuits aside in a cool place for at least an hour so that the chocolate can dry.

Yield: 3–4 dozen biscuits

Meringue Mints

2 egg whites
¼ teaspoon cream of tartar
⅔ cup confectioners' sugar
½ teaspoon mint (peppermint, spearmint, etc.) extract
About 4 ounces bittersweet chocolate

Place the oven rack about a third up from the bottom. Preheat the oven to 200°F. Line a large baking sheet with parchment paper. Warm the baking sheet in the oven while you prepare the meringue.

Make a double boiler using a medium, grease-free metal mixing bowl that fits snugly over a pan of hot water. Beat the egg whites in the mixing bowl at a slow steady speed. When they are foamy add the cream of tartar. Gradually add the confectioners' sugar and, when the meringue will form soft peaks, add the mint extract and increase to a moderate beating speed. Beat for another 4–6 minutes, until meringue forms firm peaks when the beaters are lifted.

Quickly, while the meringue is still warm, use a rubber spatula to scoop it into a pastry bag fitted with a medium (number 5 or 6) star tip. Remove the warm baking sheet from the oven. Glue the parchment paper to the baking sheet with a few pinches of meringue. Hold the pastry bag firmly with both hands, keeping it taut and closed with the top hand. With the tip directly over the parchment, press out rosettes about an inch in diameter.

Bake the mints at 200°F for about 45 minutes, until they feel firm and dry when squeezed gently. Use a small sharp knife, if necessary, to loosen the mints from the parchment.

Melt the chocolate in the top of a double boiler. Brush it onto the bottom of each mint. Set them upside down on a sheet of wax paper to dry for about an hour.

VARIATIONS
1. Melt only about 2½ ounces bittersweet chocolate and use it to glue two rosettes bottom-to-bottom—double mints. Let them dry for about an hour.

2. Melt about 6 ounces bittersweet chocolate and use a very small brush to coat the tops of each mint. After about an hour, when they are dry, turn them over and brush melted chocolate on the bottoms so that the mints are completely coated. Let them dry for another hour.

3. For Christmas, make wreath-shaped mints. Simply press out rings of meringue, each about 3 inches in diameter. Sprinkle each wreath with green granulated sugar. Bake the meringue at 200°F for about 30 minutes. Remove from the parchment carefully, using a small sharp knife.

4. Sift 2 tablespoons cocoa with the confectioners' sugar before beating it into the egg whites.
   Yield: 7–8 dozen single mints; 3½–4 dozen double mints

Meringue Mushrooms

I once made thirty baskets of these mushrooms for a Broadway opening. The cast and crew appreciated them far more than the critics liked the show. In fact the plaudits I received were well worth the time and patience it took to produce those 450 or so hand-dipped mushrooms. They do require practice to perfect, so don't be discouraged if it takes several attempts to achieve a product that pleases you.

> 3 egg whites
> ¼ teaspoon cream of tartar
> ⅓ cup sugar
> ½ teaspoon vanilla extract
> 1 tablespoon cocoa
> 1 teaspoon cinnamon
> 3 ounces semisweet chocolate
> ¼ cup chopped nuts (walnuts, pecans, almonds, etc.)

Place the oven rack about a third up from the bottom. Preheat the oven to 200°F. Line a baking sheet with parchment paper.

In a large, grease-free mixing bowl beat the egg whites at a slow steady speed. When they are foamy add the cream of tartar. Gradually add the sugar and, when the meringue will form soft peaks, increase to a moderate beating speed. Beat in the vanilla extract. Continue to beat for another 5–8 minutes, until the meringue is thick, glossy, and forms firm peaks when the beaters are lifted.

Glue the parchment paper to the baking sheet with a few pinches of meringue. Use a rubber spatula to scoop the meringue into a pastry bag, fitted with a medium (number 6) plain tip.

The mushrooms are formed in two parts—caps and stems. Hold the pastry bag firmly with both hands about ½ inch above the baking sheet and press out rounded caps of meringue about an inch in diameter, ½ inch apart. Pull the tip firmly across the top of the cap to break the meringue neatly. If the caps still have peaks, smooth them away with a cold knife. To shape the stems, press out the meringue, forming a base, and pull the bag straight up—making a stem about 1½ inches high that ends in a peak. Make approximately the same number of stems as caps; alternating rows will help you count. Don't be concerned about keeping your mushrooms uniform in size and shape. No two real mushrooms look the same. Sift

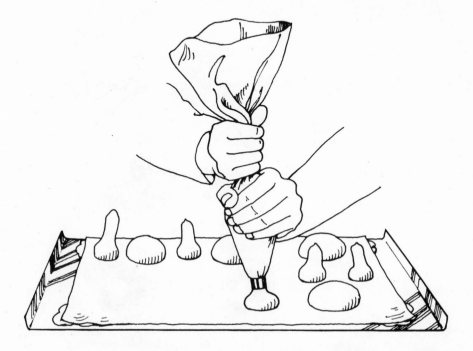

the cocoa and cinnamon over the caps to resemble dirt that's often found on fungi.

Bake at 200°F for 45–60 minutes, until the meringue feels firm and dry when squeezed gently. Use a small sharp knife to loosen the baked mushroom parts from the paper. They are ready for assembling or can be put aside in an airtight container for several weeks.

ASSEMBLING

Put the semisweet chocolate in the top of a double boiler over hot water just until it has melted. With a small sharp knife gently carve a small hollow in the flat side of each cap. Spread this side with the melted chocolate and fit the pointed end of a stem into the hollow. Dip the flat bottom of the stem in the chocolate and then in the chopped nuts. Allow at least an hour for the chocolate to dry at room temperature. These mushrooms are lovely placed in greengrocers' baskets and look remarkably like the real thing.

Yield: 3–4 dozen mushrooms

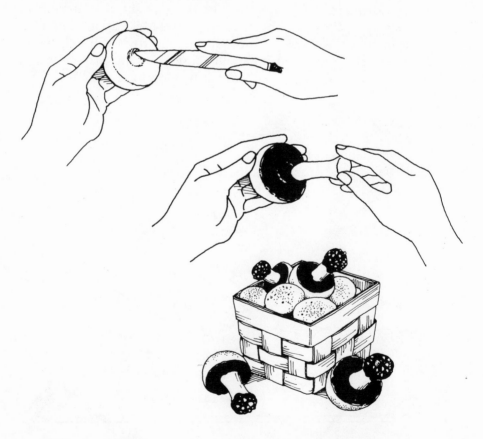

Almond Meringue Asparagus

This "asparagus" is one of my favorite creations. You'll probably want more than one recipe, but this meringue is delicate. So make it in the amount suggested and then repeat until you have enough spears.

> *1 egg white*
> *Pinch cream of tartar*
> *3 tablespoons sugar*
> *¼ teaspoon vanilla extract*
> *¼ teaspoon almond extract*
> *About 3 tablespoons finely slivered almonds*
> *Rum sauce, (page 205) or Chocolate Sauce (page 204),*
> *(optional)*

Place the oven rack about a third up from the bottom. Preheat the oven to 225°F. Line a baking sheet with parchment paper.

In a medium, grease-free mixing bowl beat the egg whites at a slow steady speed. When they are foamy add the cream of tartar. Gradually add the sugar and continue to beat until the meringue will form soft peaks. Add the vanilla extract and almond extract and increase to a moderate beating speed. Beat for about another 5 minutes, until the meringue is thick, glossy, and forms firm peaks when the beaters are lifted.

Glue the parchment paper to the baking sheet with a few pinches of meringue. Use a rubber spatula to scoop the meringue into a

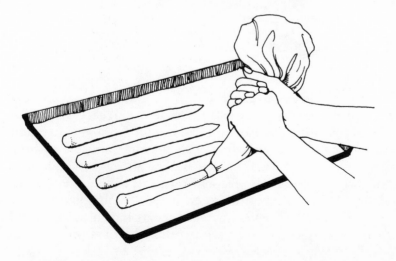

pastry bag fitted with a medium (number 5 or 6) plain tip. Hold the bag firmly with both hands, and angle the tip almost parallel to the baking sheet and just above it. Press out a strip of meringue about 7 inches long, using more pressure at first and then pulling the bag a little faster to taper the meringue and form a tip. Press out eight to ten more strips, leaving about 2 inches between each, until you've used all the meringue.

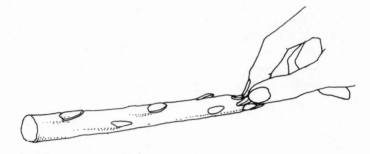

Push about a dozen almond slivers, one at a time, into the meringue tips. Keep the almond slivers close together and cover about an inch of the tip. Push another five or six almond slivers into the meringue strips, about an inch apart, alternating sides. (These almond slivers should, of course, resemble the leaflike structures on a real asparagus spear.) Work as quickly as possible to garnish all the meringue strips with almond slivers.

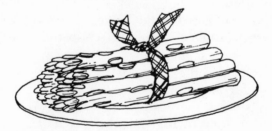

Bake the meringue at 225°F for 30–45 minutes, until it is very lightly colored and feels dry and firm when squeezed gently. Use a small sharp knife to loosen the meringue from the parchment. (These meringues are very fragile so it is not unusual to break a spear when removing it from the baking sheet. Just glue it back together with a little meringue and return it to the oven for about 10 minutes.) Trim the bottom of each spear with a knife.

Bundled, these meringue asparagus spears look astonishingly like the real thing. Arrange them with rounded fronts on the outside and tie with a ribbon, or with a clean piece of hemp for a more authentic look. They make a lovely table decoration and can be pulled one-by-one from the bundle and dipped in a dessert sauce. Or serve the spears, three or four on a plate, with a few tablespoons of sauce poured over them.

Yield: one recipe will yield only eight to eleven spears. For a dessert course, allow two servings per recipe.

Amaretto Cookies

Actually these are tiny light confections that you can serve instead of mints or chocolates. Pile them into a small, beautiful serving bowl.

> ¼ cup Amaretto
> ¾ cup ground blanched almonds
> 2 egg whites
> ¼ teaspoon cream of tartar
> ½ cup sugar
> ½ teaspoon almond extract
> About ¼ cup sliced almonds

Place the oven rack about a third up from the bottom. Preheat the oven to 325°F. Line a large cookie sheet with parchment paper.

Stir the Amaretto into the ground almonds and set the mixture aside. In a large, grease-free mixing bowl beat the egg whites at a slow steady speed. When they are foamy add the cream of tartar. Gradually add the sugar and, when the meringue will form soft peaks, beat in the almond extract and increase to a moderate beating speed. Beat for about another 5 minutes, until the meringue forms firm peaks when the beaters are lifted.

Use a rubber spatula to fold in the ground almond mixture, a heaping tablespoon at a time. Fold just until the batter is evenly blended. Drop the batter by teaspoonfuls onto the prepared cookie sheet. Press a sliced almond or two into the center of each cookie.

Bake the cookies at 325°F for about 15 minutes, until they feel dry. The cookies should color only faintly while baking; lower the heat or leave the oven door ajar if necessary.

Remove the cookies from the parchment with a spatula. They need only a few minutes to cool and then can be stored in an airtight container. They will keep nicely for a few weeks.

Yield: about 60 cookies

Snowmen

A seasonal treat that may be fun for children to make when there's no snow outside.

> 4 egg whites
> 1/2 teaspoon cream of tartar
> 3/4 cup vanilla sugar
> About 1/2 ounce bittersweet chocolate, chopped into small pieces

Place the oven rack about a third up from the bottom. Preheat the oven to 200° F. Line a large baking sheet with parchment paper.

In a large, grease-free mixing bowl beat the egg whites at a slow steady speed. When they are foamy add the cream of tartar. Gradually add the sugar and, when the meringue will form soft peaks, increase to a moderate beating speed. Beat for another 5–8 minutes, until the meringue is thick, glossy, and forms firm peaks when the beaters are lifted.

Glue the parchment paper to the baking sheet with a few pinches of meringue. Use a rubber spatula to scoop the meringue into a pastry bag fitted with a large (number 9) tip. Hold the bag firmly with both hands, keeping it closed and taut with the top one. With tip directly over the parchment-lined baking sheet, press out a ball of meringue about 1½ inches in diameter and height (the meringue should resemble a snowball). Press out two more balls of meringue next to the first one, increasing each by about ½ inch in diameter and height. Press out about five more series of meringue balls. Push chocolate pieces into the smallest balls to make eyes and a mouth and into the medium balls for buttons. Bake the meringue at 200°F for about 2 hours, until the pieces feel dry and firm when squeezed gently. The smaller balls may be done first; if so, remove them from the parchment using a small sharp knife and return the baking sheet to the oven for another 30–45 minutes.

To assemble the snowmen use a small sharp knife if necessary to carve shallow grooves so that the three balls can be stacked together. Use a pinch of unbaked meringue or a tiny pinch of melted chocolate (it shouldn't show) to glue the balls together.

Yield: about 6 snowmen

Large Meringue Case

This case is delicate and decorative. Use it to hold all kinds of desserts that are light (in weight, not necessarily calories). Some suggestions follow.

> *3 egg whites*
> *¼ teaspoon cream of tartar*
> *⅓ cup confectioners' sugar*
> *3 tablespoons ground hazelnuts (or walnuts)*

Place the oven rack about a third up from the bottom. Preheat the oven to 200°F. Line two (or three) large baking sheets with parchment paper. Trace five 9-inch circles onto the parchment.

In a large, grease-free mixing bowl beat the egg whites at a slow steady speed. When they are foamy add the cream of tartar. Gradually add the confectioners' sugar and, when the meringue will form soft peaks, increase to a moderate beating speed. Beat for another 5–8 minutes, until the meringue is thick, glossy, and forms firm peaks when the beaters are lifted.

Glue the parchment paper to the baking sheets with a few pinches of meringue. With a rubber spatula fold the ground hazelnuts into 1½–2 cups of the meringue. Set this mixture aside. Use a spatula to scoop the remaining meringue into a pastry bag fitted with a medium (number 5 or 6) star tip. Hold the bag firmly with both hands, keeping it taut and closed with the top hand. With the tip just over the parchment, press out meringue rings just inside each of the five traced circles. Spread the hazelnut meringue inside one of the meringue rings. Use the spatula to meld it carefully and make it smooth.

Bake the meringue pieces at 200°F for about 45 minutes, until the rings feel firm and dry when squeezed gently. Remove only the rings from the oven. Use a sharp knife to carefully loosen them from the parchment. Let the hazelnut layer dry in the oven for another 30 minutes or so. Test it for doneness by pressing it lightly in the center; it should feel firm and dry. Remove this layer from the oven and peel away the parchment, using the knife if necessary. Leave the oven set at 200°F.

GARNISH AND ASSEMBLING

1 egg white
Pinch of cream of tartar
2 tablespoons confectioners' sugar

Line one of the baking sheets with a fresh sheet of parchment. Place the hazelnut layer on the parchment. Stack the four meringue rings over it. Cut a piece of parchment paper the height and diameter of the meringue ring. Fit the parchment snugly inside the case as a brace so that the sides don't collapse in the oven. Staple the ends of the parchment together to secure the brace.

In a medium mixing bowl beat the egg white at a slow steady speed. When it is foamy add the cream of tartar. Gradually add the confectioners' sugar and beat for a few more minutes until the meringue forms firm peaks.

Glue the stacked meringue rings together with a few pinches of the meringue you've just made. Scoop the meringue into a pastry bag fitted with a small-medium (number 3 or 4) star tip. Hold the bag firmly with both hands and, starting at the top edge, press out a zigzag on the outside of the meringue case. Pull the bag quickly and apply a gentle even pressure to it as you move the tip steadily back and forth. When you've encircled the case, break the meringue neatly and make a crisscross pattern by pressing out a second zigzag, starting at the top edge opposite a corner of the first zigzag. With the remaining meringue make about thirty small rosettes. Hold the bag with the tip directly over the parchment, press the meringue out gently and pull the bag straight up to break it. (Save any leftover meringue; you'll need it for the final garnish.)

Bake the garnished case and rosettes at 200°F until the meringue feels firm and dry when squeezed gently. The rosettes should be done in 15–25 minutes. Loosen them from the parchment with the aid of a small knife and return the baking sheet to the oven. The garnished case should be done in another 15 minutes or so. Remove the baking sheet from the oven. Let the case cool for a few minutes, then peel the parchment brace from the inside and lift the case from the baking sheet.

Using the bits of unbaked leftover meringue, glue the rosettes around the top edge of the case. It will be fragile, but beautiful and ready to be filled.

SUGGESTED FILLINGS AND VARIATIONS
1. This case is a lovely way to serve Chocolate or Lemon Meringue Mousse (pages 46, 47). Spoon it in at the last minute.

2. Cut a half sheet of Yolk Cake (page 212) into cubes (about 2 cups). Use a melon scoop to shape about a half pint of ice cream or sherbet into small balls. Keep these ice cream balls in the freezer until the last minute. Then mix them with the cake cubes, pile the mixture into the meringue case, and sprinkle the top with a few tablespoons of Meringue Dust (page 51). Pass a dessert sauce to pour over each serving.

3. Fold about 2 cups of your favorite fruit (if you use canned fruit, drain it well) into 1 cup of whipped cream flavored with a liqueur.

4. Scoop various complementary flavors of ice cream or sherbet into the case and garnish with a few pieces fresh fruit.

5. Make a drum cake: Omit the rosettes. Fit a pastry bag with a medium (number 5 or 6) plain tip. Scoop about a cup of meringue into the bag and press out two 10-inch strips. At the end of each strip hold the bag stationary and apply a little more pressure to form the head of the drumsticks. Pull the bag away so that the meringue breaks in a blunt tip. Bake these drumsticks with the garnished case at 200°F. They should be done in about 30 minutes. When the case is done fill it with a quart or more of softened chocolate ice cream. The ice cream should fill the case to the brim. Smooth the surface and place this drum in the freezer for about an hour, until the ice cream is firm. Garnish with the drumsticks, slice it with a pie server, and pour Chocolate Sauce (page 204) over each serving.

Dessert Shells

These shells can be made ahead and stored in an airtight container for several weeks. If they have absorbed any moisture, dry them in a 200°F oven for about 15 minutes just before filling them. Serve the shells with any of a number of fillings—sherbet, ice cream, fresh fruit, custards. At the end of this recipe I suggest some variations on the shell recipe too.

> 3 egg whites
> ¼ teaspoon cream of tartar
> ½ cup sugar
> ½ teaspoon vanilla extract

Place the oven rack about a third up from the bottom. Preheat the oven to 200°F. Line a baking sheet with parchment paper. Trace six 5-inch circles onto the parchment. (For Valentine's Day trace heart shapes, or stars for Christmas.)

In a large, grease-free mixing bowl beat the egg whites at a slow steady speed. When they are foamy add the cream of tartar. Gradually beat in the sugar and, when the meringue will form soft peaks, add the vanilla extract and increase to a moderate beating speed.

Beat for about another 5 minutes, until the meringue is thick, glossy, and forms firm peaks when the beaters are lifted.

Glue the parchment paper to the baking sheet with a few pinches of meringue. Fit a pastry bag with a medium tip (I like number 5 star tip). Use a rubber spatula to fill the bag with the meringue. Hold the bag firmly with both hands, keeping it taut and closed with the top hand. With the tip just over the parchment, pipe out the meringue just inside the traced outlines. Fill in the meringue borders first, with a base about ¾-inch thick, and then pipe out a wall about 2 inches high around the edges.

Bake the meringue shells at 200°F for about 1½ hours, until they feel firm and dry when squeezed gently. Remove the baking sheet from the oven and loosen the shells from the parchment, using a small sharp knife if necessary. They are ready to be filled or you can store them in an airtight container.

Yield: 6 shells

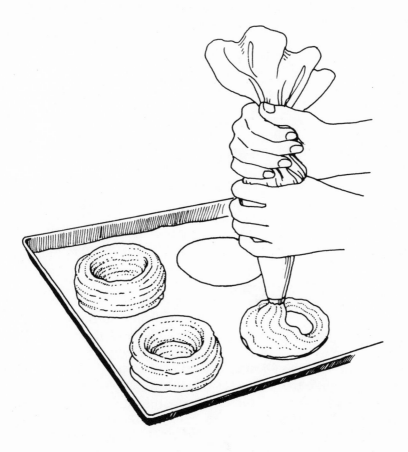

SUGGESTED FILLINGS

1. Heap sliced strawberries and bananas into each shell (about ½ cup fruit per shell). Top each with a heaping tablespoon of whipped cream and sprinkle with chopped nuts.

2. Drain the syrup from a 16-ounce can of sliced pears into a saucepan. Reserve the pears (do not chill). Heat the syrup with 2 tablespoons of cinnamon candy bits. When the candy has dissolved, remove the syrup from the heat. Put the pears into the shells and pour the heated syrup over each one. Make heart-shaped shells and use this filling for Valentine's Day.

3. Fill the shells with Basic Custard (page 198) or Chocolate Custard (page 199). Shave semisweet chocolate generously over the center of each filled shell.

4. Line the shells with mandarin oranges or seeded tangerine sections. Spoon Yolk Parfait, made with curaçao (page 200) to cover the fruit.

5. These shells are a beautiful way to serve Chocolate Meringue Mousse (page 46).

6. Pile vanilla ice cream into each shell and pour warm Rum Sauce (page 205) over the ice cream.

VARIATIONS

1. Substitute ½ teaspoon almond extract for the vanilla. Fold ¾ cup finely chopped nuts into the meringue before filling the pastry bag. These nutted shells are good filled with ice cream or Chocolate Custard (page 199).

2. For a special treat, wash, peel, and chill fresh figs. Put them into the nutted shells (allow two per shell). Cover each shell with about ⅓ cup stiffly whipped cream.

3. Substitute ½ teaspoon coconut extract for the vanilla. Shape the shells and sprinkle them generously with about ½ cup grated coconut. Fill the coconut shells with Basic Custard made with coconut extract (page 198) and folded with ½ cup whipped cream. Sprinkle a little fresh grated coconut over each filled shell. These shells are also good filled with coconut ice cream.

Meringue Cones

These cones are smaller than Dessert Shells so use them with richer fillings.

3 egg whites
¼ teaspoon cream of tartar
½ cup confectioners' sugar
½ teaspoon vanilla extract

Place the oven rack about a third up from the bottom. Preheat the oven to 200°F. Line a baking sheet with parchment paper. Trace six circles, each 2½ inches in diameter, onto the parchment.

In a large, grease-free mixing bowl beat the egg whites at a slow steady speed. When they are foamy, add the cream of tartar. Gradually add the sugar and, when the meringue will form soft peaks, add the vanilla extract and increase to a moderate beating speed. Beat for another 5 to 8 minutes, until the meringue is thick, glossy, and forms firm peaks when the beaters are lifted.

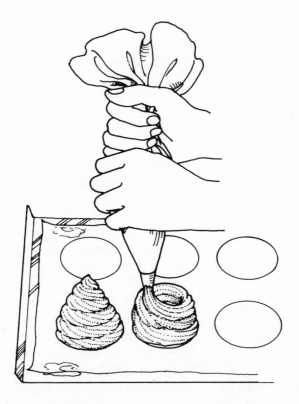

Glue the parchment paper to the baking sheet with a few pinches of meringue. Use a rubber spatula to scoop the meringue into a pastry bag fitted with a number 3B star tip. Hold the bag firmly with both hands, keeping it taut and closed with the top hand. Press out a ring of meringue just inside one of the traced circles. Do not break the meringue but continue to press it out in a spiral, gradually decreasing the diameter of the circles until the cone is closed. It should be 2½–3 inches high. Work quickly to press out the other five cones.

Bake the meringue cones at 200°F for about 2 hours, until they feel firm and dry when pressed gently. Remove them from the oven and use a small sharp knife to loosen them from the parchment.

Yield: 6 cones

SUGGESTED FILLINGS

1. Melt about 2 ounces of bittersweet chocolate in the top of a double boiler over hot water. Use a brush or very small rubber spatula to coat the inside and rim of each cone with the chocolate. Set them aside to allow the chocolate to dry. Just before serving fill a pastry bag fitted with a medium (number 5 or 6) star tip with ½ recipe Meringue Parfait (page 43). Hold the bag firmly with both hands and press out enough parfait to fill each cone and finish with a small spiral or rosette.

2. Omit the chocolate and spoon in ½ recipe Meringue Parfait that is filled with fruit or nuts.

3. About ½ recipe of Chocolate Meringue Mousse (page 46) or Lemon Meringue Mousse (page 47) will fill six cones.

4. Spoon Chestnut Pudding (about ½ recipe, page 202) into each cone and garnish with 2 tablespoons chocolate shavings.

5. Fill the cones with Chocolate Parfait pressed from a pastry bag fitted with a small or medium (number 3 or 4) star tip. About ½ recipe (page 201) is enough for six cones.

Tiny Tarts

I once prepared these for a theater party of four hundred guests. Indeed they are a great small treat to end a light supper or late-night party, especially for a large number of people. Choose fillings that are rich and colorful.

Place the oven rack about a third up from the bottom. Preheat the oven to 200°F. Line a large baking sheet (or two small sheets) with parchment paper.

Make the meringue recipe for Dessert Shells (page 32). Glue the parchment paper to the baking sheet(s) with a few pinches of meringue. Fit a pastry bag with a small (number 0) star tip and, using a rubber spatula, fill it with the meringue. Press out a base about 1 inch in diameter and encircle it with two rings of meringue piping, making a wall about ¾ inch high. Fill the baking sheet(s) with these little shells.

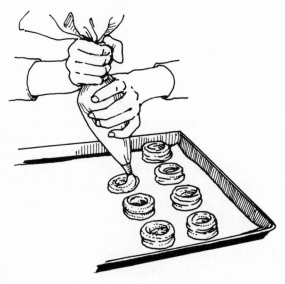

Bake the tart shells at 200°F for 45–60 minutes, until the meringue is firm and the shells lift easily from the paper. Store them in an airtight container until just before time to serve. They will keep for several weeks.

Yield: about 100 shells

SUGGESTED FILLINGS

1. One recipe of Whole Lemon Custard (page 200) will fill about 100 tart shells. Place all the shells on a serving tray and spoon a scant teaspoonful into each.

2. Rich Nut Mix is an elegant filling for these shells. One recipe (page 224) is enough for 100 of them. Make the mix and spoon it into the shells while it's quite warm.

3. Put ½ recipe Chocolate Parfait (page 201) into a pastry bag fitted with a small (number 1 or 2) star tip. Press out a mound of filling that comes just above the edge of the shell.

Stuffed Eggs

These are small elegant treats—just right after a rich meal, served with a pot of flavored coffee. Or add them to a tray of petit fours.

> 3 egg whites
> ½ teaspoon cream of tartar
> ¼ cup sugar
> ½ teaspoon vanilla extract
> ¼ cup finely chopped walnuts or pecans
> ¼ cup grated coconut

Place the oven rack about a third up from the bottom. Preheat the oven to 200°F. Line a baking sheet with parchment paper.

In a large, grease-free mixing bowl beat the egg whites at a slow steady speed. When they are foamy, add the cream of tartar. Gradually add the sugar and continue to beat until the meringue will form soft peaks. Add the vanilla extract and increase to a moderate beating speed. Beat for another 5 to 8 minutes, until the meringue is thick, glossy, and forms firm peaks when the beaters are lifted. Use a rubber spatula to fold in the chopped nuts and grated coconut.

Glue the parchment paper to the baking sheet with a few pinches of meringue. With the rubber spatula scoop the meringue into a pastry bag fitted with a large (number 9) plain tip. Hold the bag firmly with both hands and, with the tip slightly at an angle to the parchment paper, press out an oval or egg shape 2½–3 inches long and about ¾-inch thick. Break the meringue. Press out eggs at 1-inch intervals until you've used all the meringue.

Bake the meringue eggs at 200°F for about an hour. They should be dry on the surface but not yet firm. Remove the baking sheet from the oven. With the back of a tablespoon make a gentle depression in each of the meringue eggs. Return the baking sheet to the oven and let the meringue bake at 200°F for about another hour, until it feels firm when squeezed gently. Remove the eggs from the oven and use a small sharp knife to loosen them from the parchment paper. They will cool in about 10 minutes and can be stored in an airtight container for several weeks or filled right away.

Yield: about a dozen eggs

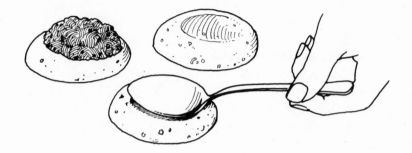

SUGGESTED FILLINGS

1. My favorite filling for these eggs is Chocolate Parfait (for a dozen eggs make ½ recipe, page 201). Use a pastry bag fitted with a small or medium (number 3 or 4) plain tip and press out a heaping mound of parfait in each egg. After filling put them in the freezer for 1 or 2 hours before serving.

2. Spread a thick coat of Rum, Kirsch, or Chocolate Butter Cream (page 205, 207, 208) into each egg and garnish with a few attractive pieces of candied fruit.

3. Fill them with spirals of flavored cream. Whip about 1½ cups of heavy cream with 2 tablespoons of any dessert liqueur until it is quite stiff, then press it from a pastry bag fitted with a small or medium (number 3 or 4) star tip.

Meringue Basket

This is pure whimsy and more for looks than eating. It certainly can be made larger than the one in this recipe. Just keep tracing circles that increase by ½ inch and repeat the meringue recipe.

> 2 egg whites
> ¼ teaspoon cream of tartar
> ⅓ cup sugar

Place the oven rack about a third up from the bottom. Preheat the oven to 200°F. Line two baking sheets with parchment paper. Trace two 3-inch circles, one each at 3½, 4, 4½, 5, 5½ inches, and two at 6 inches onto the parchment. These sizes are approximate, but the idea is to make a series of circles, increasing the diameter of each circle by ½ inch. If you want a handle on your basket, trace two horseshoes that measure about 4½ inches across the bottom and loop about 5 inches high.

In a medium, grease-free mixing bowl beat the egg whites at a slow steady speed. When they are foamy add the cream of tartar. Gradually add the sugar and, when the meringue will form soft peaks, increase to a moderate beating speed. Beat for another 5–8 minutes, until the meringue forms firm peaks when the beaters are lifted.

Glue the parchment paper to the baking sheets with a few pinches of meringue. Fit one pastry bag with a medium (number 5 or 6) star tip and another with a smaller (number 2 or 3) star tip. Use a rubber spatula to scoop all but a cup of the meringue into the bag with the larger tip. Fill the other bag with the remaining meringue. Take up the first bag and hold it firmly with both hands,

keeping it taut and closed with the top hand. With the tip just over the parchment, press out meringue rings, all of the same thickness, just inside each of the traced circles. Fill in one of the 3-inch rings with meringue. Use the spatula to smooth it. With the other bag press out meringue just inside the traced horseshoes. Save any left-over meringue; you'll need it for assembling the basket.

Bake the meringue pieces at 200°F for about 30 minutes, until they feel firm and dry when squeezed gently. Remove the baking sheets from the oven and loosen the meringue from the parchment with a small sharp knife. Stack the meringue rings, beginning with the filled-in base, in increasing diameter. The two 6-inch rings make a finishing border. Glue the rings together with pinches of the unbaked leftover meringue.

If you have made a handle, glue the horseshoes back to back and fit the handle inside the basket. (I suggest winding a thin ribbon around the handle which is not only decorative but also binds it together.) With the knife, gently carve out shallow notches in the basket sides so that it fits securely. Glue it in place with some of the unbaked meringue. Let the basket dry at room temperature for a few hours. Then it will be ready for filling.

I advise against using any custards, sauces, or even ice cream with this basket. It is a lovely vessel for dry meringues such as Amaretto Cookies (page 27), Meringue Mints (page 21), or Divinity (page 50). You can also fill it with jelly beans or other small egg-shaped candy.

Meringue Parfait

Here is one of the most versatile of all meringue recipes. My lists of variations and serving suggestions could be expanded endlessly.

> 1⅓ *cups sugar*
> ⅓ *cup water*
> 4 *egg whites*
> ½ *teaspoon vanilla extract*
> 1½ *cups heavy cream*
> 2 *tablespoons kirsch, Grand Marnier, Amaretto, curaçao, or*
>   *other liqueur (optional)*

In a saucepan combine the sugar and water over medium heat. Bring the mixture to a boil and let this sugar syrup boil for a few minutes to 234°F (soft-ball stage). Remove the saucepan from the heat. Quickly, in a large, grease-free bowl beat the egg whites at a slow steady speed. When they are stiff pour in the warm sugar syrup in a thin stream. Continue to beat for another 5 to 8 minutes, until the meringue is thick, glossy, and cool. It should almost form firm peaks when the beaters are lifted. Beat in the vanilla extract.

In a large chilled bowl with chilled beaters whip the heavy cream until it just begins to stiffen. Add the liqueur if desired. With a rubber spatula fold the whipped cream into the meringue in six to eight additions, blending the parfait well after each addition.

Fold in any other ingredients (see Variations below) and then scoop the parfait into a covered container and freeze it for 2 or 3 hours before serving. It will keep in the freezer for a week or so.

Yield: about 6 cups parfait

VARIATIONS
1. Make the parfait with kirsch and fold in about a cup of chopped candied cherries. Serve it in clear dishes.

2. Make the parfait with Grand Marnier. Line a shallow serving dish with fresh peaches that have been peeled and sliced. Chill the dish. Spread the frozen parfait over the peaches and serve the dessert very cold.

3. Make the parfait with Amaretto and fold in about ¾ cup slivered almonds.

4. Fold in a cup of fresh raspberries or sliced strawberries.

5. Fold about ½ cup Praline Powder (page 223) into plain parfait or parfait made with Amaretto.

SERVING SUGGESTIONS

1. Use a long serrated knife to split a layer of Génoise (½ recipe, page 227) into three sheets. The sheets will be very thin. Spread parfait frozen with cherries over each sheet. Stack them and ice the outside with parfait. Freeze this parfait cake. Let it thaw at room temperature for only about 15 minutes before slicing (use the serrated knife) and serving.

2. Alternate layers of parfait with layers of Chocolate Meringue Mousse (page 46) in tall clear parfait glasses.

3. Line clear serving glasses with fruit, nuts, or a combination. Fill a pastry bag fitted with a medium (number 5 or 6) star tip with the parfait. Press it out into the glasses and keep them in the freezer until time to serve.

Grand Soufflé

3 tablespoons sweet butter
¼ cup ground pecans or almonds
3 tablespoons sugar
⅔ cup milk
2 ounces bittersweet chocolate, broken into small pieces
6 egg yolks, lightly beaten
3 tablespoons Grand Marnier
8 egg whites
3 tablespoons sugar
1 teaspoon vanilla extract

Place the oven rack in the lowest quarter of the oven. Preheat the oven to 375°F. Butter a 2-quart soufflé dish and dust it with sugar.

In a heavy saucepan over low heat melt the butter. Stir in the ground nuts and 3 tablespoons sugar. Gradually add the milk, stirring to blend it well. Add the chocolate and stir until it has melted and blended with the mixture. Gently and slowly beat in the egg yolks. When the mixture has thickened slightly, remove the sauce-pan from the heat and stir in the Grand Marnier. Set the saucepan aside so that the mixture can cool.

In a very large, grease-free mixing bowl beat the egg whites at a slow steady speed. When they begin to stiffen, gradually add the remaining 3 tablespoons sugar. Beat in the vanilla extract. Continue to beat just until the egg whites are quite stiff but not dry.

A little at a time, fold the chocolate mixture into the egg whites. Fold only until the chocolate is barely blended. Gently pour the soufflé batter into the prepared dish.

Bake the soufflé at 375°F for 30–45 minutes, until it is puffed and the top feels almost firm when pressed very lightly.

Serve the soufflé immediately from the oven with Grand Marnier Sauce (page 206) poured over each portion.

Yield: 10–12 servings

Prune Whip

This baked meringue dessert seems to have southern origins. At least it was popularized by several generations of home cooks in the South. It's a mock soufflé if you bake it in one large dish.

> ½ *pound pitted prunes*
> ½ *cup Madeira or port wine*
> ½ *cup water*
> 2 *tablespoons sugar*
> 3 *egg whites*
> ¼ *teaspoon cream of tartar*
> ¼ *cup sugar*

Put the prunes into a saucepan, pour the Madeira or port over them, and set them aside to marinate for at least 30 minutes.

Preheat the oven to 325°F. Lightly butter six individual baking (or custard) cups or a 1½- or 2-quart soufflé dish.

Add the water and 2 tablespoons sugar to the mixture in the saucepan and place it over medium heat. Bring the mixture to a boil and let it boil for 5 minutes, until most of the liquid has been ab-sorbed or boiled away. Remove the saucepan from the heat and drain the prunes. Force the warm prunes through a food mill or purée them in a blender and set them aside.

In a large, grease-free mixing bowl beat the egg whites at a slow steady speed. When they are foamy add the cream of tartar. Gradually add the ¼ cup sugar and continue to beat for a few more minutes until the meringue will form soft peaks.

Use a large spoon or rubber spatula to fold the puréed prunes, about a tablespoon at a time, into the meringue. Spoon the mixture into the prepared baking cups or soufflé dish, piling it slightly above the rim(s). Bake the prune whip at 325°F for 20–30 minutes in the baking cups, about 15 minutes longer in the soufflé dish, until it is firm and the top is lightly browned. Remove the prune whip from the oven and serve warm.

Yield: (either preparation) 6 servings

Chocolate Meringue Mousse

¼ cup sweet butter, cut into tablespoons
4 ounces bittersweet chocolate, broken into pieces
2 egg yolks, lightly beaten
⅔ cup sugar
⅓ cup water
3 egg whites
¼ teaspoon cream of tartar

In a small saucepan over very low heat or in the top of a double boiler, melt the butter and the chocolate. Stir to blend these ingredients and beat in the egg yolks. Remove the saucepan from the heat and set it aside on a trivet to cool.

In another small saucepan combine the sugar and water. Over medium heat, bring the mixture to a boil. Let the sugar syrup boil for 5 to 8 minutes, until it reaches 234°F (soft-ball stage). Remove the saucepan from the heat. Immediately begin to beat the egg whites in a large, grease-free bowl at a slow steady speed. When they are foamy add the cream of tartar. Continue to beat and pour in the sugar syrup in a slow thin stream. When the meringue is well blended increase beating speed to moderate and beat for another 5 minutes, until it is thick, glossy, and cool.

Fold about a third of the meringue into the cooled chocolate mixture. When it is blended enough that none of the white shows, fold in another third. Fold the chocolate mixture into the remaining meringue, using broad regular strokes from the bottom of the bowl, until the texture and color are smooth and even. Spoon into individual serving dishes or one large bowl. Chill in the refrigerator for at least an hour before serving.

Yield: 4–6 servings

Lemon Meringue Mousse

An actor friend, one of the best Tevyes in "Fiddler on the Roof," asks for this mousse almost every time I invite him for supper.

6 egg yolks, lightly beaten
¾ cup heavy cream
¾ cup lemon juice
1 teaspoon lime juice
1 cup sugar
⅓ cup water
6 egg whites
¼ teaspoon cream of tartar

In a heavy saucepan over low heat or in the top of a double boiler, combine the egg yolks, heavy cream, and lemon juice. Stir continuously, with vigor if necessary to keep the yolks from curdling, until the mixture thickens enough to coat the spoon. Stir in the lime juice and remove the pan from the heat. Set it aside to cool to room temperature.

In another saucepan combine the sugar and water. Over medium heat, bring the mixture to a boil. Let this sugar syrup boil for 3 to 5 minutes, until it reaches 234°F (soft-ball stage). Remove the saucepan from the heat. Immediately begin to beat the egg whites in a large, grease-free mixing bowl at a slow steady speed. When they are foamy add the cream of tartar. Pour in the sugar syrup in a thin stream. When the meringue is thoroughly blended, increase beating speed to moderate and beat for at least another 5 minutes, until it is thick, glossy, and cool.

Fold the cooled lemon mixture, a heaping tablespoon at a time, into the meringue. Use a rubber spatula and gentle strokes, folding until the color and texture are smooth and even. Spoon the mousse into individual serving dishes or a large shallow tray. Chill in the refrigerator for at least an hour before serving.

Yield: about 6 servings

Pavlova

It may be apocryphal, but the story is that this dessert was indeed created in honor of the legendary dancer Anna Pavlova. Whatever the origin, it's an exquisite meringue and has won its own fame and tradition in the culinary world.

> 6 egg whites
> 1 teaspoon cream of tartar
> 1 cup sugar
> 1 teaspoon vanilla extract
> 6 kiwi, pared and sliced (kiwi is the usual fruit in a Pavlova;
>   peaches, bananas, or pineapple can be substituted)
> 1 cup heavy cream
> 1 recipe Raspberry Sauce (page 225)

Place the oven rack about a third up from the bottom. Preheat the oven to 375°F. Line a small baking sheet or shallow 9-inch round cake pan with parchment paper. Trace an 8-inch circle onto the parchment.

In a very large, grease-free mixing bowl beat the egg whites at a slow steady speed. When they are foamy add the cream of tartar. Gradually add the sugar and, when the meringue will form soft peaks, add the vanilla extract and increase to a moderate beating speed. Beat for about another 10 minutes, until the meringue is thick, glossy, and forms firm peaks when the beaters are lifted.

Use a large rubber spatula to pile the meringue onto the prepared baking sheet (or into the cake pan). Cover the area inside the traced circle and then shape the meringue like a mountain, several inches high in the center.

Bake the meringue at 375°F for only about 3 minutes, just until the surface feels dry. (If it starts to color, turn the oven down to 200° and leave the door ajar.) Turn the oven down to 200°F and leave the oven door open for 20–30 minutes. Bake the Pavlova at 200°F for 2 to 3 hours, until the surface feels not only dry but firm and crispy. (The inside should remain soft.)

Remove the meringue from the oven and let it cool for a few minutes. As soon as you can handle it, lift it from the baking sheet and peel away the parchment. The meringue can be stored for a day or two in an airtight container kept in a cool place. When you are ready to assemble the Pavlova, place the meringue on a serving platter and arrange the sliced kiwi around it.

In a large chilled bowl with chilled beaters whip the cream just until it will hold soft shapes. Pile the whipped cream over the meringue and swirl it down the sides. Drizzle a little of the raspberry sauce on top.

Slice the Pavlova with a pie server and pour more raspberry sauce over each serving.

Yield: about 8 servings

Divinity

¼ cup water
¼ cup corn syrup
⅔ cup sugar
1 egg white
1 cup chopped nuts (or candied fruit, or ½ cup of each)

In a small saucepan combine the water and corn syrup. Over medium heat bring the mixture to a boil and stir in the sugar until it has dissolved. Cover the boiling syrup for 3 minutes. Uncover and let it cook for a few minutes to 260°F (hard-ball stage). Quickly beat the egg white in a medium, grease-free mixing bowl at a slow steady speed. When it is quite stiff, pour the syrup, in a thin stream, over the stiffened egg white, as you continue to beat. Increase to a moderate beating speed for about 1 minute.

Use a large spoon to fold in the chopped nuts and/or fruit. Hand beat this mixture with the spoon for a few minutes. Drop the divinity from a tablespoon onto a lightly buttered baking sheet or piece of foil. Let the patties cool to room temperature. Remove them from the baking sheet, using a knife if necessary, and store the divinity in an airtight container.

Yield: about 2 dozen pieces

Maple Divinity

3 tablespoons water
½ cup maple syrup
1 cup light brown sugar
2 egg whites
About 1½ cup pecan halves

Butter a baking sheet or piece of foil and set it aside.

In a small saucepan over medium heat combine the water and maple syrup. Bring the mixture to a boil, then gradually stir in the sugar. When the sugar has dissolved cover the pan and let the mixture boil for 3 minutes. Uncover the pan and swirl it occasionally over the heat, letting the sugar syrup boil another few minutes. As soon as it reaches 260°F (hard-ball stage) remove the saucepan from the heat.

Quickly, in a large, grease-free mixing bowl, beat the egg whites at a slow steady speed. When they are stiff, gradually beat in the boiled sugar syrup, pouring it in a thin stream. As soon as the meringue will form soft peaks, increase to a moderate beating speed. Beat for another 3 to 5 minutes, until the meringue is thick, glossy, and cool.

Drop tablespoonfuls of the meringue onto the prepared baking sheet. Press a pecan half into the center of each. Let the divinity dry for several hours (overnight is best) in a cool, dry place. Loosen the pieces from the baking sheet using a spatula or knife if necessary. Keep the divinity cool and dry.

Yield: about 40 pieces

Meringue Dust

Keep this all-purpose meringue garnish in an airtight container where it will stay fresh for months. If you should ever chip a meringue pie crust or vacherin layer beyond repair or shatter a rosette, just add the damaged goods to your dust collection.

> *2 egg whites*
> *¼ teaspoon cream of tartar*
> *3 tablespoons sugar*
> *¼ teaspoon extract or flavor (vanilla, coconut, almond, black walnut, etc.)*
> *½ cup chopped walnuts, pecans, or grated coconut (or a mixture)*

Place the oven rack about a third up from the bottom. Preheat the oven to 200°F. Line a baking sheet with parchment paper.

In a medium, grease-free mixing bowl beat the egg whites at a slow steady speed. When they are foamy add the cream of tartar. Gradually add the sugar and, when the meringue will form soft peaks, add the extract or flavor and increase to a moderate beating speed. Beat for another 3 to 5 minutes, until the meringue is thick, glossy, and forms firm peaks when the beaters are lifted. Use a rubber spatula to fold in the chopped nuts or grated coconut, about a tablespoon at a time. Spread the meringue onto the prepared baking sheet with the spatula.

Bake the meringue at 200°F for 2 to 3 hours until it feels firm and dry when pressed gently in the center. Remove the baking sheet from the oven and peel the paper away from the meringue. You need no tools except your fingers to crumble the meringue into powder. Store the meringue dust airtight in a cool place.

Use this garnish instead of nuts, or it's an excellent way to flavor nuts to complement a special dessert.

Yield: about 1¼ cups dust

Honey Meringue

⅔ *cup honey*
2 *egg whites*
¼ *teaspoon cream of tartar*

In a small saucepan heat the honey for several minutes to 234°F (soft-ball stage). Remove the pan from the heat but keep it warm. In a medium, grease-free mixing bowl beat the egg whites at a slow steady speed. When they are foamy add the cream of tartar. When the egg whites are stiff, gradually beat in the warm honey, pouring it in a thin stream. Beat the meringue for about another 5 minutes until it is thick, glossy, and cool.

This meringue is more of a soft topping than an icing. Use it on individual servings of cakes, breads, and over chilled fresh fruit. Several recipes in this book call for it.

Yield: about 2 cups meringue

Quick Icing

This basic icing is an Italian meringue. It requires no baking since the boiling syrup cooks the egg whites. However, if you prefer a crisper texture, brown your iced cake in the oven at 350°F for about 5 minutes.

1½ *cups sugar*
⅓ *cup water*
2 *egg whites*
¼ *teaspoon cream of tartar*
1 *teaspoon vanilla extract (or substitute rum, lemon, almond,*
   etc., extract according to the cake recipe you've selected)

In a small saucepan stir the sugar into the water and, over medium heat, bring the mixture to a boil. Let it boil for 3 minutes. Remove the saucepan to very low heat. In a large, grease-free mixing bowl beat the egg whites at a slow steady speed. When they are foamy add the cream of tartar. When the egg whites are stiff, gradually beat in the boiled syrup, pouring it in a thin stream. Beat the meringue for another 5 minutes, until it is thick, glossy, and cool. Beat in the vanilla extract. This icing does not keep well and therefore should be used right away.

Several recipes in this book specifically call for Quick Icing. Also check the Basic Dessert Recipes chapter for other cakes and tortes that go well with it.

Yield: about 3 cups icing

Quicker Icing

This is one of those recipes to use when there is no time for elaborate preparation.

> 2 egg whites
> 2 tablespoons lemon juice (or substitute pineapple, lime, cherry juice; select a flavor that complements your cake)
> 1¼ cups confectioners' sugar

In a large, grease-free mixing bowl beat the egg whites at a moderate speed until foamy. Add 1 tablespoon of the lemon juice. Gradually sift in the confectioners' sugar and continue to beat for about 5 minutes, until the meringue is smooth, thick, and will almost form firm peaks when the beaters are lifted. Fold in the remaining tablespoon of lemon juice.

For best results apply a thin coat of the icing to the cake. Allow about an hour for it to dry, then use the remaining icing for a second coat.

In the Basic Dessert Recipes chapter, I suggest cakes and tortes to use with this icing.

Yield: about 2 cups icing

Chocolate Meringue Icing

1½ cups sugar
⅓ cup water
3 egg whites
¼ teaspoon cream of tartar
⅓ cup cocoa

In a saucepan combine the sugar and water and bring the syrup to a boil. Let it boil over medium heat for 2 to 3 minutes until it reaches 234°F (soft-ball stage). Remove the saucepan from the heat. Quickly, in a large, grease-free mixing bowl, beat the egg whites at a slow steady speed. When they are foamy add the cream of tartar. When the egg whites are stiff, gradually beat in the boiled syrup, pouring it in a thin stream. As soon as the meringue is blended and will form soft peaks, add the cocoa, sifting it in 1 tablespoon at a time. Continue to beat for a few minutes until the meringue is thick, glossy, and cool.

In the Basic Dessert Recipes chapter, I suggest cakes and tortes to use with this icing.

Yield: about 3½ cups icing

Cakes and Tortes

Some cakes have meringue in the batter. Others are topped with meringue. And then there are the lightest of all—vacherins, layers of meringue laced with butter cream, delicate fruit, sauces, or whipped cream.

Spanish Wind Torte

This dessert is one of the airiest and most beautiful of all. It is a traditional delicacy in any chef's meringue repertory.

> 1 dry quart strawberries
> 3–4 tablespoons maraschino or kirsch
> 3 egg whites
> ½ teaspoon cream of tartar
> ⅓ cup vanilla sugar
> ¼ cup ground blanched almonds
> 1 cup heavy cream
> 2 tablespoons vanilla sugar

Place the oven rack about a third up from the bottom. Preheat the oven to 200°F. Line two (or three) large baking sheets with parchment paper. Trace five 8-inch circles onto the parchment.

Wash, dry, and hull the strawberries. Slice them in half and place them in a shallow dish. Pour the maraschino or kirsch over the strawberry halves and set them aside to marinate while you prepare the meringue.

In a large, grease-free mixing bowl beat the egg whites at a slow steady speed. When they are foamy add the cream of tartar. Gradually add the ⅓ cup vanilla sugar and, when the meringue will form soft peaks, increase to a moderate beating speed. Beat for another 5–8 minutes, until the meringue is thick, glossy, and forms firm peaks when the beaters are lifted.

With a rubber spatula fold the ground almonds into about 1½ cups of the meringue and reserve it. Glue the parchment paper to the baking sheets with a few pinches of meringue. Scoop the rest of the meringue into a pastry bag fitted with a medium (number 5 or 6) star tip. Hold the bag firmly with both hands, keeping it taut and closed with the top hand. With the tip just over the parchment press out rings of meringue just inside each of the traced circles.

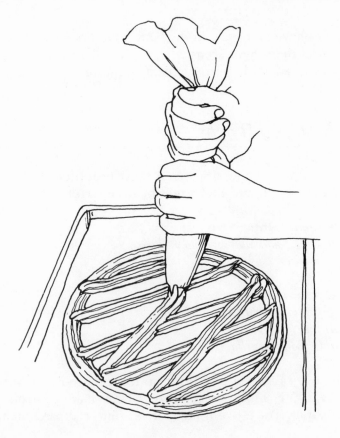

Then make a lattice top: Starting at the inside edge of one of the meringue rings press out a 2-inch strip of meringue. Break the meringue neatly where it meets the opposite side of the ring. Press out three or four more strips parallel to the first one. Then, with the tip at the beginning of the first strip, press out three or four strips across the inside of the ring in the opposite direction. (Save any leftover meringue; you'll need it for assembling.)

Use a rubber spatula to spread an even layer of the reserved almond meringue inside another ring.

Bake the meringue at 200°F for about 45 minutes, until the three plain rings feel firm and dry when squeezed gently. Use a small sharp knife to remove them from the parchment. The lattice top will be dry in another 15–30 minutes and should be removed from the oven then. Bake the almond layer yet another 15–30 minutes. Test it for doneness by pressing it gently in the center. When it feels firm and dry, remove it from the oven and peel away the parchment.

Stack the three plain rings over the almond meringue base and glue the pieces together with pinches of the leftover meringue. Set this case aside. In a chilled bowl with chilled beaters whip the cream, gradually adding the 2 tablespoons vanilla sugar, until it is stiff. Drain the strawberries. Reserve about a cup of the most beautiful strawberry halves and fold the rest into the whipped cream. Fill the meringue case with this mixture. Arrange reserved strawberries on top and then cover the torte with the lattice top. Chill the torte in the refrigerator for at least 30 minutes and then serve.

Yield: 6–8 servings

Mont Blanc

This is named for its appearance—the generous pile of whipped cream in the center. Bases and fillings for this classic dessert vary from chef to chef. This recipe reflects my fondness for the complementary flavors of chestnut and chocolate.

MERINGUE BASE

4 egg whites
½ teaspoon cream of tartar
½ cup vanilla sugar
¼ cup bittersweet chocolate shavings

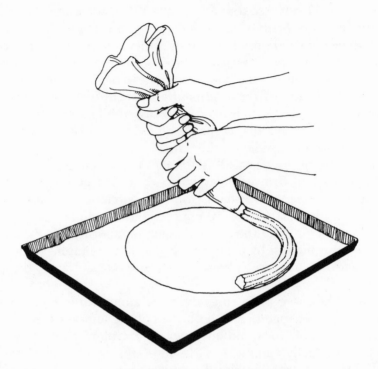

Place the oven rack about a third up from the bottom. Preheat the oven to 200°F. Line a baking sheet with parchment paper. Trace a circle, about 10 inches in diameter, onto the paper.

In a large, grease-free mixing bowl beat the egg whites at a slow steady speed. When they are foamy add the cream of tartar. Gradually add the sugar and, when the meringue will form soft peaks, increase to a moderate beating speed. Continue to beat for another 5–8 minutes, until the meringue is thick, glossy, and forms firm peaks when the beaters are lifted.

Glue the parchment paper to the baking sheet with a few pinches of meringue. Fit a pastry bag with a medium (number 5 or 6) star tip and fill it with about 1½ cups of meringue, reserving the rest. Hold the bag firmly with both hands, using one to keep it closed and taut. Press out a ring of meringue onto the paper just inside the traced circle. Put the pastry bag aside; it should still be partially filled. Quickly fold the chocolate chips into the reserved meringue. Use a rubber spatula to spread this chocolate chip meringue inside the circle, melding it with the meringue ring. Take up the pastry bag and press out a second ring of plain meringue on top of the first, making a shallow well. Make this second ring thick enough so that from the outside the chocolate chips don't show.

Bake the meringue at 200°F for about 2½ hours, until it feels firm and dry when pressed lightly in the center. Remove it from the oven and, when it is cool enough to handle, peel the paper away. This meringue base can be stored in an airtight container for several weeks.

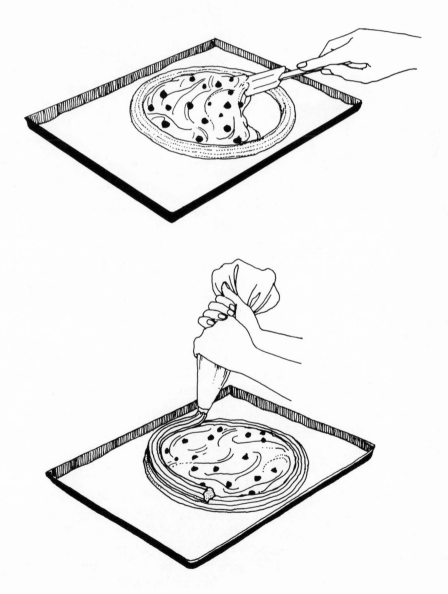

CHESTNUT FILLING

> *1 pound fresh chestnuts*
> *About 2 quarts boiling water*
> *1 cup milk*
> *1 inch vanilla bean, split*
> *¼ cup sugar*
> *3 tablespoons water*

Use a sharp knife to slash crosses in the flat side of each chestnut. Put them into a saucepan of boiling water and let them boil for about 20 minutes, until the shells and skins can be easily removed. Leave them soaking in hot water and remove them one at a time to peel away the shells and inner skins.

In a saucepan scald the milk with the vanilla bean. Add the peeled chestnuts and let the mixture simmer over low heat for 20–30 minutes, stirring occasionally to break the chestnuts apart. When most of the milk has been absorbed, remove the vanilla bean and purée the chestnuts in a blender or force them through a strainer or food mill. Set the chestnut purée aside in a mixing bowl.

In another small saucepan combine the sugar and 3 tablespoons water over medium heat. Bring to a boil and let the syrup boil for 3 minutes. Remove the saucepan from the heat and blend the boiled syrup into the puréed chestnuts. Set the chestnut filling aside to cool.

ASSEMBLING

> 1 cup heavy cream, whipped
> 2 tablespoons bittersweet chocolate shavings

Use your fingertips to press all but about a cup of the chestnut filling into the well of the meringue base. Put the remaining cup of filling into a pastry bag fitted with a large (number 9) star tip. Push out a chestnut border just inside the filled well. Pile the whipped cream inside the chestnut border, making the mound quite high in the center. Sprinkle the chocolate shavings over the center. Keep the Mont Blanc cool until time to serve. Slice it in wedges, using a serrated knife.

Yield: about 8 servings

Dacquoise

MERINGUE LAYERS

> 5 egg whites
> ¼ teaspoon cream of tartar
> ½ cup vanilla sugar
> ⅓ cup ground blanched almonds

Place the oven rack about a third up from the bottom. Preheat the oven to 200°F. Line a large baking sheet with parchment paper. Trace two 9-inch circles onto the parchment.

In a large, grease-free mixing bowl beat the egg whites at a slow steady speed. When they are foamy add the cream of tartar. Gradually add the vanilla sugar and, when the meringue will form soft peaks, increase to a moderate beating speed. Continue to beat for another 5 to 8 minutes, until the meringue is thick, glossy, and forms firm peaks when the beaters are lifted. Use a rubber spatula to fold in the ground almonds, 1 tablespoon at a time.

Glue the parchment paper to the baking sheet with a few pinches of meringue. With the spatula scoop about 1½ cups of the meringue into a pastry bag fitted with a large (number 9) star tip. Hold the bag firmly with both hands, keeping it taut and closed with the top hand. Press out a ring of meringue on the parchment inside each of the traced circles. Divide the remaining meringue and, with the spatula, spread it evenly inside the meringue rings. Press the meringue filling down as you meld it with the rings, making a shallow well.

Bake the meringue layers at 200°F for about 2 to 3 hours, until the centers feel firm and dry when pressed gently. Remove the baking sheet from the oven and use a small sharp knife to loosen the layers from the parchment. These layers can be assembled or stored in an airtight container for several weeks.

FILLING

> ¾ pound dried apricots
> 3 cups water
> 2 tablespoons curaçao (optional)
> 2 cups heavy cream
> ⅔ cup vanilla sugar

In a saucepan cover the apricots with water and bring to a boil over medium heat. Let the mixture boil gently for 10 to 15 minutes, until the apricots have softened and most of the water has been absorbed. Remove the saucepan from the heat and let the apricots cool for a few minutes. Purée the warm apricots in a food mill or blender and blend in the curaçao if desired. Place the purée in a mixing bowl and refrigerate.

In a large chilled bowl with chilled beaters whip the heavy cream. Gradually add the vanilla sugar. Whip only until it will hold soft shapes. Leave about a fourth of the whipped cream in the bowl, and with a spatula quickly fold the rest of it, in five additions, into the chilled apricot purée. Fold using broad strokes. I rather like this filling not so thoroughly blended—so that it has a marbled look. And there are pleasant contrasts in texture and tart and sweet tastes. Reserve about ⅓ cup of this filling and use the spatula to gently spread the remainder of it into the well of one meringue layer. Place the other layer on top. (The apricot filling should not show. If it does, lift the layer away and use the spatula to press the filling down. Replace the top layer.)

Whip the remaining cream a little, until it is stiff. Scoop it into a pastry bag fitted with a medium (number 5 or 6) star tip. Put the reserved apricot filling into another pastry bag with a slightly smaller (number 3 or 4) tip. Garnish the top of the dacquoise with rosettes. Hold the bag filled with whipped cream firmly with both hands, keeping it taut and closed with the top hand. Press rosettes, each about 1½-inches in diameter and about an inch apart, just inside the well. Keep the bag close to the surface as you begin to force the cream out; then pull it straight up for a neat finish. Press out smaller apricot rosettes (you'll have to use a little more force to shape these) in the 1-inch spaces between the whipped cream rosettes. Chill the dacquoise for at least 30 minutes. It slices best with a serrated knife.

Yield: about 8 servings

Orange Angel Cake

Angel food cakes were my favorite dessert when I was a child. I eschewed fancy layer cakes, requesting angel food for most of my birthday parties.

> *1 cup flour*
> *¼ cup sugar*
> *10 egg whites*
> *2 tablespoons fresh orange juice*
> *2 tablespoons orange juice concentrate*
> *1 teaspoon cream of tartar*
> *1 cup sugar*
> *½ teaspoon vanilla extract*
> *Grated rind of 1 orange (about 2 tablespoons)*

Place the oven rack on the lowest rung. Preheat the oven to 325°F.

Sift the flour and ¼ cup sugar together several times. Set the mixture aside. In a very large, grease-free mixing bowl beat the egg whites at a slow steady speed, gradually adding the orange juice and orange juice concentrate. When the mixture is foamy add the cream of tartar. Gradually beat in the cup of sugar and beat for 3–5 minutes, until the meringue will form soft peaks. Beat in the vanilla extract. Use a rubber spatula to fold the flour mixture, 1 tablespoon at a time, into the meringue. Fold in the grated orange rind.

Spread the batter evenly in a grease-free 9-inch tube pan. With a fork puncture the batter around the center at 1-inch intervals to allow any air pockets to escape. Bake the cake at 325°F for 35–40 minutes, until it is golden brown and springs back when touched lightly. Remove the cake from the oven, leave it in the pan, and hang it upside down on the neck of a bottle to cool. After about 30 minutes remove the cake from the pan, using a fork to gently loosen it from the sides and center of the tube. Place the cake on a baking sheet or in a shallow ovenproof dish.

GLAZE

> *¼ cup lemon juice*
> *½ cup confectioners' sugar*
> *2 tablespoons butter*

Preheat the broiler.

In a small saucepan combine the lemon juice and confectioners' sugar. Over high heat add the butter, stirring as it melts. Boil the mixture for about 5 minutes, swirling the pan over the heat occasionally. Remove the saucepan from the heat when the mixture begins to thicken. Drizzle the glaze over the top of the cake. Place the cake under the broiler for 5 minutes, watching that it doesn't burn. If your broiler is too shallow, bake the cake in the oven at 500°F for about 5 minutes. Serve warm or at room temperature.

Yield: about 8 servings

Angel Fruit Cake

Don't expect a traditional dense fruit cake. This one is light and flavorful.

>   8 egg whites
>   1 teaspoon cream of tartar
>   ¾ cup light brown sugar, sifted
>   ½ teaspoon vanilla extract
>   ½ teaspoon black walnut flavor (or maple, almond, rum)
>   1 cup ground walnuts (or almonds)
>   2 cups candied fruit
>   1 cup chopped walnuts (or almonds)

Place the oven rack about a third up from the bottom. Preheat the oven to 325°F.

In a very large, grease-free mixing bowl beat the egg whites at a slow steady speed. When they are foamy add the cream of tartar. Gradually add the sugar and, when it is thoroughly blended, increase to a moderate beating speed and beat for a few minutes until the meringue will form soft peaks. Beat in the vanilla extract and black walnut flavor. With a rubber spatula fold in the ground walnuts, ¼ cup at a time. Use the spatula to fold in the candied fruit and chopped walnuts.

Spoon the batter evenly into a grease-free 9-inch tube pan and bake at 325°F for about an hour and 20 minutes, until the top springs back when touched lightly. Remove the cake from the oven, leave it in the pan, and hang it upside down on the neck of a bottle or large funnel to cool. After about 20 minutes remove the cake from the pan, using a fork to loosen it gently from the sides and center of the tube.

This cake slices best with a serrated knife. If desired, you can pour warm Rum Sauce (page 205) over each slice.

Yield: 8–10 slices

Chocolate Angel Cake

1 cup sugar
½ cup cocoa
¾ cup cake flour
8 egg whites
1 teaspoon cream of tartar
1 ounce any chocolate liqueur or 3 tablespoons chocolate milk

Place the oven rack about a third up from the bottom. Preheat the oven to 325°F.

Sift together the sugar and cocoa. Resift it so that it is thoroughly blended. Sift about a fourth of this mixture with the flour and set both mixtures aside.

In a very large, grease-free mixing bowl beat the egg whites at a slow steady speed. When they are foamy add the cream of tartar. Gradually add the sugar/cocoa mixture and, just when the meringue will form soft peaks, beat in the liqueur (or chocolate milk), ½ teaspoon at a time. Beat the meringue only another minute or so, until it is thoroughly blended. Sprinkle a heaping tablespoon of the flour mixture over the meringue batter and fold it in with a rubber spatula. Continue to sprinkle and fold until all ingredients are thoroughly blended.

Spread the batter evenly in a grease-free 9-inch tube pan. Puncture it with a fork around the center at 1-inch intervals to release any air pockets. Bake the cake at 325°F for about 35 minutes, until the top springs back when touched lightly. Remove the cake from the oven, leave it in the tube pan, and hang it upside down on a funnel or the neck of a bottle to cool. After about 20 minutes remove the cake from the pan, using a fork to gently loosen it from the sides and center of the tube pan.

This cake is moist and flavorful without being rich. If you wish to garnish it, melt about 3 ounces of bittersweet chocolate (coating chocolate is best) and brush a thin coat over the cooled cake. Let it dry before slicing.

Yield: 8–10 servings

Peach Folly

One Fourth of July I returned to Folly Beach, South Carolina, where I was christened, for a weekend of sun and the freshest native-grown food. Our host and master chef requested a dessert that was not too sweet. So while the "pantry help" cleaned the morning catch and shelled butter beans, I dug into our bushel barrel of peaches—glowing, sweet, and ripe from a South Carolina orchard—to present them this dish.

ANGEL CAKE BASE

> 1 cup flour
> ¼ cup sugar
> 8 egg whites
> 1 teaspoon cream of tartar
> ½ cup sugar
> 1 teaspoon vanilla extract

Place the oven rack on the lowest rung. Preheat the oven to 325°F.

Sift the flour and ¼ cup sugar together several times and set aside. In a large, grease-free mixing bowl beat the egg whites at a slow steady speed. When they are foamy add the cream of tartar. Gradually add the ½ cup sugar and increase to a moderate beating speed. Add the vanilla extract. When the meringue will form soft peaks, use a rubber spatula to fold in the flour/sugar mixture, a heaping ⅓ cup at a time. With the spatula spread the batter in a grease-free 8-inch tube pan. Use a fork to puncture the batter around the center at 1½-inch intervals, so that any air pockets will be released. Bake at 325°F for 20–30 minutes, until the top is lightly but evenly golden.

Remove the cake from the oven and hang the pan upside down on the neck of a bottle to cool. After about 15 minutes use a sharp knife to gently loosen the cake from the outer rim of the pan. Leave it on the bottle for another 30 minutes or so. When the cake is cool loosen it from the center rim with the knife and remove it from the pan. Place it upside down on a cutting board and, with a small serrated knife, carefully trim the brown edges from the outside of the cake only.

Leaving about a ¾-inch border on each side, cut a well in the center of the cake: use the serrated knife to cut concentric circles around the top, no more than 1 inch into the cake. Make six to eight cuts across the center section (between the concentric circles only!) and lift out the chunks of cake with a fork. (Freeze these cake pieces or store them airtight for another dessert, page 198.)

ASSEMBLING

> 6 large, ripe sweet peaches
> ½ cup brandy
> 2 cups heavy cream

Peel the peaches. Chop 2 peaches into chunks and place the chunks in a medium bowl with about 2 tablespoons of the brandy. Section the other 4 peaches lengthwise, as uniformly as possible, and pour the remaining brandy over the sections in a shallow dish. Set them aside, with the peach chunks, to marinate for an hour or so.

In a large chilled mixing bowl using chilled beaters, whip the pint of heavy cream. Drain the bowl of peach chunks and fold in about a third of the whipped cream. Fill the well of the cake base with this mixture. Spoon half of the remaining whipped cream over the top of the cake and place the sectioned peaches, overlapping, to cover the cream. Ice the outside and center of the cake with the last of the whipped cream. Chill in the refrigerator until time to serve.

Yield: about 8 servings

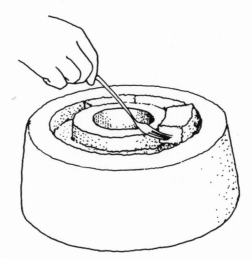

Black Forest Kirsch Torte

There are many versions of this dessert. This one is exceedingly simple to prepare.

9 egg whites
½ cup sugar
1 teaspoon vanilla extract
1½ cups ground blanched almonds
5 ounces bittersweet chocolate
1 tablespoon kirsch
2 cups heavy cream
½ cup sugar
2 tablespoons kirsch
¼ cup bittersweet chocolate shavings

Place the oven rack on the lowest rung. Preheat the oven to 300°F. Line the bottoms of three 9-inch round cake pans with parchment or waxed paper.

In a very large, grease-free mixing bowl beat the egg whites at a slow steady speed. When they begin to stiffen, gradually add the sugar. Add the vanilla extract. Continue to beat until the meringue will form soft peaks. Use a rubber spatula to fold in the ground almonds, about ¼ cup at a time. Divide the batter and use the spatula to spread it evenly in the three prepared pans.

Bake the meringue layers at 300°F for 30–40 minutes, until the centers spring back when touched lightly. Remove the layers from the oven and loosen the sides from the pans with a fork. Invert the pans over a wire rack, lift them away, and peel off the paper. Leave the meringue layers on the rack to cool for 20–30 minutes.

In the top of a double boiler, over hot water, melt the 5 ounces of chocolate. Remove the pan from the heat and use a rubber spatula to stir in the tablespoon of kirsch. Spread this mixture over the sides and tops of the cooled meringue layers. Set them aside to allow the chocolate to dry.

In a chilled bowl with chilled beaters whip the heavy cream. Gradually add the ½ cup sugar while beating and, just as the cream will hold soft shapes, add the 2 tablespoons kirsch, 1 tablespoon at a time. Use a rubber spatula to spread the cream over two of the layers. Stack them and put the plain layer on top. Ice the top and sides of the torte with the remaining cream. Garnish it with the chocolate shavings. Chill the torte in the refrigerator for at least an hour before serving.

Yield: 8–10 servings

Coconut Layer Torte

FILLING

> 3 tablespoons sugar
> 1 tablespoon water
> 1 egg white
> 1/4 teaspoon coconut extract
> 1/2 recipe Basic Custard, made with coconut extract and chilled (page 198)

In a small saucepan combine the sugar and water and bring the mixture to a boil over medium heat. Let it boil for just a few minutes to 234°F (soft-ball stage). Remove the saucepan from the heat. Quickly, beat the egg white in a medium grease-free mixing bowl at a slow steady speed. When it is stiff beat in the boiled sugar mixture, pouring it in a thin stream. Continue to beat for another few minutes until the meringue is thick, glossy, and cool. Chill the meringue in the refrigerator for about 30 minutes.

Using a rubber spatula, fold the chilled custard, about a tablespoon at a time, into the chilled meringue. Fold just until the color is even and the texture is like that of a thick mousse. Chill the filling in the refrigerator while you make the layers.

LAYERS

> 6 egg whites
> 1 cup vanilla sugar
> 1 1/2 teaspoons coconut extract
> 1/3 cup flour
> 1 cup grated or shredded coconut (fresh is best; if you use sweetened coconut, reduce vanilla sugar to 3/4 cup)
> 3 tablespoons sweet butter, melted

Place the rack in the center of the oven. Preheat the oven to 300°F. Line three 7-inch pans with parchment paper.

In a large, grease-free mixing bowl beat the egg whites at a slow steady speed. When they begin to stiffen, gradually add the vanilla sugar. Beat in the coconut extract. Continue to beat for a few more minutes, until the meringue will form soft peaks.

With a large rubber spatula fold in the flour and then the grated coconut, 1 heaping tablespoon at a time. Drizzle in the melted butter in a thin stream while you fold it into the batter. Spread the batter evenly in the prepared pans.

Bake the cake layers at 300°F for about 25 minutes, until the tops spring back when touched lightly in the center. (Test each layer for doneness.) Remove the layers from the oven, invert the pans over a wire rack, and lift them away. Peel the parchment from the layers and leave them on the rack to cool for about 20 minutes.

Spread a thin layer of the chilled filling over two of the cooled layers and stack them. Add the third layer to the top and spoon a thick covering of filling over it. The filling should run down the sides of the torte. Keep the torte in the refrigerator and serve it very cold. Any leftover filling can be spooned over individual slices as you serve them.

Yield: about 6 slices

White Layer Cake

This basic cake is made with meringue in the batter. I suggest baking it in deep pans so that the top stays white. Chocolate Meringue Icing (page 54) makes this a perfect layer cake. You might like to top single sheets or squares of the cake with Chocolate Meringue Mousse (page 46).

> 8 egg whites
> 1/4 teaspoon salt
> 2 cups vanilla sugar
> 2 cups sifted cake flour
> 3/4 teaspoon baking powder
> 1/4 teaspoon cinnamon
> 1 1/2 cups half-and-half
> 3/4 cup vegetable shortening, melted
> 6 tablespoons sweet butter, melted

Place the rack in the center of the oven. Preheat the oven to 325°F. Lightly grease three 9-inch cake pans that are 1 1/2–2 inches deep. Line the bottoms of the pans with waxed paper, grease it, and dust the pans with flour.

In a large, grease-free mixing bowl beat the egg whites at a slow steady speed. When they are foamy add the salt. Gradually beat in the vanilla sugar. Continue to beat for a few minutes until the meringue will form soft peaks. Set this meringue aside.

In another large mixing bowl sift together the cake flour, baking powder, and cinnamon. Stir the half-and-half, about 1/3 cup at a time, into this dry mixture. Spoon the melted vegetable shortening and butter, 1 tablespoon at a time, over the batter and fold it in.

With a large rubber spatula fold the meringue, about 1/2 cup at a time, into the main batter. Fold just until the color and texture are smooth. Divide the batter and pour it into the prepared pans. Bake the layers at 325°F for 30–40 minutes, until the tops spring back when touched lightly in the center. Remove the cake layers from the oven and loosen the sides from the pans with a knife. Invert the pans over a wire rack, lift the pans away, and peel off the waxed paper. Let the layers cool for about 30 minutes before icing them.

Yield: about 10 slices as a layer cake; about 24 slices in single sheets

Roll Cake

3/4 cup sifted flour
1/4 cup sugar
8 egg whites
1/2 teaspoon cream of tartar
1/2 cup sugar
1 teaspoon vanilla extract
2 tablespoons milk

Place the rack in the center of the oven. Preheat the oven to 325°F. Line the bottom of a 9 × 13-inch pan with parchment or wax paper. Lightly grease the paper (but not the sides of the pan). Lightly dust a cotton or linen towel with confectioners' sugar.

Sift together the flour and 1/4 cup sugar. Set the mixture aside. In a large, grease-free mixing bowl beat the egg whites at a slow steady speed. When they are foamy add the cream of tartar. Gradually beat in the 1/2 cup sugar and beat for 3–5 minutes, until the meringue will form soft peaks. Beat in the vanilla extract and then the milk, 1 tablespoon at a time. With a rubber spatula fold the flour mixture into the meringue batter in four additions. Fold just until the mixture is an even consistency.

Using the spatula, spread the batter into the prepared pan. Bake the cake at 325°F for 25–30 minutes. The edges should be brown, and a toothpick inserted into the center will come out easily but not quite clean. Remove the cake from the oven and invert the pan over a wire rack. Let the cake cool for about 10 minutes, then loosen the sides from the pan with a fork and turn the cake onto the prepared towel. Lift the paper around the edges enough to trim around it with a serrated knife. Peel the paper away and roll the cake into the towel. Wrap it snugly and place it on a rack, seam side down, to cool for at least 30 minutes. Carefully unroll it and spread one of the following fillings (or your own favorite) over the cooled cake. Re-roll the cake and place it on a platter, seam side down. Keep it covered with a damp cloth in the refrigerator. Let the cake warm to room temperature and then slice it with a serrated knife to serve.

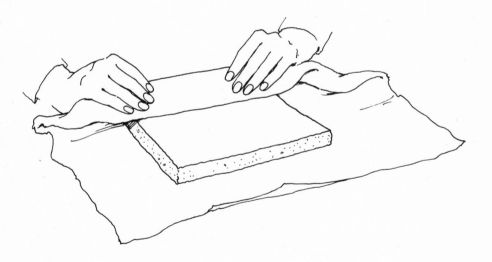

SUGGESTED FILLINGS
1. Whip 4 ounces of cream cheese with an electric mixer until it is smooth and has a light texture. Melt and cool ⅓ cup raspberry, strawberry, or currant jelly. Use a rubber spatula to spread the cream cheese over the cake and then cover it evenly with the cooled jelly. Gently reroll the cake and refrigerate it.

2. In the top of a double boiler over hot water melt 4 ounces of bittersweet chocolate with 2 tablespoons sweet butter. Stir to blend the ingredients and then beat in 2 egg yolks with 2 tablespoons of heavy cream. Stir in 2 tablespoons of confectioners' sugar and leave the mixture over the heat, beating it gently, for a few minutes, just until it is blended. Place the pan on a trivet and let the filling cool for about 10 minutes before spreading it over the cake. Keep this roll cake in the refrigerator but let it warm to room temperature for at least 30 minutes before serving it. The filling becomes quite firm when chilled.

3. In a chilled bowl with chilled beaters whip 1 cup of heavy cream. Gradually whip in 2 tablespoons of Grand Marnier, curaçao, or other liqueur and 2 tablespoons of sugar. Whip the cream just until it is stiff. Fold in ½ cup chopped pecans or slivered almonds. Reroll the cake and keep it in the refrigerator until you are ready to serve it.
     Yield: 6–8 slices (any filling)

Log Cake

Yule Cake and Bûche de Noël are other names for this traditional Christmas dessert. You might like to arrange it on a serving platter with meringue Snowmen (page 28).

> ¾ cup strawberry or raspberry preserves (or jam), melted and
>   cooled to lukewarm
> 1 Roll Cake, unfilled (page 72)
> 2 egg whites
> 3 tablespoons sugar
> ½ teaspoon vanilla extract

Place the oven rack about a third up from the bottom. Preheat the oven to 375°F. Line a baking sheet with foil.

Reserve about 3 tablespoons of the preserves. Unroll the cake and spread the remaining preserves evenly over it. Reroll the cake and place it, seam underneath, on the baking sheet. Spread the reserved preserves over the outside of the cake. Set it aside.

In a medium, grease-free mixing bowl beat the egg whites at a slow steady speed. When they begin to stiffen, gradually add the sugar. Beat in the vanilla extract. Continue to beat for a few minutes until the meringue will form soft peaks. Use a rubber spatula to spread the meringue over the cake. (Do not cover the ends.) Draw a fork through the meringue along the length of the cake to make streaks that will resemble tree bark. Turn up the foil just to cover the ends of the cake so that they don't dry out too much while the cake is in the oven.

Bake the cake at 375°F for 5 to 8 minutes, just until the meringue is browned. Remove the cake from the oven and carefully remove the foil from the ends. Lift the cake onto a serving platter. Serve it warm or at room temperature. This cake should be eaten as soon after baking as possible. It slices best with a serrated knife.

Yield: 6–8 slices

Spice Vacherin

½ teaspoon cinnamon
¼ teaspoon allspice
2 tablespoons sugar
4 egg whites
½ teaspoon cream of tartar
⅓ cup sugar
½ teaspoon vanilla extract
2 cups heavy cream
3 tablespoons sugar
Double recipe Raspberry Sauce, chilled (page 225)
½ recipe (1 9-inch layer) Génoise (page 227; sift ½ teaspoon cinnamon, ¼ teaspoon allspice, and a pinch of ground cloves into the flour)
A few fresh raspberries for garnish

Place the oven rack about a third up from the bottom. Preheat the oven to 225°F. Line a large baking sheet with parchment paper. Trace two 9-inch circles (use the pan in which you baked the génoise as a guide) onto the parchment.

Sift together the cinnamon, allspice, and 2 tablespoons sugar. Reserve this spice mixture.

In a large, grease-free mixing bowl beat the egg whites at a slow steady speed. When they are foamy add the cream of tartar. Gradually add the ⅓ cup sugar and then the reserved spice mixture. When the meringue will form soft peaks, beat in the vanilla extract and increase to a moderate beating speed. Beat for another 5 to 8 minutes, until the meringue is thick, glossy, and forms firm peaks when the beaters are lifted.

Glue the parchment paper to the baking sheet with a few pinches of meringue. Use a rubber spatula to scoop about 2 cups of the meringue into a pastry bag fitted with a medium (number 5 or 6) tip. Hold the bag firmly with both hands, keeping it taut and closed with the top hand. With the tip just over the parchment, press out a ring of meringue just inside each of the traced circles. With the spatula spread the remaining meringue inside each of the meringue rings, making smooth even layers.

Bake the meringue at 225°F for 1 to 2 hours, until it feels firm and dry when pressed lightly in the center. Remove the baking sheet from the oven and peel the parchment away from the meringue as soon as it is cool enough to handle.

In a large chilled bowl with chilled beaters whip the heavy cream, gradually adding 3 tablespoons sugar, until it is stiff. Pour a very thin layer of raspberry sauce over one of the meringue layers and then spread whipped cream over it. Add the génoise layer on top and pour a little raspberry sauce over it. (It's fine if the raspberry sauce runs down the sides of the vacherin.) Spread whipped cream over the génoise and stack the second meringue layer over it. Ice the sides and top of the vacherin with the remaining whipped cream. Add the fresh raspberry garnish in the center. Chill the vacherin in the refrigerator for at least 30 minutes. It should be served as soon as possible after assembling. Use a large serrated knife to slice it. Pass around the remaining raspberry sauce to pour over each serving.

Yield: about 8 servings

Individual Vacherins

MERINGUE LAYERS

> *4 egg whites*
> *½ teaspoon cream of tartar*
> *½ cup sugar*
> *1 teaspoon vanilla extract*

Place the oven rack about a third up from the bottom. Preheat the oven to 200°F. Line a large baking sheet with parchment paper. Trace twelve circles, each 3 inches in diameter, onto the paper.

In a large, grease-free mixing bowl beat the egg whites at a slow steady speed. When they are foamy add the cream of tartar. Gradually beat in the sugar and, when the meringue will form soft peaks, add the vanilla extract and increase to a moderate beating speed. Beat for another 5–8 minutes, until the meringue is thick, glossy, and forms firm peaks when the beaters are lifted.

Glue the parchment paper to the baking sheet with a few pinches of meringue. Use a rubber spatula to scoop about three-quarters of the meringue into a pastry bag fitted with a medium (number 5 or 6) plain tip. Hold the bag firmly with both hands, keeping it taut and closed with the top hand. Press out a ring of meringue just inside one of the traced circles. Do not break the meringue but fill in the circle by continuing to press out meringue rings. Repeat this process to fill in all twelve traced circles. If necessary use a rubber spatula to smooth the surfaces of these meringue layers.

Scoop the remaining meringue into a pastry bag fitted with a small or medium (number 3 or 5) star tip. Hold the bag firmly with both hands and press out a rosette in the centers of six of the meringue layers. Press out smaller rosettes, at ¾-inch intervals, around each of these layers. Bake the meringue layers at 200°F for about an hour, until they feel dry and firm when squeezed gently. The layers trimmed with rosettes may require another 20–30 minutes of baking. Just use a small sharp knife to remove the plain layers from the parchment and return the baking sheet to the oven, still at 200°F. When all the layers are done they can be assembled right away or stored in an airtight container for several weeks.

ASSEMBLING

> 1 recipe Kirsch Butter Cream (page 208)
> ½ recipe Génoise (page 227), baked in a 9-inch pan and cut into 6 circles, each 3 inches in diameter (I suggest using a jar lid as a guide, and a serrated knife cuts best.)
> About 1 cup confectioners' sugar
> About ⅓ cup maraschino cherry halves

Spread the plain meringue layers and the génoise with butter cream. Stack them, meringue on the bottom, and top each with a decorated meringue layer. Ice the sides of each vacherin with butter cream and dust with a coat of confectioners' sugar. Use a pinch of butter cream to secure cherry halves between the smaller rosettes. Chill in the refrigerator for at least 30 minutes.

VARIATION
Substitute about ½ cup walnut halves for the cherries and use Rum Butter Cream or Praline Butter Cream (page 208).
Yield: 6 vacherins

Butter Cream Layer Cake

Here is my version of a meringue band cake I first tasted at a restaurant in Los Angeles. It was just about the most wonderful dessert I had ever enjoyed, and that restaurant became a regular stop on my way home from ballet class. I still think this cake to be quite special—heavenly, light, full of rich flavors—and certainly worth all the time and care required to produce it.

MERINGUE LAYERS

¾ cup ground hazelnuts
¾ cup ground almonds
1¼ cups sugar
8 egg whites

Place the oven rack about a third up from the bottom. Preheat the oven to 250°F. Line a 12 × 16-inch pan with parchment paper.

Combine the ground hazelnuts, almonds, and sugar and set the mixture aside. In a large, grease-free mixing bowl beat the egg whites at a slow steady speed. Gradually add the nut mixture and, when the meringue will form soft peaks, increase to a moderate beating speed. Beat for another 8–10 minutes, until the meringue is thick and forms firm peaks when the beaters are lifted.

Secure the parchment paper to the pan with a few pinches of meringue. With a rubber spatula spread the mixture evenly into the prepared pan. Bake at 250°F for 45–50 minutes, until it feels dry when touched lightly in the center. Remove the pan from the oven and let it cool for a few minutes. Use a very sharp knife to cut the meringue into four pieces, each measuring 4 × 12 inches. Peel off the paper and put the layers aside in a cool, dry place. They can be stored in an airtight container for several weeks.

ASSEMBLING

> 1½ recipe Vanilla Butter Cream (page 206)
> ½ recipe Praline Butter Cream (page 208)
> 1 recipe Chocolate Butter Cream (page 207)
> ⅓ cup blanched ground almonds
> About 1 cup confectioners' sugar

Ice three of the meringue layers, each with a different butter cream, reserving half of the chocolate butter cream. Stack the iced layers and put the plain layer on top. Ice the sides of the cake with the reserved chocolate butter cream and garnish the sides and top with the ground almonds and a dusting of confectioners' sugar. Keep the cake in the refrigerator. When serving, it will slice best with a serrated knife.

Yield: about 8 servings

Almond Vacherin

This dessert is light, elegant, and a delight to make. It is one of my favorites for small dinner parties. The meringue layers can be made as much as several weeks ahead, so there's not much to do at the last minute.

MERINGUE LAYERS

> *4 egg whites*
> *½ teaspoon cream of tartar*
> *⅓ cup sugar*
> *1 teaspoon almond extract*

Place the oven rack about a third up from the bottom. Preheat the oven to 200°F. Line a very large baking sheet (or two smaller sheets) with parchment paper. Trace three 8-inch circles onto the parchment.

In a large, grease-free mixing bowl beat the egg whites at a slow steady speed. When they are foamy beat in the cream of tartar. Gradually beat in the sugar and, when the meringue will form soft peaks, add the almond extract and increase to a moderate beating speed. Beat for another 5 to 8 minutes, until the meringue is thick, glossy, and forms firm peaks when the beaters are lifted.

Glue the parchment paper to the baking sheet with a few pinches of meringue. Use a rubber spatula to spread the meringue evenly onto the parchment inside the traced circles, making uniform layers about ½ inch thick. Bake the layers at 200°F for about 2 hours, until the meringue feels dry and firm when pressed gently. The meringue should not color at all while it's drying in the oven. Watch carefully or leave the oven door ajar to be sure of a low enough temperature.

Remove the meringue layers from the oven and loosen them from the parchment paper using a small sharp knife. The vacherin can be assembled now, or store the meringue layers between waxed paper in an airtight container for up to three weeks.

ASSEMBLING

> *2 cups sliced strawberries (or cherries or peaches)*
> *1 cup sliced almonds*
> *2 cups heavy cream, whipped*

Reserve the most attractive pieces of fruit (about ½ cup), ⅓ cup of almonds, and about half of the whipped cream for garnishing. Fold the remaining fruit and almonds into the other half of the whipped cream. With a rubber spatula spread this mixture on two of the meringue layers and stack them. Place the uniced layer on top. Use the spatula to ice the top and sides of the cake with the reserved whipped cream. Arrange the reserved fruit in a concentric circle on top of the cake and sprinkle the almonds over the top and sides. Chill the vacherin in the refrigerator for about an hour and serve it cool.

Yield: about 6 servings

Grand Marnier Tiers

5 egg whites
½ teaspoon cream of tartar
½ cup vanilla sugar
½ cup blanched whole almonds
¼ cup maraschino cherries
1 medium-size ripe peach, peeled and sliced thinly
1 cup heavy cream, whipped
1 recipe Grand Marnier Sauce (page 206)

Place the oven rack about a third up from the bottom. Preheat the oven to 200°F. Line two baking sheets with parchment paper. Trace five circles—one 5-inch, two 6½-inch, one 8-inch, and one 9½-inch—onto the parchment.

In a large, grease-free bowl beat the egg whites at a slow steady speed. When they are foamy add the cream of tartar. Gradually add the vanilla sugar and, when the meringue will form soft peaks, increase to a moderate beating speed. Beat for another 5 to 8 minutes, until the meringue is thick, glossy, and forms firm peaks when the beaters are lifted.

Glue the parchment paper to the baking sheets with a few pinches of meringue. Use a rubber spatula to scoop the meringue into a pastry bag fitted with a medium (number 5 or 6) star tip. Hold the bag firmly with both hands, keeping it taut and closed with the top hand. With the tip just over the parchment, press out a scallop outline inside the two largest traced circles and one of the 6½-inch circles, three scallop outlines in all. (I find it quite easy to make these scallops free-form. If you prefer, trace the scallops onto the parchment before making them in meringue.) Press out rings of meringue inside the two remaining circles.

Fill in the scallop designs and the rings by spreading meringue with the spatula. Meld it carefully so that the grooves in the outline remain. Use the spatula to pull up meringue peaks and make swirls on the three scalloped tiers. Their surfaces should be quite rough and piled a little higher in the center. The two meringue circles, however, should be as smooth and even as possible. (Save any left-over meringue; you'll need it later for assembling.)

Bake the meringue pieces at 200°F for about 2 hours, until they feel firm and dry when pressed gently in the center. The smaller pieces may be dry in less than an hour and should be removed from the oven as soon as they are done. Just loosen them from the parchment with a small sharp knife and return the baking sheet to the oven. Watch carefully that the meringue stays white. If it starts to color, or you're not sure of your oven, leave the door ajar. When all the meringue pieces are done you can assemble the torte or store the meringue in an airtight container for several weeks.

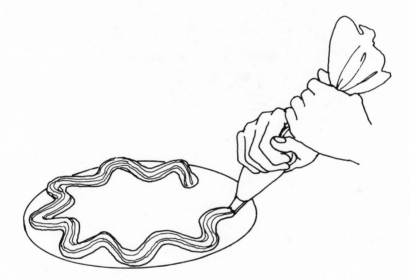

Place the largest scalloped layer on a serving platter. Place the larger plain circle on top, then the second scalloped tier, the smaller circle, and the smallest scalloped tier. Secure the pieces together with pinches of unbaked leftover meringue. (This assembled meringue can also be stored airtight for several weeks.)

Arrange the almonds, cherries, and peach slices on the two lower tiers, tucked into the gap between layers as much as possible. Pile the whipped cream onto the top tier and let a little of it spill onto the other tiers. At this point you can refrigerate the torte for an hour or so. Just before serving pour about a cup of the Grand Marnier sauce over the top of the torte.

Cut the meringue with a pie server or serrated knife and spoon individual servings into shallow bowls. Add a little more sauce to each serving.

Yield: 12–15 servings

Banana Torte

MERINGUE LAYERS

> 3 egg whites
> 1/4 teaspoon cream of tartar
> 6 tablespoons light brown sugar
> 1/2 teaspoon vanilla extract
> 1/2 cup graham cracker crumbs
> 1/2 cup chopped walnuts

Place the oven rack about a third up from the bottom. Preheat the oven to 200°F. Line a 9 × 13-inch pan or baking sheet with parchment paper.

In a large, grease-free mixing bowl beat the egg whites at a slow steady speed. When they are foamy add the cream of tartar. Gradually add the sugar and, when the meringue will form soft peaks, add the vanilla extract and increase to a moderate beating speed. Beat for another 5 to 8 minutes, until the meringue is thick, glossy, and forms firm peaks when the beaters are lifted. Glue the parchment paper to the pan with a few pinches of meringue. With a rubber spatula fold in the graham cracker crumbs and chopped walnuts. Use the spatula to spread the meringue evenly in the prepared pan.

Bake at 200°F for about 1 hour and 15 minutes, until the meringue feels dry and firm when pressed lightly. Remove from the oven and use a very sharp knife to slice it into three pieces of equal size. As soon as the slices are cool enough to handle, peel away the paper. These meringue layers will keep, stored in an airtight container, for a week or two.

FILLING

> 3 egg yolks, lightly beaten
> 3 tablespoons sugar
> ¼ cup milk
> ½ teaspoon vanilla extract
> ⅓ cup heavy cream
> 1–2 tablespoons liqueur, such as curaçao, Grand Marnier, or
>   Amaretto (optional)
> 2 or 3 bananas

In the top of a double boiler or heavy saucepan over low heat combine the egg yolks with the sugar. Blend in the milk and continue to cook, stirring gently for about 15 minutes, until the custard begins to coat the spoon and sides of the pan. Add the vanilla extract and remove from the heat. Let the custard cool for about 10 minutes, then transfer it to a small bowl and put it in the refrigerator to chill for at least 30 minutes.

In a chilled mixing bowl with chilled beaters whip the heavy cream. When it will hold a soft shape add the liqueur if desired. Fold the chilled custard into the whipped cream in three additions. Slice the bananas into pieces ½-inch thick and place them in rows on two of the meringue layers. Spoon the filling over these layers, stack one on top of the other, and place the plain layer on top. Keep the torte in the refrigerator until time to serve.

Yield: about 6 slices

Lemon Meringue Vacherin

MERINGUE LAYERS

> 4 egg whites
> ½ teaspoon cream of tartar
> ⅓ cup sugar
> ½ teaspoon lemon extract
> 2 tablespoons grated lemon rind

Place the oven rack about a third up from the bottom. Preheat the oven to 200°F. Line a large baking sheet with parchment paper. Trace two 9-inch circles onto the paper.

In a large, grease-free mixing bowl beat the egg whites at a slow steady speed. When they are foamy add the cream of tartar. Gradually add the sugar and, when the meringue will form soft peaks, add the lemon extract and increase to a moderate beating speed. Beat for another 5 to 8 minutes, until the meringue is thick, glossy, and forms firm peaks when the beaters are lifted. With a rubber spatula, fold in the grated lemon rind.

Use the rubber spatula to scoop the meringue into a pastry bag fitted with a medium (number 5 or 6) tip. Hold the bag firmly with both hands, keeping it taut and closed with the top hand. Press out a ring of meringue on the parchment paper just inside each of the traced circles. Fill in the circles by continuing to press out meringue—use a rubber spatula as necessary to spread it smoothly. Bake the meringue layers at 200°F for 2 to 3 hours, until they feel firm and dry when pressed gently in the center. Remove them from the oven and, as soon as they are cool enough to handle, peel away the paper. These meringue layers are ready for assembling or can be stored airtight for several weeks.

ASSEMBLING

> 1 recipe Lemon Butter Cream (page 207)
> ½ recipe Lemon Meringue Mousse (page 47)

Spread one of the meringue layers with the butter cream. Stack the other layer on top of it. Use a rubber spatula to cover the entire vacherin with the mousse, piling it quite high on top. Chill the vacherin for at least 30 minutes before serving. It should be served as soon as possible.

Yield: 6–8 servings

Pecan Vacherin

5 egg whites
½ teaspoon cream of tartar
⅔ cup vanilla sugar
About ½ cup pecan halves
½ cup chopped pecans

Place the oven rack about a third up from the bottom. Preheat the oven to 200°F. Line two large baking sheets with parchment paper and trace three 9-inch circles onto the parchment.

In a large, grease-free mixing bowl beat the egg whites at a slow steady speed. When they are foamy add the cream of tartar. Gradually add the sugar and, when the meringue will form soft peaks, increase to a moderate beating speed. Beat for another 5–8 minutes, until the meringue is thick, glossy, and forms firm peaks when the beaters are lifted.

Glue the parchment paper to the baking sheets with a few pinches of meringue. Use a rubber spatula to scoop about 2 cups of the meringue into a pastry bag fitted with a medium (number 5 or 6) star tip. Hold the bag firmly with both hands, keeping it taut and closed with the top hand. Press out a circle of meringue inside each of the three traced circles on the parchment.

With a rubber spatula spread about a third of the remaining meringue inside one of the circles. Mold carefully so that the grooved edges remain. Take up the pastry bag again and press out a second circle of meringue directly on top of the first. Place a ring of pecan halves just inside this meringue border. Press out another ring of meringue below the pecans. Add a second ring of pecan halves. Finish with a third ring of meringue.

Fold the chopped pecans into the remaining meringue and use the spatula to spread it inside the other two meringue circles. Again, meld carefully so that the grooved edges remain.

Bake the meringue layers at 200°F for about 1½–2 hours, until they feel firm and dry when squeezed gently. The layer garnished with pecan halves may need an extra 30 minutes of baking. Remove the layers from the oven and loosen them from the parchment with a small sharp knife. You can assemble the vacherin now or store the meringue layers in an airtight container for several weeks.

ASSEMBLING

> 1 recipe Rum Butter Cream (page 208)
> 1 small peach, peeled and sliced very thinly (optional)

Spread the butter cream over the two plain meringue layers, inside the grooved edges. If desired, add one layer of peach slices to each. Stack these layers and put the garnished meringue layer on top. Refrigerate the vacherin for about an hour, until the butter cream is firm. To serve, it slices best with a serrated knife.

Yield: 6–8 servings

Chocolate Chip Vacherin

4 egg whites
½ teaspoon cream of tartar
⅓ cup vanilla sugar
⅓ cup semisweet chocolate shavings (or miniature chips)
1 recipe Chocolate Meringue Icing (page 54)

Place the oven rack about a third up from the bottom. Preheat the oven to 200°F. Line a large baking sheet with baking parchment. Trace two 9-inch circles onto the parchment.

In a large, grease-free mixing bowl beat the egg whites at a slow steady speed. When they are foamy add the cream of tartar. Gradually add the vanilla sugar and, when the meringue will form soft peaks, increase to a moderate beating speed. Beat for another 5 to 8 minutes, until the meringue is thick, glossy, and forms firm peaks when the beaters are lifted.

Glue the parchment paper to the baking sheets with a few pinches of meringue. Reserve about 2 tablespoons of the chocolate shavings (or chips). With a rubber spatula fold the remaining chocolate into the meringue.

Use the spatula to spread the meringue onto the parchment inside the traced circles. Make the layers as thick as possible and keep them smooth and even. Bake the meringue at 200°F for about 3 hours, until it feels firms and dry when pressed lightly in the center. Remove the baking sheet from the oven and peel the parchment away from the meringue layers.

Spread one of the layers generously with the meringue icing. Put the uniced layer on top. Ice the sides and top of the vacherin with the remaining icing. Garnish it with the reserved chocolate shavings.

Chill the vacherin in the refrigerator for at least 30 minutes and serve it cold. It slices best with a serrated knife.

Yield: about 8 slices

Chocolate Vacherin

MERINGUE LAYERS

> ½ cup sugar
> ¼ cup cocoa
> 6 egg whites
> ½ teaspoon cream of tartar
> ¾ cup chopped walnuts (optional)

Place the oven rack about a third up from the bottom. Preheat the oven to 250°F. Line two large baking sheets with parchment paper and trace three 9-inch circles onto the parchment.

Sift together the sugar and cocoa several times and set the mixture aside. In a large, grease-free mixing bowl beat the egg whites at a slow steady speed. When they are foamy add the cream of tartar. Gradually add the sugar/cocoa mixture and, when the meringue will form soft peaks, increase to a moderate beating speed. Continue to beat for another 5–8 minutes, until the meringue is thick, glossy, and forms firm peaks when the beaters are lifted. If you are using the walnuts, use a rubber spatula to fold them in.

Glue the parchment paper to the baking sheets with a few pinches of meringue. Divide the meringue into three equal parts and, with the spatula, spread each inside the traced circles on the parchment paper. Smooth away any ragged edges or unevenness so that the layers are as uniform as possible.

Bake the meringue layers at 250°F for about an hour, until they feel firm and dry when pressed gently in the centers. Remove them from the oven and lift the parchment paper from the baking sheets onto a wire rack. After a few minutes, when the meringue layers are cool enough to handle, peel the paper away. Use a small sharp knife to loosen the meringue if necessary. These layers can be stored in an airtight container for several weeks.

ICING

> ½ cup bittersweet chocolate, broken into pieces
> ½ cup preserves (strawberry, raspberry, or apricot)

Melt the chocolate in the top of a double boiler. Add the preserves and stir with a rubber spatula. When the icing is blended, remove from the heat and set it aside to cool to lukewarm. Spread the icing over two of the meringue layers. Put them in a cool, dry place and let the icing harden.

CHOCOLATE CREAM

> 1¼ cups heavy cream
> ¼ cup bittersweet chocolate, melted and cooled

In a large chilled mixing bowl with chilled beaters, whip the cream until it holds a soft shape. Whip in the chocolate, 1 table-spoon at a time. Spread a thin layer of the chocolate cream on the two iced meringue layers. Stack them and then put the plain layer on top. Cover the top and sides of the vacherin with the remaining chocolate cream. Chill the vacherin in the refrigerator for at least 30 minutes before serving.

Yield: 6–8 servings

Chocolate Fudge Torte

MERINGUE LAYERS

> ½ cup sugar
> ⅓ cup cocoa
> 5 egg whites
> ½ teaspoon cream of tartar

Place the oven rack about a third up from the bottom. Preheat the oven to 250°F. Line a large baking sheet with parchment or brown paper. Trace three 7-inch circles onto the paper.

Sift the sugar and cocoa together several times and set the mixture aside. In a large, grease-free mixing bowl beat the egg whites at a slow steady speed. When they are foamy add the cream of tartar. Gradually beat in the sugar/cocoa mixture and, when the meringue will form soft peaks, increase to a moderate beating speed. Beat for another 5–8 minutes, until the meringue is thick, glossy, and forms firm peaks when the beaters are lifted.

Use a rubber spatula to scoop the meringue into a pastry bag fitted with a medium (number 5 or 6) plain tip. Hold the bag firmly with both hands, keeping it taut and closed with the top hand. Press out a border of meringue about ¼ inch inside each of the traced circles. Press out meringue to fill in the circles, and use a rubber spatula as necessary to spread it smoothly.

Bake at 250°F for about an hour, until the meringue feels firm and dry when pressed gently in the center. Remove from the oven and, when it is cool enough to handle, peel away the paper. Use a small sharp knife to loosen the meringue if necessary. Set the meringue layers aside in a cool, dry place. They may be stored airtight for several weeks.

TORTE LAYERS

> 4 tablespoons butter
> 2 ounces bittersweet chocolate
> 1 ounce unsweetened chocolate
> ½ cup sugar
> 5 egg yolks, lightly beaten
> 1 cup ground walnuts
> ¼ teaspoon baking soda
> ¼ teaspoon baking powder
> ¼ cup buttermilk
> ¼ teaspoon vanilla extract

Reset the oven to 325°F. Lightly grease a 7-inch round cake pan that is 2 inches deep. Line the bottom with wax paper, grease it, and dust the pan lightly with flour.

In a small saucepan (or in the top of a double boiler) over very low heat, melt the butter and both chocolates. Stir a little to blend and set the mixture aside. In a large mixing bowl beat the sugar into the egg yolks. When thoroughly blended, add the melted ingredients. Combine the ground walnuts, baking soda, and baking powder. Stir in half of this dry mixture, then add the buttermilk. Stir in the remaining dry mixture, beat just until blended, and add the vanilla extract. Pour the batter into the prepared pan.

Bake the torte at 325°F for 30–45 minutes, until a toothpick inserted in the center comes out clean. Remove it from the oven, and loosen the side with a fork or small knife. Let it cool for about 10 minutes on a rack, then remove the torte from the pan, peel the paper away, and put the torte back on the rack to cool completely. When the torte has reached room temperature, split it into two layers, using a large serrated knife. Wrap the layers in foil or plastic to keep them moist.

FUDGE ICING

> 1 cup sugar
> 1½ tablespoons light corn syrup
> ½ cup milk
> 2 ounces unsweetened chocolate
> 4 tablespoons butter, cut into 8–10 pieces
> 1 teaspoon vanilla extract

In a small saucepan over medium heat, combine the sugar, corn syrup, milk, and chocolate. Stir until blended, then let the mixture boil gently to 234°F (soft-ball stage). Add the pieces of butter and remove saucepan from the heat. When the butter has melted, add the vanilla extract and beat the mixture with a large wooden spoon. Beat until the fudge is smooth and cool.

ASSEMBLING

Put about ½ cup of the fudge icing into a pastry bag fitted with a very small (number 0) plain tip. Hold the bag firmly with both hands, keeping it taut and closed with the top hand. Pipe out a looping circle on top of one of the meringue layers. Control the thickness of the icing by pulling the bag along rather quickly. (You will not need this much icing for the loop trim, but it's easier to control with a fuller bag.) Use a knife to spread the remaining icing, including that in the pastry bag, in equal amounts over the other meringue layers and the torte layers. Stack the iced layers alternately, beginning with a meringue and ending with the decorated layer. Keep the torte in a cool place. Cover the sides (not the top!) securely with plastic wrap until you serve it.

Yield: 6–8 servings

Black and White Layers

This cake is visually stunning and will serve a large group.

MERINGUE LAYERS

> 5 egg whites
> ½ teaspoon cream of tartar
> ⅔ cup vanilla sugar

Place the oven rack about a third up from the bottom. Preheat the oven to 200°F. Line two large baking sheets with parchment paper. Trace three 9-inch circles onto the paper.

In a large, grease-free mixing bowl beat the egg whites at a slow steady speed. When they are foamy add the cream of tartar. Gradually add the sugar and, when the meringue will form soft peaks, increase to a moderate beating speed. Beat for another 5 to 8 minutes, until the meringue is thick, glossy, and forms firm peaks when the beaters are lifted.

Glue the parchment paper to the baking sheets with a few pinches of meringue. Use a rubber spatula to put about a third of the meringue into a pastry bag fitted with a medium (number 5 or 6) tip. Hold the bag firmly with both hands, keeping it taut and closed with the top hand. Press out a ring of meringue on the parchment paper just inside each of the traced circles. Fill in the circles with remaining meringue, spreading it smoothly with a rubber spatula. Bake the meringue layers at 200°F for about an hour and a half, until they feel firm and dry when squeezed gently. (Watch carefully that the meringue does not color even faintly. Leave the oven door open if necessary.) Remove from the oven and carefully peel the parchment away.

ASSEMBLING

> 4 ounces bittersweet chocolate (coating chocolate is best), melted
> 1 recipe Rich Chocolate Layers (page 213) baked in three
>   9-inch round pans
> 1 cup sugar
> ⅔ cup cocoa
> 5 egg yolks, lightly beaten
> 1¼ cups milk
> 1 teaspoon vanilla extract

Spread a thin coat of the bittersweet chocolate over the tops and sides of the chocolate layers. Set them aside to dry.

Sift together the sugar and cocoa. In a saucepan over very low heat or in the top of a double boiler gradually combine the dry ingredients with the beaten egg yolks. When the mixture is thoroughly blended and warm, stir in the milk. The sauce will begin to thicken to the texture of a light custard after about 15 minutes. Stir in the vanilla extract and remove the pan from the heat.

Stack the six layers alternately, beginning with chocolate, and spoon about ¼ cup of the warm chocolate sauce over each meringue layer. Let the sauce run down the sides of the cake. Put the remaining sauce into a dish and pour it over individual slices as you serve them.

Yield: 12–15 servings

Ice Cream Cake

This festive cake is simple to put together, especially if you prepare the meringue layers well ahead of time.

>8 egg whites
>1 teaspoon cream of tartar
>¾ cup confectioners' sugar
>1 teaspoon vanilla extract
>½ cup ground hazelnuts
>¼ cup graham cracker or vanilla wafer crumbs
>¼ cup ground walnuts (or pecans)
>3 pints ice cream, softened (I like to use three different flavors—
>   usually vanilla, chocolate, and banana)
>2–3 tablespoons sliced almonds for garnish
>½ recipe Chocolate Sauce (page 204) or other dessert sauce
>about ½ cup heavy cream, whipped for garnish

Place the oven rack(s) in the lower third of the oven. Preheat the oven to 200°F. Line two baking sheets with parchment paper. Trace two 9-inch circles onto each piece of parchment (total four circles).

In a very large, grease-free mixing bowl beat the egg whites at a slow steady speed. When they are foamy add the cream of tartar. Gradually add the confectioners' sugar and, when the meringue will form soft peaks, add the vanilla extract and increase to a moderate beating speed. Beat for another 5 to 8 minutes, until the meringue is thick, glossy, and forms firm peaks when the beaters are lifted.

Glue the parchment paper to the baking sheets with a few pinches of meringue. Divide the meringue in half. Reserve one of the halves and, with a rubber spatula, fold the ground hazelnuts into the remaining meringue. Scoop about a cup of this hazelnut meringue into a pastry bag fitted with a medium-small (number 3 or 4) plain tip. Hold the bag firmly with both hands, keeping it taut and closed with the top hand. With the tip just over the parchment, press out rings of meringue on one baking sheet just inside the two traced circles. Use the rubber spatula to spread the remaining hazelnut meringue inside the outlined circles. Put this sheet of meringue layers into the oven at 200°F while you make the other layers.

Divide the reserved meringue into two equal parts. Again, with a spatula, fold the cracker (or wafer) crumbs into one part. Scoop about a cup of this meringue into the pastry bag. (No need to clean the bag, just discard any leftover hazelnut meringue.) Press out a ring of meringue inside one of the traced circles on the remaining baking sheet. With the spatula spread all the cracker crumb meringue inside the outline.

Fold the ground walnuts (or pecans) into the last of the meringue. Discard any leftover crumb meringue in the pastry bag and scoop about a cup of the walnut meringue into the bag. Press out a circle of meringue just inside the fourth traced circle and spread all the walnut meringue inside the outline.

Put this baking sheet into the oven and bake the meringue layers at 200°F for 1 to 2 hours, until they feel dry and firm when pressed gently in the center. (Test each layer for doneness.) Remove the baking sheets from the oven and, as soon as they are cool enough to handle, peel the parchment from the layers. (These meringue layers can be stored in an airtight container for several weeks.)

Reserve one hazelnut layer. Spread one pint of the softened ice cream over each of the three other layers and stack them, hazelnut layer on the bottom. Place the reserved hazelnut layer on top. Put the cake in the freezer for at least an hour, or until the ice cream is firm.

When you are ready to serve it, remove the cake from the freezer and place it on a serving platter. Drizzle chocolate sauce over the top and let it run down the sides. Scoop the whipped cream onto the center and sprinkle the sliced almonds over the cake. This cake should be eaten at once. It slices best with a large serrated knife.

Yield: about 8 servings

Neapolitan Surprise

4 egg whites
1/2 teaspoon cream of tartar
1/2 cup vanilla sugar
1 tablespoon cocoa
3 tablespoons sugar
2 egg whites
1/4 teaspoon cream of tartar

Place the oven rack about a third up from the bottom. Preheat the oven to 200°F. Line two small baking sheets with parchment paper. Trace a 9-inch circle onto each piece of parchment.

In a large, grease-free mixing bowl beat the 4 egg whites at a slow steady speed. When they are foamy add the cream of tartar. Gradually add the vanilla sugar and, when the meringue will form soft peaks, increase to a moderate beating speed. Continue to beat for 5 to 8 minutes, until the meringue is thick, glossy, and forms firm peaks when the beaters are lifted.

Glue the parchment paper to one of the baking sheets with a few pinches of meringue. Use a rubber spatula to scoop the meringue into a pastry bag fitted with a medium-large (I like number 7A) star tip. Hold the bag firmly with both hands, keeping it taut and closed with the top hand. With the tip just over the parchment, press out a ring of meringue just inside the traced circle. Continue to press out the meringue in rings to fill in the circle. Use the spatula to gently meld any rings together if necessary. Press out a ring of meringue directly over the second ring from the outside. Do not break the meringue but press out two more rings of meringue directly above the first one, building a shallow wall. You should have at least 1 cup

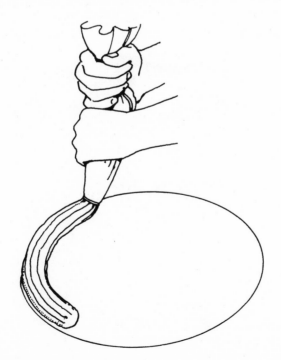

of vanilla meringue left over; leave it in the pastry bag. Put this meringue case into the oven at 200°F to begin baking while you make the meringue top.

Sift together the cocoa and sugar. In a medium, grease-free mixing bowl beat the 2 egg whites at a slow steady speed. When they are foamy add the cream of tartar. Gradually add the cocoa/sugar mixture and, when the meringue will form soft peaks, increase to a moderate beating speed. Continue to beat until the meringue is thick, glossy, and forms firm peaks when the beaters are lifted.

Glue the parchment paper to the second baking sheet with a few pinches of meringue. Use a rubber spatula to scoop the cocoa meringue into a pastry bag fitted with a medium-large star tip (number 7 or 8—I prefer one slightly larger than the tip used for the meringue case). With the tip just over the parchment press out a ring of meringue just inside the traced circle. Set the bag of cocoa meringue aside and take up the other pastry bag. Right next to the cocoa ring press out a ring of vanilla meringue. Break the meringue neatly and fill in the circle with cocoa meringue rings, pressing them out so that they are melded. Again take up the bag of vanilla meringue and, with the tip directly over the center of the cocoa layer, press out a large rosette. If you have any remaining vanilla meringue, garnish the layer with a zigzag or scallop around the edge.

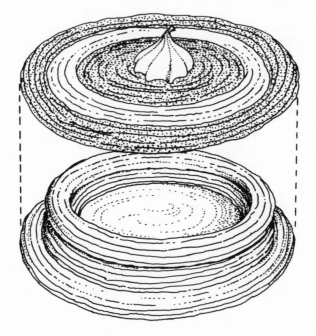

Place the cocoa top in the oven at 200°F. After about an hour the cocoa top should be done. Press it gently to check that it is firm and dry. Leave the vanilla case in for another hour or two. Test it for doneness by gently squeezing or pressing. As each piece is done, remove the baking sheets from the oven and peel away the parchment. These meringue pieces can be stored for several weeks in an airtight container.

ASSEMBLING

> 1½ cups sliced fresh strawberries, chilled (If strawberries are not in season, omit the heavy cream below and use 1 quart strawberry ice cream, softened)
> 1 cup heavy cream, whipped
> 1 recipe Chocolate Sauce, warm (page 204)

Fold the strawberries into the whipped cream and spoon the mixture (or the softened ice cream) into the vanilla meringue case. (If you are using ice cream, put the filled case in the freezer for about an hour.) Place the cocoa meringue piece on top when you are ready to serve. Slice the Neapolitan Surprise with a serrated knife and pass the chocolate sauce to spoon over each serving.

Yield: about 6 servings

Cinnamon-Rum Torte

CAKE BASE

> ½ cup sweet butter
> ½ cup sugar
> 4 egg yolks, lightly beaten
> 1 cup flour
> 1 teaspoon baking powder
> ¼ teaspoon salt
> ½ cup milk
> 1 teaspoon vanilla extract

Place the oven rack about a third up from the bottom. Preheat the oven to 350°F. Lightly grease and flour a 9 × 13-inch pan.

In a large mixing bowl cream the butter, gradually adding the sugar. Beat this mixture until it is light and fluffy, then beat in the egg yolks. Sift together the flour, baking powder, and salt. Add these dry ingredients to the butter mixture alternately with the milk. Blend thoroughly and stir in the vanilla extract. Spread the batter evenly in the prepared pan. Bake the cake base at 350°F for 20–25 minutes, until the top springs back when touched lightly in the center. Remove the cake from the oven and from the baking pan. Place it on a wire rack to cool. Reset the oven to 325°F.

FILLING

> 1 cup sugar
> 3 tablespoons cornstarch
> 1 egg, beaten
> 1 cup hot water
> 3 tablespoons rum
> 1 teaspoon vanilla extract
> 1 tablespoon sweet butter

In a saucepan combine the sugar and cornstarch. Add the beaten egg and blend thoroughly. Over medium heat gradually stir in the hot water. Continue to stir gently for about 20 minutes, until the mixture thickens. Remove the pan from the heat and stir in the rum, vanilla extract, and butter. Place the cake base on a cookie sheet and spread this filling on top. Set it aside.

MERINGUE

> 1 tablespoon cinnamon
> ¼ cup sugar
> 4 egg whites
> ⅓ cup sugar

Sift together the cinnamon and ¼ cup sugar and set the mixture aside. In a large, grease-free mixing bowl beat the egg whites at a slow steady speed until foamy. Gradually beat in the ⅓ cup sugar. Add the cinnamon/sugar mixture, 1 tablespoon at a time. Continue to beat until the meringue will form soft peaks.

Use a rubber spatula to ice the torte with the meringue, bringing it over the sides of the cake base. Bake at 325°F for about 15 minutes, until the meringue is evenly browned. Cool to room temperature and slice before serving.

Yield: 16–20 slices

Pecan Torte

1 cup butter or margarine
2 cups brown sugar
4 egg yolks
2½ cups flour
1½ teaspoons baking powder
1 teaspoon salt
1 cup milk
1 teaspoon vanilla extract
1 cup pecan pieces
4 egg whites
4 tablespoons sugar
2 cups heavy cream, whipped
⅓ cup pecan halves

Place the oven rack about a third up from the bottom. Preheat the oven to 325°F. Lightly grease and flour two 9-inch round cake pans.

In a large mixing bowl cream the butter and gradually add the brown sugar, using your fingertips to break up any lumps. Add the egg yolks, 1 at a time, and blend thoroughly. Sift together the flour, baking powder, and salt. Add these dry ingredients alternately with the milk to the main batter. Blend well, stirring in the vanilla extract and the cup of pecan pieces. Spread the batter into the prepared pans. Set them aside.

In a large, grease-free mixing bowl beat the egg whites at a slow steady speed until foamy. Gradually beat in the sugar and continue to beat until the meringue will form soft peaks.

With a rubber spatula spread the meringue evenly on top of the cake batter. Bake the layers at 325°F for 20–30 minutes, until the meringue is golden brown and a toothpick inserted into the centers of the layers comes out clean.

Remove the torte layers from the oven and let them cool slightly before lifting them out of the baking pans and placing them on a wire rack to cool to room temperature. Spread a thin coat of whipped cream on one layer. Place the second layer on top and ice the whole cake with the remaining whipped cream. Garnish the top with the pecan halves. Keep the torte cool until time to serve.

Yield: 8–10 servings

Cranberry Layers

I adapted this layer cake from one of my favorite bread recipes. The cake itself is quite tart, a pleasant contrast to the sweet meringue.

> *4 egg yolks*
> *2 eggs*
> *1 cup brown sugar*
> *¼ cup milk*
> *⅔ cup ground walnuts*
> *⅔ cup whole-wheat flour*
> *Pinch salt*
> *½ cup butter or margarine, melted*
> *1 cup chopped (or minced) cranberries*
> *2 egg whites*
> *2 tablespoons sugar*
> *2 tablespoons chopped walnuts*

Place the oven rack about a third up from the bottom. Preheat the oven to 350°F. Grease two 9-inch cake pans that are 1½ to 2 inches deep. Line them with greased wax paper and dust lightly with flour.

In a large mixing bowl beat the egg yolks and eggs with an electric mixer at medium speed until they are frothy. Gradually add the brown sugar, sifting it through your fingertips to make sure it's free of lumps. After about 5 minutes, when the mixture has thickened slightly, beat in the milk. Use a large rubber spatula to fold in the ⅔ cup ground walnuts and whole-wheat flour, in a half dozen additions. Sprinkle the salt over the batter and beat gently. Pour in the butter in a thin stream and fold just until the batter is thoroughly blended. Fold in the chopped cranberries, ⅓ cup at a time. Leave the cake batter in the mixing bowl while you make the meringue.

In a medium, grease-free mixing bowl beat the egg whites at a slow steady speed. When they begin to stiffen, gradually add the 2 tablespoons of sugar. Continue to beat for a few minutes until the meringue will form soft peaks. Use a rubber spatula to fold in the 2 tablespoons of chopped walnuts.

Use a spatula to fold the cake batter with a few broad strokes from the bottom of the bowl just to remix any butter that may have separated. Then pour the batter into the two prepared pans. Spread the meringue over each layer. Cover the cake pans snugly with foil.

Bake the cake layers at 350°F for about 30 minutes, until an inserted toothpick comes out clean. Remove the cake pans from the oven and uncover them. Loosen the sides of the layers from the pans with a knife and place them, still in the baking pans, on a wire rack to cool for about 15 minutes. Lift the layers from the pans with a large spatula. Stack them and set them aside while you make the meringue garnish. Reset the oven to 375°F.

MERINGUE GARNISH

> 3 egg whites
> 1/4 teaspoon cream of tartar
> 1/4 cup sugar
> 1/2 cup chopped walnuts

In a large, grease-free mixing bowl beat the egg whites at a slow steady speed. When they are foamy add the cream of tartar. Gradually add the sugar and continue to beat for a few more minutes until the meringue forms soft peaks. With a rubber spatula fold in the chopped walnuts, 1 tablespoon at a time. Spread this meringue garnish over the top and sides of the layer cake.

Return the cake to the oven at 375°F for 5 to 8 minutes, until the meringue begins to color. Serve the cake warm or at room temperature.

Yield: 8–10 servings

Ginger Torte

Here is one of my eclectic recipes: the ginger layers are based on an old southern gingerbread recipe. I discovered lemon curd in England. The meringue icing gives a light and sweet contrast to the tart lemon filling and spicy torte layers. And when sliced there is a lovely display of dark and bright color bands.

GINGER LAYERS

> 2 1/2 cups flour
> 1/2 teaspoon baking powder
> 2 teaspoons baking soda
> 2 teaspoons ground ginger
> 1/2 teaspoon ground cloves
> 1/2 teaspoon allspice

    1 teaspoon cinnamon
    ¾ cup brown sugar, loosely packed
    ¾ cup dark molasses
    ¾ cup butter or margarine, melted
    2 eggs, lightly beaten
    1 cup boiling water

Place the oven rack about a third up from the bottom. Preheat the oven to 350°F. Grease two 8-inch (square or round) pans. Line the bottoms with wax paper and grease again. Dust lightly with flour.

Sift together the flour, baking powder, baking soda, ginger, cloves, allspice, and cinnamon. Set this dry mixture aside. In a large mixing bowl beat together the sugar and molasses. Gradually beat in the melted butter and then the eggs. Stir in the dry ingredients, in four additions, alternately with the boiling water. Beat for about a minute to blend thoroughly. Pour the batter into the two prepared pans.

Bake the ginger layers at 350°F for about 30 minutes, until the center springs back when touched lightly. Remove from the oven and loosen from the sides of the pans using a knife. Turn the layers onto a wire rack to cool, and peel away the wax paper. Reset the oven to 400°F.

ASSEMBLING

    1 recipe Lemon Curd (page 224)
    5 egg whites
    ½ teaspoon cream of tartar
    ⅓ cup sugar

Spread the cooled ginger layers with the lemon curd and stack them. In a large, grease-free mixing bowl beat the egg whites at a slow steady speed. When they are foamy add the cream of tartar. Gradually add the sugar and continue to beat for a few minutes until the meringue will form soft peaks. Use a rubber spatula to ice the torte with the meringue, piling it higher on top. Bake at 400°F for 5 to 8 minutes, until the meringue peaks are golden. Serve hot or cool.

Yield: 8–10 servings

Monticello Cake

This tall layer cake is a visual delight as well as a taste treat. I created it to celebrate the beginning of restoration on my brother's Victorian estate in Monticello, Georgia. We enjoyed it in true southern style—in the wisteria-laden solarium after a meal of fried chicken, potato salad, fresh stewed okra, and lots of iced tea.

> ¼ cup sweet butter
> 2 cups sugar
> 3 eggs
> 3 cups flour
> ¼ teaspoon salt
> 2 teaspoons baking soda
> 1 cup buttermilk
> 2 ounces unsweetened chocolate, grated or broken into small
>   pieces
> 1 cup milk
> 2 teaspoons vanilla extract

Place the oven rack in the center. Preheat the oven to 325°F. Lightly butter and flour three 9-inch round pans.

In a large mixing bowl cut the butter into the sugar using a tablespoon. Beat in the eggs, one at a time, and blend thoroughly. Sift together the flour, salt, and baking soda, and stir these dry ingredients into the egg mixture in six additions, alternately with the buttermilk. When the ingredients are mixed thoroughly, beat for 1 minute. Set this batter aside.

In a saucepan over low heat stir the chocolate pieces into the milk. Continue to stir so that the milk does not scald, until the chocolate has melted. Remove the saucepan from the heat and allow the milk mixture to cool for a few minutes before stirring it into the cake batter. Beat in the vanilla extract. Pour the batter into the prepared pans. Bake the layers at 325°F for 30–35 minutes, until the centers spring back when touched lightly. (Test each layer for doneness.) Remove the layers from the oven, invert the pans over a wire rack, and lift them away. Leave the layers on the rack to cool to room temperature.

ASSEMBLING

> ½ cup chopped maraschino cherries
> 1 recipe Quick Icing (page 52)
> About 1 cup maraschino cherry halves

Use a rubber spatula to fold the chopped cherries into 1 cup of the icing. Spread this mixture on two of the cake layers. Stack the layers, placing the uniced layer on top. Cover the cake with the remaining icing and garnish the top with cherry halves placed in concentric circles.

Yield: 10–12 servings

Apple Torte

> 3 egg yolks
> 2 eggs
> ½ cup light brown sugar
> ½ teaspoon vanilla extract
> 2 tablespoons milk
> ¾ cup ground walnuts
> 3 tablespoons sweet butter, melted
> 2 tart apples (Cortlands, MacIntosh)
> 3–4 tablespoons lemon juice

Place the oven rack about a third up from the bottom. Preheat the oven to 350°F. Lightly butter a 9-inch round cake pan and line it with buttered wax paper. Dust it with a few pinches of ground walnuts.

Beat the egg yolks and eggs with an electric mixer at a high speed in a large mixing bowl which has been fitted snugly over a pan or bowl of hot water. (Ideally this pan or bowl should be of copper since it retains heat well.) When the mixture is a light color, add the light brown sugar by sifting it in steadily as you beat. Continue to beat at a high speed for 10–15 minutes, until the batter is quite thick. Beat in the vanilla extract and milk.

With a rubber spatula fold in the ground walnuts, in three additions. Add the melted butter a few drops at a time, still folding the batter with the spatula.

Pour the batter into the prepared pan and bake it at 350°F for about 30 minutes, until the center springs back when touched lightly. Remove this torte base from the oven and loosen the sides from the pan (use a fork or knife if necessary). Invert the pan over a wire rack and lift it away. Peel off the wax paper and leave the torte base to cool. Reset the oven to 375°F.

Meanwhile, peel, core, and slice the apples thinly. Brush the slices with lemon juice so that they don't discolor. In a saucepan with water just to cover, boil the apple slices for 2–3 minutes, until they are almost tender. Drain the apple slices and set them aside to cool while you make the meringue and glaze.

MERINGUE AND GLAZE

3 egg whites
¼ teaspoon cream of tartar
¼ cup sugar
2 tablespoons water
3 tablespoons sugar

Line a baking sheet with foil or parchment paper. Place the torte base on it. Set it aside.

In a large, grease-free mixing bowl beat the egg whites at a slow steady speed. When they are foamy add the cream of tartar. Gradually beat in the ¼ cup sugar and beat for a few more minutes, until the meringue will form firm peaks when the beaters are lifted.

Combine the water with the 3 tablespoons sugar in a small saucepan over medium heat. Let it boil for a few minutes to 234°F (softball stage) while you start to garnish the torte. Spread the meringue over the torte base. Arrange the apple slices, overlapping, in two concentric circles on top of the torte. Drizzle the boiled sugar syrup over the apples for a glaze.

Bake the torte at 375°F for 5–8 minutes, just until the meringue starts to color. Serve the torte warm.

Yield: 6–8 servings

Orange Marmalade Cake

This cake is a dense, moist, tall single layer covered with an Italian meringue.

3 cups flour
2 teaspoons baking powder
1 teaspoon baking soda

Pinch salt
½ cup sweet butter, softened
¾ cup sugar
5 egg yolks, lightly beaten
¾ cup milk
1 teaspoon vanilla extract
3 egg whites
½ cup orange marmalade
⅓ cup orange marmalade for coating (optional)

Place rack in the center of the oven. Preheat the oven to 350°F. Grease and flour a 9-inch springform pan that is at least 2 inches deep.

Sift together the flour, baking powder, baking soda, and salt. Set this dry mixture aside. In a large mixing bowl cream the butter, gradually adding the sugar. Beat in the egg yolks until the mixture is thoroughly blended. Stir in the dry ingredients, in five additions, alternately with the milk. Beat in the vanilla extract.

In a large, grease-free mixing bowl beat the egg whites until they are quite stiff. With a large rubber spatula, fold these beaten whites, a third at a time, into the main batter. Use broad strokes and fold just until the color and texture are even. Pour the batter into the prepared pan. Spoon the ½ cup marmalade around the batter, about an inch from the edge of the pan. With the spatula gently turn the batter over the marmalade, just until it is covered, and smooth the batter so that the top is even.

Bake the cake at 350°F for 30–40 minutes, until the top springs back when touched lightly. Remove the cake from the oven, and loosen the sides from the pan with a knife. Place the pan on a wire rack, and release the rim. With the knife, loosen the cake from the bottom of the pan; do not remove it but leave it on the rack to cool slightly for 15–20 minutes. If desired, spread ⅓ cup marmalade over the top of the warm cake. Place the cake on a serving platter.

MARMALADE MERINGUE ICING

⅔ cup orange marmalade
2 egg whites
¼ teaspoon cream of tartar

In a small saucepan over medium heat, melt the marmalade. Stir it gently and let it bubble for a few minutes to 234°F (soft-ball stage). Remove the saucepan from the heat. Quickly, in a medium, grease-free mixing bowl beat the egg whites at a slow steady speed. When they are foamy add the cream of tartar. When the egg whites are stiff, add the orange marmalade, 1 tablespoon at a time. Continue to beat for another 5–8 minutes, until the meringue is thick, glossy, and cool.

Using a large rubber spatula, spread the icing over the cooled cake. There should be enough icing for a generous thick coat. Keep the cake cool until you are ready to serve it. Serve warm (return it to the oven at 350°F for 8–10 minutes) or at room temperature.

Yield: 10–12 slices

Meringue Cheesecake

The secret to making this a velvety smooth cheesecake is whipping the cream-cheese mixture until it is as light and airy as the meringue. That means when you think you have whipped it enough, give it another few minutes. You may like to garnish the cake with fresh strawberries or Raspberry Sauce (page 225). It is a perfectly wonderful cake on its own.

> 1½ pounds cream cheese, softened
> ½ cup sour cream
> 2 egg yolks, lightly beaten
> 4 egg whites
> ½ cup sugar
> 1 teaspoon vanilla extract

Place the rack in the center of the oven. Preheat the oven to 350°F.

In a large mixing bowl whip the cream cheese for at least 5 minutes, until it is quite light and airy (use an electric mixer). Add the sour cream, ¼ cup at a time. Beat in the egg yolks. Continue to beat for another few minutes, until the mixture is thoroughly blended and very light in texture. Set it aside.

In a large, grease-free mixing bowl beat the egg whites at a slow steady speed. When they begin to stiffen, gradually add the sugar. Beat in the vanilla extract. Continue to beat for a few minutes until the meringue will form soft peaks.

Whip the cream-cheese mixture for another minute, just to be sure. (The texture should be similar to that of the meringue.) Use a large rubber spatula to fold the cream-cheese mixture, about ½ cup at a time, into the meringue. Fold with broad strokes until the batter is smooth and thoroughly blended. Spoon the cake batter into a grease-free 9-inch springform pan.

Bake the cheesecake at 350°F for about 30 minutes, until a toothpick inserted in the center comes out almost clean. (Watch carefully toward the end of baking time. If this cake bakes too long the top will shrink and split.)

Remove the cake from the oven and place it, still in the pan, on a wire rack. Gently loosen the sides of the cake with a knife and then carefully release the pan and lift it away. Leave the cake in the bottom of the pan to cool on the rack. When the cake is room temperature it can be removed carefully with a large spatula, but I suggest leaving it on the bottom of the baking pan which can then be placed on a serving platter. Keep the cheesecake cool until you are ready to serve it. It can be refrigerated with a damp cloth draped over it. Add any garnish just before serving the cake.

Yield: 10–12 servings

Bourbon Pound Cake

Pound cakes are usually not iced because they are so rich and moist, but a light cover of nutted meringue is just the right garnish. This cake was large and festive enough to feed the cast of a Broadway musical on opening night.

> 2½ cups flour
> ¼ teaspoon baking soda
> ¼ teaspoon baking powder
> ¾ pound sweet butter, softened
> 1¾ cups light brown sugar, packed
> 4 eggs
> 4 egg yolks, lightly beaten
> ⅓ cup bourbon liqueur (or ⅓ cup bourbon and increase
>   sugar to 2 cups)
> ¼ cup milk
> Freshly grated nutmeg (about ½ teaspoon)

Place the oven rack about a third up from the bottom. Preheat the oven to 350°F. Butter a 9-inch tube pan and line the bottom with wax paper. Lightly butter the paper and dust it with flour.

Sift together the flour, baking soda, and baking powder and set the mixture aside. Cream the butter (I usually use an electric mixer) and gradually add the sugar, beating it in at a medium speed. When the mixture is smooth, beat in the eggs, 1 at a time, and then the egg yolks. Add about half of the dry ingredients by sprinkling 2 tablespoons at a time over the batter and folding in with the electric mixer set at the lowest speed. Use a rubber spatula to scrape the sides of the bowl from time to time. Pour in the bourbon liqueur, still using a low mixer speed, and fold in the remaining dry ingredients, 2 tablespoons at a time. Add the milk. Scrape the batter into the prepared tube pan. Cut around the pan through the center of the batter with the spatula to release any air pockets and level the batter. Grate about ½ teaspoon nutmeg over the top.

Bake the cake at 350°F for about an hour, until the top springs back when touched lightly. Remove the cake from the oven and loosen the outside and center from the pan using a knife. Place it upside down on a rack, lift the pan away, and peel off the paper. Leave the cake on the rack to cool. Reset the oven to 375°F.

NUTTED MERINGUE

> *3 egg whites*
> *¼ teaspoon cream of tartar*
> *¼ cup sugar*
> *½ cup chopped nuts (walnuts, pecans, or almonds)*

In a large, grease-free mixing bowl beat the egg whites at a slow steady speed. When they are foamy add the cream of tartar. Gradually add the sugar. When the meringue will form soft peaks use a rubber spatula to fold in the chopped nuts. With the spatula spread the nutted meringue evenly over the outside and top of the cooled cake and cover as much of the center as possible. Return the cake to the oven and bake at 375°F for about 15 minutes, until the meringue is golden.

Yield: 18–24 servings

Pies and Tarts

Some of these pies are baked in meringue crusts. Some are made in dough or crumb crusts with meringue Chantilly on top. One pie is encased in meringue. "Double crust" in this book means a crumb or dough crust lined with meringue, slow-baked, and then filled.

Vanilla Meringue Crust

4 egg whites
½ teaspoon cream of tartar
⅓ cup vanilla sugar

Place the oven rack about a third up from the bottom. Preheat the oven to 200°F.

In a large, grease-free mixing bowl beat the egg whites at a slow steady speed. When they are foamy add the cream of tartar. Gradually add the sugar and, when the meringue will form soft peaks, increase beating speed to moderate. Continue to beat for another 5–8 minutes, until the meringue is thick, glossy, and forms firm peaks when the beaters are lifted.

With a rubber spatula, scoop the meringue into a 9-inch pie pan. Pile it higher on the sides and make sure the bottom is evenly covered. Use the spatula to pull up some peaks of meringue on the crust edge. Bake the crust at 200° for 3 to 4 hours, until it feels firm and dry when squeezed gently. To partially bake, leave the crust in the oven for 1½ hours. (Watch that it doesn't color while baking; leave the oven door open if necessary.) Remove the crust from the oven and put it aside to cool. It is ready for filling or can be stored in an airtight container for several weeks.

Nutted Meringue Crust

3 egg whites
½ teaspoon cream of tartar
¼ cup sugar
¼ teaspoon vanilla extract (or other flavoring)
½ cup chopped walnuts (or pecans)

Place the oven rack about a third up from the bottom. Preheat the oven to 200°F. Line a 9-inch pie pan with foil.

In a large, grease-free mixing bowl beat the egg whites at a slow steady speed. When they are foamy add the cream of tartar. Gradually add the sugar and, when the meringue will form soft peaks, add the vanilla extract and increase to a moderate beating speed. Beat for another 5 to 8 minutes, until the meringue is thick, glossy, and forms firm peaks when the beaters are lifted. Use a rubber spatula to fold in the chopped nuts.

Scoop the meringue into the prepared pan and, with the spatula, spread it evenly, making the sides only slightly thicker than the bottom. The edge should be even and about a half inch higher than the pan. Use the spatula to pull up peaks of meringue around the crust edge.

Bake the crust at 200°F for 3 to 4 hours, until it feels dry and firm when pressed gently in the center. Remove it from the oven, lift the crust—still in the foil—out of the pan and place it on a rack. When the crust is cool enough to handle, peel away the foil. Keep the crust in an airtight container until you are ready to fill it.

Coconut Meringue Crust

4 egg whites
½ teaspoon cream of tartar
½ cup sugar
½ teaspoon coconut extract
½ teaspoon vanilla extract
⅓ cup grated coconut (fresh is best; if you use sweetened
coconut, reduce sugar to ⅓ cup)

Place the oven rack about a third up from the bottom. Preheat the oven to 200°F. Line a 9-inch pie pan with foil.

In a large, grease-free mixing bowl beat the egg whites at a slow steady speed. When they are foamy add the cream of tartar. Gradually beat in the sugar and, when the meringue will form soft peaks, add the coconut and vanilla extracts, and increase to a moderate beating speed. Beat for another 5 to 8 minutes, until the meringue will form firm peaks when the beaters are lifted.

With a rubber spatula scoop the meringue into the prepared pan. Pile it higher on the sides and make sure the bottom is evenly covered. Use the spatula to pull up some peaks of meringue on the crust edge. Sprinkle the grated coconut into the bottom of the crust and generously around the edge.

Bake the crust at 200°F for 3 to 4 hours, until it feels firm and dry when pressed gently in the center. Remove it from the oven, lift the crust—still in the foil—out of the pan, and place it on a rack. When the crust is cool enough to handle, peel away the foil. Keep the crust in an airtight container until you are ready to fill it.

Lime (or Lemon) Meringue Crust

4 egg whites
½ teaspoon cream of tartar
½ cup sugar
1½ teaspoons lime (or lemon) extract
About 10 lime (or lemon) slices

Place the oven rack about a third up from the bottom. Preheat the oven to 200°F. Line a 9-inch pie pan with foil.

In a large, grease-free mixing bowl beat the egg whites at a slow steady speed. When they are foamy add the cream of tartar. Gradually beat in the sugar and, when the meringue will form soft peaks, add the lime (or lemon) extract and increase to a moderate beating speed. Beat for another 5 to 8 minutes, until the meringue is thick, glossy, and forms firm peaks when the beaters are lifted.

With a rubber spatula scoop the meringue into the prepared pie pan. Cover the bottom evenly and shape a shallow nest, finishing with a band about 1½ inches thick around the edge. Use the spatula to smooth away any peaks of meringue.

Bake the crust at 200°F for 3 to 4 hours, until it feels firm and dry when squeezed gently. (Watch that it doesn't color while baking; leave the oven door ajar if necessary.) Remove the crust from the oven and let it cool for a few minutes.

When it is cool enough to handle, lift the crust from the pan and peel away the foil. Use a small sharp knife to carve slots, about 1¼ inches long at 1-inch intervals, around the edge of the crust. Fit the lime (or lemon) slices into these slots. The crust is ready for filling. (You can bake the crust, carve the slots, and store this crust in an airtight container for several weeks. Then insert the lime or lemon slices just before you are ready to serve it.)

Ice Cream Pie

I offer several ideas for an easy, elegant change from "just ice cream" for dessert. The crusts and sauces can be made well ahead of time, so there isn't much to do at the last minute but assemble them. Select a flavor combination from my suggestions or experiment to find your own favorite. The meringue crusts go well with many other ice creams and sauces. Amounts and preparation will always be the same.

1 Nutted Meringue Crust, made with vanilla extract (page 113)
1 pint chocolate or vanilla ice cream, softened
1 recipe Chocolate Sauce, warm (page 204)
About ½ cup Meringue Dust (page 51)

Place the meringue crust in a pie pan. Scoop the softened ice cream into the crust and use a spatula or the back of a large spoon to spread it smoothly. Place the filled pie crust in the freezer for about an hour, until the ice cream is firm.

When you are ready to serve it, remove the pie from the freezer and spoon about ½ cup of the chocolate sauce over it. Sprinkle the top with meringue dust. Slice the pie with a sharp knife and pour more sauce over each piece.

Yield: 6–8 slices

VARIATIONS

1. 1 Nutted Meringue Crust made with black walnut flavor (page 113)
   1 pint maple walnut ice cream, softened
   ½ recipe Honey Meringue (page 52)

2. 1 Nutted Meringue Crust, made with vanilla extract or butterscotch flavor (page 113)
   1 pint butter pecan ice cream, softened
   1 recipe Butterscotch Sauce, warm (page 205)

3. 1 Coconut Meringue Crust (page 114)
   1 pint coconut ice cream, softened
   1 recipe Rum Sauce, warm or cold (page 205)
   About ½ cup Meringue Dust (page 51)

Sherbet Alaska Pie

> 1 pint sherbet (orange, lime, or raspberry), softened
> 1 9-inch Chocolate Wafer Crumb Crust, baked then frozen
>   (page 221)
> 4 egg whites
> ½ teaspoon cream of tartar
> ⅓ cup sugar
> ½ cup fresh fruit (orange or lime slices or raspberries)

Scoop the sherbet into the frozen pie crust. Smooth it out so that about a ½-inch border of the crust shows. Place the pie in the freezer for an hour or more, until the sherbet is firm again. (It can be stored, covered tightly with plastic wrap, in the freezer for up to ten days.)

Place the rack in the center of the oven. Preheat the oven to 500°F. Spread ice cubes evenly in the bottom of a shallow ovenproof dish that is at least 10 inches in diameter.

In a large, grease-free mixing bowl beat the egg whites at a slow steady speed. When they are foamy add the cream of tartar. Gradually add the sugar and continue to beat for a few minutes until the meringue will form soft peaks.

Remove the frozen pie from the freezer and place it on the ice-filled dish. Use a rubber spatula to cover the pie with the meringue, piling it higher in the center and sealing in the sherbet. Pull up some meringue peaks with the spatula.

Bake the pie at 500°F for 3 to 5 minutes, until the meringue peaks are golden. Remove the pie from the oven, still on the ice-filled dish. (Keep the pie on ice cubes until it is served.) Garnish with fruit around the edge and serve immediately.

Yield: 6–8 servings

Chocolate Custard Pie

DOUBLE CRUST

> 3 tablespoons sugar
> 1 tablespoon cocoa
> 3 egg whites

> *½ teaspoon cream of tartar*
> *1 Chocolate Wafer Crumb Crust, partially baked (page 221)*

Place the oven rack about a third up from the bottom. Preheat the oven to 325°F.

Sift together the sugar and cocoa and set the mixture aside. In a medium, grease-free mixing bowl beat the egg whites at a slow steady speed. When they are foamy add the cream of tartar. Gradually add the sugar/cocoa mixture and, when the meringue will form soft peaks, increase beating speed to moderate. Beat for another 5 to 8 minutes, until the meringue is thick, glossy, and forms firm peaks when the beaters are lifted.

With a rubber spatula scoop the meringue into the crumb crust. Cover the bottom evenly, making the sides a little thicker and using the spatula to pull up some meringue peaks around the edge.

Bake the crust at 325°F for 3 minutes. Turn the oven down to 225°F and leave the door open for about 20 minutes. Bake the crust at 225°F for another hour or more, until the meringue feels firm and dry when pressed gently in the center. Remove the crust from the oven and let it cool to room temperature.

CUSTARD FILLING

> *⅔ cup sugar*
> *2 tablespoons cornstarch*
> *2 egg yolks*
> *1½ cups milk*
> *1 ounce unsweetened chocolate, broken into small pieces*
> *1 teaspoon vanilla extract or 1 tablespoon of any chocolate liqueur*

In a medium saucepan sift together the sugar and cornstarch. In a separate bowl beat the egg yolks, one at a time, into the milk. Over medium heat gradually stir the liquid mixture into the dry ingredients. When it is blended add the chocolate pieces. Continue to stir as the custard cooks. After about another 5 minutes the chocolate should be melted and the mixture will become quite thick. Still stirring, a little less gently now, let it bubble for about 1 minute.

Remove the saucepan from the heat and stir in the vanilla extract or liqueur. Set the custard aside to cool. When it is lukewarm, spoon the custard into the cooled pie shell. Keep the pie at room temperature or cooler.

Yield: about 8 servings

Summer Chocolate Pie

This pie is good any season, but it is an especially cool dessert for a hot day. You can bake the meringue pieces even three weeks ahead, store them in an airtight container, and assemble the pie at almost the last minute.

> ½ cup strong freshly brewed coffee, cooled to room temperature
> 1 tablespoon unflavored gelatin
> 2 ounces bittersweet chocolate, melted and cooled slightly
> 3 egg yolks, lightly beaten
> ¼ cup sugar
> 1 cup heavy cream
> 2 tablespoons sugar
> 1 9-inch Chocolate Wafer Crumb Crust, baked and chilled
>   (page 221)

In a small bowl combine half of the coffee with the gelatin and set it aside. In another small bowl combine the melted chocolate with the remaining coffee and set it aside.

In the top of a double boiler over hot water, beat together the egg yolks and ¼ cup sugar. When thoroughly blended, add the gelatin mixture. Stir over low heat for 5–8 minutes, until the gelatin has dissolved. Add the chocolate mixture, scraping it from the bowl with a rubber spatula. Stir a minute or so to blend the mixture, then remove the pan from the heat. Set it aside on a trivet to cool to room temperature.

When the gelatin mixture has cooled, whip the cup of heavy cream in a chilled bowl with chilled beaters, gradually adding the 2 tablespoons of sugar. When the cream is stiff, fold it into the gelatin mixture and pour this filling into the chilled pie crust. Refrigerate the pie for at least 2 hours, until it is firm.

MERINGUE

> 3 tablespoons sugar
> 2 tablespoons cocoa
> 2 egg whites
> ¼ teaspoon cream of tartar

Place the rack in the center of the oven. Preheat the oven to 200°F. Line a baking sheet with parchment paper and trace a 9-inch circle onto the parchment. Fit one pastry bag with a number 3B star tip and a second bag with a number 5 star tip.

In a small bowl or on wax paper, sift together the sugar and cocoa. In a medium, grease-free mixing bowl beat the egg whites at a slow steady speed. When they are foamy add the cream of tartar. Gradually add the sugar/cocoa mixture and, when the meringue will form soft peaks, increase to a moderate beating speed. Beat for about another 5 minutes, until the meringue is thick, glossy, and forms firm peaks when the beaters are lifted.

Glue the parchment paper to the baking sheet with a few pinches of meringue. Divide the meringue and use a rubber spatula to fill each pastry bag. Start with the bag fitted with the larger tip. Hold it firmly with both hands, keeping it taut and closed with the top hand. About an inch inside the traced circle, press out the meringue to form a circular zigzag pattern. Keep the meringue rather thick (about ¾ inch in diameter). Break the meringue neatly as you complete the circle, using a small sharp chilled knife if necessary to smooth it.

On the inside of the zigzag pattern, make rosettes at each point: Hold the pastry bag directly above the paper and press the meringue out until it is about an inch in diameter. Then pull the bag gently but firmly up from the paper so that the meringue breaks forming a point. Repeat the rosettes around the zigzag and make a few extra ones outside the traced circle.

With the second pastry bag, again holding it firmly and keeping it closed, form smaller rosettes, two inside each of the zigzag corners. Begin with the tip close to the paper, press the meringue out, and pull straight up to break it. Make a few extra rosettes outside the circle.

Bake the meringue at 200°F. Use a small sharp knife to carefully remove the rosettes from the paper after 20–30 minutes, or when they are firm and dry. (Test by squeezing gently.) Bake the zigzag 15–20 minutes, until it is done. Remove the zigzag from the paper with great care. Use a small sharp knife to loosen it gently. (If the zigzag breaks, which is not unusual, just glue it back together with a little meringue and return it to the oven for about 10 minutes.)

This pie should not be garnished until just before serving. Place the zigzag concentrically on top of the pie. Arrange the rosettes, larger ones at the inside points and two smaller ones between each of these, in the zigzag corners. Serve the pie cold.

Yield: 8–10 servings

Citrus Pie

1 grapefruit, peeled, sectioned, and seeded
1 large orange, peeled, sectioned, and seeded
2 tangerines, peeled, sectioned, and seeded (Use clementines if
    you can get them; they're seedless.)
4 egg yolks, lightly beaten
1/2 cup lemon juice
1/2 cup sugar
1/2 teaspoon allspice
1 Lime Meringue Crust, fitted with lemon slices (page 114)
2 or 3 kumquats with leaves, for garnish (optional)

In a large bowl combine the grapefruit, orange, and tangerine
sections. Chill this mixture in the refrigerator for about an hour.

In a heavy saucepan over low heat or in the top of a double boiler
beat the egg yolks with the lemon juice. Gradually beat in the sugar.
Stir the mixture vigorously over low heat for another 15 minutes,
until it is thick enough to coat the spoon and sides of the pan. Stir in
the allspice and remove the pan from the heat. Chill the sauce in the
refrigerator for at least 2 hours. (You can also make this lemon
sauce several days ahead and keep it in the refrigerator. If you've
also prepared the crust ahead of time, assembling this pie will take
only a few minutes.)

Spread a thin layer of the chilled lemon sauce in the bottom of
the prepared pie crust. Turn the chilled fruit mixture into the crust
and pour the remaining sauce over it. Chill the pie briefly before
serving it. If desired, garnish with kumquats in the center. Use a
sharp or serrated knife to slice the pie.

Yield: 6–8 servings

Cantaloupe Tart

FROZEN LEMON CREAM

2 egg yolks
1/2 cup heavy cream
1/4 cup lemon juice
1/4 cup sugar

In a medium mixing bowl whisk the yolks, 1 at a time, into the cream. Whisk in the lemon juice. Beat only until blended. Put the sugar into a small or medium saucepan over medium heat and stir in the liquid, pouring it in a slow steady stream. When the mixture is thoroughly blended reduce the heat to low and continue to cook, stirring, for about 15 minutes. The custard will start to coat the sides of the pan and thicken slightly. Remove pan from the heat and pour the custard into a small container. Cover it and freeze for 2 to 3 hours.

ASSEMBLING

> 1 small cantaloupe, rind and seeds removed, sliced lengthwise
>   into ½-inch pieces
> 1 Lemon Meringue Crust (page 114)

Spread about half of the lemon cream into the bottom of the crust. Arrange the cantaloupe pieces as spokes, overlapping them at the center if necessary. You may need to trim the ends to make the slices fit. Spoon the remaining lemon cream onto the center of the tart as a garnish. Serve immediately.

Yield: about 6 servings

Tropical Tart

> ½ recipe Basic Custard, made with coconut extract and
>   chilled (page 198)
> ½ cup heavy cream, whipped
> 1 large ripe mango, pared and sliced
> 1 small banana, sliced
> 1 Coconut Meringue Crust (page 114)
> 2 or 3 kiwi, pared and sliced (or use star fruit or other exotic
>   fresh fruit)

In a medium mixing bowl fold the chilled custard, 1 tablespoon at a time, into the whipped cream. Place the mixture in the freezer for at least an hour.

Combine the mango and banana in another bowl and chill this mixture in the refrigerator.

Fold about half of the frozen custard mixture into the bowl of fruit. Turn this filling into the coconut crust. Arrange the sliced kiwi as a garnish around the edge of the tart.

Serve the tart cold and slice it with a pie server. Spoon a little of the remaining frozen custard over each piece.

Yield: 6–8 servings

Fresh Fruit Tart

1 cup seedless grapes
1 cup melon (cantaloupe, honeydew, etc.) chunks
1 medium orange or tangerine, sectioned and seeded
½ cup sliced strawberries
2 egg whites
¼ teaspoon cream of tartar
2 tablespoons sugar
2 tablespoons semisweet chocolate chips or shavings
1 Sweet Pie Crust (page 222) or Almond Pie Crust (page
    222), baked in a 9-inch tart ring and chilled
1 recipe Raspberry Sauce, chilled (page 225)

In a large bowl combine the grapes, melon chunks, orange (or tangerine) sections, and sliced strawberries. Put the bowl in the refrigerator for several hours (until you've made the meringue).

Place the oven rack in the center. Preheat the oven to 200°F. Line a baking sheet with parchment paper.

In a medium, grease-free bowl beat the egg whites at a slow steady speed. When they are foamy add the cream of tartar. Gradually add the sugar and, when the meringue will form soft peaks, increase to a moderate beating speed. Beat for another 3 or 4 minutes, until the meringue is thick, glossy, and forms firm peaks when the beaters are lifted. With a rubber spatula fold in the chocolate chips or shavings.

Use a few pinches of meringue to secure the parchment to the baking sheet. Spread the meringue onto the parchment, roughly in a square shape, about ¼ inch thick.

Bake the meringue at 200°F for 1 to 2 hours. Make sure that the meringue stays white; if it starts to color, leave the oven door open. Test for doneness by squeezing or pressing gently; it should feel firm and dry. Remove the meringue from the oven and, while it is still warm, use a small sharp knife to loosen it from the parchment and slice it into 1-inch squares. (Don't discard broken or uneven meringue pieces. They can be used in this recipe.)

Remove the bowl of fruit from the refrigerator and fold in the meringue squares and any broken pieces. Turn this mixture into the chilled tart shell. Spoon the raspberry sauce over the tart. Serve immediately.

Yield: 6–8 servings

Italian Strawberry Tart

This is a strikingly sweet, rich dessert that is easy to prepare. I think it particularly elegant when made as individual tarts.

> *1 dry pint strawberries*
> *¼ cup kirsch*
> *2 tablespoons water*
> *¾ cup sugar*
> *1 egg white*
> *Pinch cream of tartar*
> *½ teaspoon vanilla extract*
> *1 Almond Pie Crust, baked in a 9- or 10-inch tart ring (page 222)*

Select several well-shaped whole strawberries for garnishing. Wash them, leaving their green tops on, and set them aside.

Clean and hull the remaining strawberries. Slice them evenly and place them in a shallow dish. Pour the kirsch over the strawberry pieces and set them aside to marinate for at least 20 minutes.

Place the rack in the center of the oven. Preheat the oven to 375°F.

In a small saucepan combine the water and sugar and, over medium heat, bring this syrup to a boil. Let it boil for about 2 minutes. Remove the saucepan to very low heat.

In a medium, grease-free mixing bowl beat the egg white at a slow steady speed. When it is foamy add the cream of tartar. Gradually beat in the hot sugar syrup, pouring it in a continuous stream. Beat the meringue for another few minutes, until it is thick, glossy, and cool. Beat in the vanilla extract.

Drain the strawberry pieces and fold them into the meringue. Place the baked tart shell on a baking sheet. Spoon the filling into the tart shell. Bake the tart only about 5 minutes at 375°F, just long enough for the meringue to feel dry when touched lightly. It should look dull but do not allow it to brown. Remove the tart from the oven, carefully lift it from the baking sheet, and place it on a wire rack to cool slightly.

Garnish the tart with the reserved whole strawberries in the center, and serve it warm or at room temperature.

Yield: 6–8 servings

INDIVIDUAL TARTS

Place the oven rack about a third up from the bottom. Preheat the oven to 350°F. Lightly butter six small (3- or 4-inch) tart rings and place them on a large baking sheet.

Prepare one recipe of Almond Pie Crust dough (page 222). Roll it out and divide the dough into six pieces. Fit them snugly into the prepared tart rings and trim away the edges with a knife. Bake the tart shells at 350°F for about 8 minutes, until they are dry and lightly browned. Remove the baking sheet from the oven and place it on a wire rack.

Reset the oven to 375°F and place the rack in the center.

With a small sharp knife loosen the shells from the baking rings while they cool. After 15–20 minutes, when they are cool enough to handle, remove the rings but leave the shells on the baking sheet.

Fill each cooled tart shell with the strawberry-meringue mixture and bake at 375°F for 3 to 4 minutes. Garnish each tart with one beautiful strawberry. Serve them warm or at room temperature.

Yield: 6 tarts

Fresh Lime Pie

8–10 very thin lime slices without rind (I suggest slicing the whole lime with a very sharp paring knife or in a food processor and then snipping the rind away with scissors.)
¾ cup sugar
2 tablespoons sweet butter, melted
2 eggs
¼ cup lime juice
¼ cup water
½ teaspoon ground ginger
1 9-inch Basic Pie Crust, partially baked (page 219)

Place the oven rack about a third up from the bottom. Preheat the oven to 350°F.

In a large mixing bowl combine the sugar with the melted butter. Beat in the eggs, 1 at a time. Add the lime juice and, when thoroughly blended, the water. Beat the mixture about 1 minute.

Arrange the lime slices in the partially baked pie crust. Sprinkle the ginger over them. Pour the egg mixture into the shell and bake the pie at 350°F for 30–35 minutes, until it appears firm when tilted gently from side to side. Remove the pie from the oven and place it on a wire rack to cool. Reset the oven to 375°F.

LIME MERINGUE TOPPING

> *3 egg whites*
> *½ teaspoon cream of tartar*
> *3 tablespoons sugar*
> *1½ teaspoons lime juice*

In a medium, grease-free mixing bowl beat the egg whites at a slow steady speed. When they are foamy add the cream of tartar. Gradually add the sugar and increase to a moderate beating speed. When the meringue will almost form soft peaks, beat in the lime juice, ½ teaspoon at a time. Beat about 1 minute longer, until the lime juice is blended and the meringue will form soft peaks.

With a rubber spatula cover the top of the cooled pie with the meringue. The topping should touch the edge of the crust all the way around. Bake the pie at 375°F for 8–10 minutes, until the meringue peaks are brown. Serve warm from the oven or at room temperature.

Yield: 8–10 servings

Lime Chiffon Pie

2 egg yolks
¼ cup sugar
¼ cup lime juice
½ cup heavy cream
1 Lime Meringue Crust (page 114)

In the top of a double boiler or in a mixing bowl which has been fitted snugly over a saucepan of hot water, beat the egg yolks. Beat in the sugar 1 tablespoon at a time. Gradually beat in the lime juice. Place the pan over low heat and beat with an electric mixer at a moderate speed. Continue to beat for about 10 minutes, until the mixture is quite thick and has about doubled in volume. Remove it from the heat and beat another 5 minutes or so, until the custard has cooled to room temperature.

In a chilled mixing bowl with chilled beaters whip the heavy cream. When the cream is stiff, fold it into the lime custard in three additions. Cover the filling tightly and freeze it for about 4 hours.

Soften the filling at room temperature for about 10 minutes, spoon it into the prepared shell, and serve immediately.

Yield: 8–10 servings

Orange Cream Pie

This dessert might also be called Park Slope Pie, since I created the recipe for the housewarming of my friends' Brooklyn brownstone. It was a lovely spring evening for a small dinner party, followed by flute duets. Those who weren't performing finished the pie.

3 egg yolks
3 tablespoons sugar
5 tablespoons orange juice concentrate

1 cup heavy cream, whipped
1 orange, peeled and sectioned (Valencia or Temple are best)
1 Vanilla Meringue Crust, baked (page 112)

In the top of a double boiler over hot water beat the egg yolks, adding the sugar 1 tablespoon at a time. Stir in the orange juice concentrate, 1 tablespoon at a time, and continue to stir gently for about 15 minutes, until the custard thickens. Remove the pan from the heat and allow the custard to cool to room temperature before folding in about two-thirds of the whipped cream. Pour this mixture into the meringue crust.

Put the remaining whipped cream into a pastry bag, fitted with a small (number 0) star tip. Hold the bag firmly with both hands and pipe the whipped cream around the outer edge of the custard and on the very center of the pie. Arrange the orange sections on top of the whipped cream. Put the pie in the freezer for 45 minutes before serving.

Yield: 6–8 servings

Tart Lemon Meringue Pie

Here is a classic recipe for what is probably the most popular meringue dessert in America.

½ cup sugar
2 tablespoons cornstarch
Pinch salt
1 cup water
3 egg yolks
¼ cup sweet butter, softened
½ cup lemon juice (I prefer fresh lemon juice for this recipe. You'll need about 3 lemons)
3 tablespoons grated lemon rind
1 9-inch Basic Pie Crust, baked and cooled (page 219)
3 egg whites
¼ teaspoon cream of tartar
3 tablespoons sugar

Place the rack in the center of the oven. Preheat the oven to 375°F.

In a medium saucepan sift together the ½ cup sugar, cornstarch, and salt. Stir in the water and cook over low heat, stirring for a few minutes until the mixture boils. Let it boil for about 8 minutes, stirring occasionally. Then cover and cook over very low heat until the mixture thickens. Remove the pan from the heat and beat in the egg yolks, 1 at a time. Return the uncovered saucepan to low heat for another 5 to 8 minutes, stirring occasionally so that it thickens evenly. When the mixture is a thick, smooth custard remove the saucepan from the heat and beat in the softened butter and lemon juice. Stir in the lemon rind. Spoon this filling into the baked pie crust and set it aside.

In a large, grease-free bowl beat the egg whites at a slow steady speed. When they are foamy add the cream of tartar. Gradually add the 3 tablespoons sugar and continue to beat for a few minutes, until the meringue will form soft peaks.

Use a rubber spatula to spread the meringue over the lemon filling in the pie crust. Make sure the meringue completely covers the pie filling. Bake the pie at 375°F for about 10 minutes, until the meringue peaks are golden. Serve warm or at room temperature.

Yield: 6–8 servings

Upside-down Lemon Meringue Pie

4 egg yolks, lightly beaten
¾ cup sugar
6 tablespoons lemon juice (juice of about 2 lemons)
Grated rind of 2 lemons (about 2 tablespoons)
1 tablespoon sweet butter
2 tablespoons cornstarch
1 Vanilla Meringue Crust, baked (page 112)

In a heavy saucepan over low heat combine the beaten egg yolks and sugar. Stir in the lemon juice and grated lemon rind and add the butter. When the butter has melted, add the cornstarch, 1 tablespoon at a time. Cook, stirring occasionally, for another 20–30 minutes, until the mixture thickens. Remove the saucepan from the heat and put it aside on a trivet to cool. When the custard reaches room temperature, spoon it into the vanilla meringue crust. Keep the pie at room temperature or cooler; it is best consumed right away.

Yield: 6–8 servings

Strawberry Cream Pie

1 tablespoon unflavored gelatin
2 tablespoons dry sherry
1 dry quart whole strawberries, cleaned and hulled
½ cup water
½ cup sugar
½ cup heavy cream
1 tablespoon dry sherry
1 Vanilla Meringue Crust, baked (page 112)

Soften the gelatin in the 2 tablespoons of sherry and set aside. Slice enough strawberries to equal 2 cups. (Reserve the remaining whole strawberries.) In a saucepan over medium heat combine the water with the sugar and bring the mixture to a boil. When the sugar has dissolved, add the sliced strawberries. After a few minutes, when the mixture reaches the consistency of light syrup, add the softened gelatin. Remove the saucepan from the heat as soon as the gelatin has dissolved. Set this mixture aside to cool to room temperature.

When the gelatin mixture has cooled, whip the heavy cream in a chilled bowl with chilled beaters. As the cream begins to hold a soft shape, add the tablespoon of sherry. Fold the whipped cream into the gelatin mixture and pour it into the baked pie crust. Cover the top with the reserved whole strawberries, placing them as close together as possible in concentric circles from the outside edge. Chill the pie in the refrigerator for at least an hour.

Yield: 6–8 servings

Raspberry-Yogurt Pie

2 tablespoons cream cheese, softened
1½ cups plain yogurt
2 egg yolks, lightly beaten
⅓ cup sugar
2 teaspoons unflavored gelatin
½ teaspoon vanilla extract
1 cup fresh raspberries
1 9-inch Graham Cracker Crust (page 220) or Vanilla Wafer
    Crumb Crust (page 220), baked

In a large saucepan over very low heat blend the cream cheese into the yogurt. When the mixture is smooth, gently beat in the egg yolks, pouring them in a thin stream. Sift the sugar and gelatin together and stir these dry ingredients into the yogurt custard. Cook, stirring, just until the sugar and gelatin have dissolved. Remove the saucepan from the heat and stir in the vanilla extract. Reserve ¼ cup of the raspberries, and fold the remainder into the yogurt custard. Spoon this filling into the baked pie crust and place the pie in the refrigerator for at least an hour, until it is firm.

JELLY MERINGUE

2 egg whites
¼ teaspoon cream of tartar
3 tablespoons raspberry jelly, melted and cooled

Place the rack in the center of the oven. Preheat the oven to 350°F. Remove the pie from the refrigerator and place it in a shallow dish lined with ice cubes.

In a medium, grease-free mixing bowl beat the egg whites at a slow steady speed. When they are foamy add the cream of tartar. Beat in the jelly 1 tablespoon at a time and then increase to a moderate beating speed. Beat for another 3 to 5 minutes, until the meringue is thoroughly blended and smooth. (This meringue will have a softer consistency than a sugar meringue at soft-peak stage.)

Use a rubber spatula to spread the meringue over the pie. Bake it, in the ice-filled dish, at 350°F for about 3 minutes, until the top of the meringue feels dry when touched lightly. Do not let the meringue brown; it should remain a pink or rosy color.

Remove the pie from the oven and lift it from the ice-filled dish. Garnish the pie with the reserved raspberries and chill it in the refrigerator for about an hour. Serve the pie cold.

Yield: 6–8 servings

Blueberry Cream Pie

⅓ cup sugar
2 tablespoons water
2 cups fresh blueberries
2 teaspoons lemon juice
3–4 tablespoons cassis (optional)

1 cup sour cream
2 egg whites
1 Vanilla Meringue Crust (page 112)
About ¼ cup sour cream for garnish
About ¼ cup blueberries for garnish
Cassis for garnish

In a medium saucepan over medium heat, combine the sugar and water. When the mixture begins to boil, stir in the blueberries and lemon juice. Cook, stirring, for another 10 minutes. The syrup should now be quite dark in color and thin but coating the sides of the pan. Stir in the 3–4 tablespoons cassis, if desired, and remove the pan from the heat. Set it aside to cool to room temperature.

In a large mixing bowl beat the sour cream gently with a spoon for about a minute. Blend in the cooled blueberry mixture. In a separate mixing bowl, using an electric mixer, beat the egg whites at a slow steady speed until they are stiff. Fold the stiffened egg whites into the blueberry mixture. Transfer the filling to a small container, cover it tightly, and freeze it for at least 3 hours.

Let the pie filling soften for 10–15 minutes, then spoon it into the baked crust. Garnish with a generous scoop of sour cream, ¼ cup fresh blueberries, and a drizzle of cassis over the center of the pie. Serve immediately.

Yield: about 8 servings

Deep-dish Blueberry Pie

This pie was once dessert for a houseful of hungry people on Fire Island where blueberries grow in abundance. It is simple to prepare and packed with luscious fresh fruit.

CRUST
Although there is only one deep-dish pie in this book, this crust is excellent with many other fresh fruit filling recipes. Try it with your favorite.

1 heaping cup flour
1 tablespoon sugar
3 tablespoons butter or margarine
1 egg yolk, lightly beaten
5 tablespoons half-and-half

Place the rack in the center of the oven and preheat the oven to 375°F.

In a large mixing bowl sift together the flour and sugar. Use two knives or a pastry blender to cut the butter into the dry mixture until the lumps are coarse but more or less even. Beat the egg yolk into the half-and-half. Gradually stir the liquid into the dry mixture. As soon as the dough is evenly moistened, gather it into a ball and place it on a lightly floured board or pastry cloth. With a rolling pin or the heel of your hand, press the dough out to a diameter of 11–12 inches.

Fit the crust into a 1½-quart casserole that is at least 2 inches deep. The crust should be slightly thicker at the bend around the bottom of the dish: push the sides of the crust down slightly and press it with your fingertips around the bottom edge at the same time. Use a knife to trim the crust neatly about ¾ inch from the top of the dish. Prick the crust with a fork and line it snugly with foil. The foil should come above the top of the crust and fit over the sides of the casserole.

Partially bake the crust at 375°F for 5–7 minutes, until it is dry but not browned. Remove it from the oven, lift out the foil, and place the casserole on a wire rack to cool for about 30 minutes. Reset the oven to 350°F.

FILLING

> ¼ *cup sugar*
> ¼ *cup sweet butter, softened*
> 3 *tablespoons flour*
> ¼ *teaspoon cinnamon*
> 2 *tablespoons lemon juice*
> 2 *tablespoons water*
> 5 *cups fresh blueberries, washed and dried*

In a large mixing bowl combine the sugar and butter. Add the flour, 1 tablespoon at a time, and the cinnamon and blend well. Stir in the lemon juice and water, 1 tablespoon at a time. When the ingredients are blended, add the blueberries, 1 or 2 cups at a time. Spoon the filling into the cooled crust. It should just fill the crust; pack it down, if necessary, so that the top of the filling meets the crust edge.

Bake the pie at 350°F for about 45 minutes, until it is almost firm. Remove it from the oven and place it on a wire rack to cool slightly. Reset the oven to 400°F.

VANILLA MERINGUE TOPPING

> 4 egg whites
> 1/2 teaspoon cream of tartar
> 1/4 cup sugar
> 2 teaspoons vanilla extract

In a large, grease-free mixing bowl beat the egg whites at a slow steady speed. When they are foamy add the cream of tartar. Gradually add the sugar and beat for a few minutes until the meringue will form soft peaks. Beat in the vanilla extract, 1/2 teaspoon at a time.

Use a rubber spatula to spread the meringue evenly over the cooled pie. Pull up some meringue peaks with the spatula. Bake the pie at 400°F for 8–10 minutes, until the meringue peaks are golden. This pie is best served right from the oven. (Or let it cool to room temperature and reheat it at 350°F for 10 minutes before serving.)

Yield: 8–10 servings

Peach Meringue Pie

I first made this pie for a friend as a thank you for his weekend of cat sitting. It has since become my standard treat for friends all over the world.

> 1/2 cup sweet butter, softened
> 1/2 cup sugar
> 3 egg yolks, lightly beaten
> 3 tablespoons flour
> 4 medium-size ripe peaches, peeled and chopped
> 1 9-inch Basic Pie Crust, unbaked (page 219)
> 3 egg whites
> 1/2 teaspoon cream of tartar
> 3 tablespoons sugar

Place the oven rack about a third up from the bottom. Preheat the oven to 350°F.

In a medium mixing bowl cream the softened butter. Add the 1/2 cup sugar gradually and beat the mixture about 3 minutes, until the texture is fluffy. Beat in the egg yolks alternately with the flour. Blend well, then fold in the chopped peaches so that the pieces are well-coated with the custard. Spoon this mixture into the unbaked pie crust.

Bake the pie at 350°F for about 45 minutes, until it is firm and golden brown. Remove the pie from the oven and let it cool on a wire rack for about 15 minutes. Reset the oven to 375°F.

In a large, grease-free mixing bowl beat the egg whites at a slow steady speed. When they are foamy add the cream of tartar. Gradually add the 3 tablespoons sugar and continue to beat for a few minutes until the meringue forms soft peaks.

Use a rubber spatula to top the cooled pie evenly with the meringue, pulling up a few peaks. Place it in the oven at 375°F for about 10 minutes, until the meringue peaks are golden. Serve warm or at room temperature.

Yield: 6–8 servings

Pear-Almond Pie

3 cups peeled, cored, sliced firm Bartlett or Bosc pears (about 3 pears)
About 3 tablespoons lemon juice
6 tablespoons sweet butter, softened
⅓ cup sugar
3 egg yolks, lightly beaten
2 tablespoons flour
½ cup heavy cream
¼ cup sliced almonds
1 9-inch Sweet Pie Crust, partially baked (page 222)

Place the oven rack about a third up from the bottom. Preheat the oven to 350°F.

Place the sliced pears in a shallow dish and sprinkle them generously with lemon juice to prevent discoloring. Set the dish aside.

In a medium mixing bowl combine the softened butter with the sugar. Blend well, then beat in the egg yolks. Stir in the flour, 1 tablespoon at a time. Add the heavy cream in two or three additions, beating the mixture after each addition.

Drain the lemon juice from the sliced pears. Spread them in the bottom of the partially baked crust and sprinkle the sliced almonds evenly over the pear pieces. Spoon the custard over, making sure the pears are well covered.

Bake the pie at 350°F for about 30 minutes, until it is firm and golden brown. Remove the pie from the oven and place it on a wire rack to cool. Reset the oven to 400°F.

ALMOND MERINGUE TOPPING

  2 egg whites
  ¼ teaspoon cream of tartar
  3 tablespoons sugar
  ¼ teaspoon almond extract
  2 tablespoons sliced almonds

In a medium, grease-free mixing bowl beat the egg whites at a slow steady speed. When they are foamy add the cream of tartar. Gradually add the sugar and continue to beat for a few more minutes, until the meringue will form soft peaks. Beat in the almond extract. Use a rubber spatula to fold 1 tablespoon of sliced almonds into the meringue.

With the spatula, spread the meringue evenly over the cooled pie, covering it to the edge of the crust. (The meringue layer will be thin.) Garnish the top with the remaining tablespoon of almonds. Bake at 400°F for 3 to 5 minutes, until the meringue is slightly brown. Serve warm from the oven or at room temperature.

Yield: about 8 servings

Cherries in a Double Crust

DOUBLE CRUST

  2 egg whites
  3 tablespoons sugar
  1 9-inch Graham Cracker Crust, unbaked (page 220)

Place the oven rack about a third up from the bottom. Preheat the oven to 325°F.

In a medium, grease-free mixing bowl beat the egg whites at a slow steady speed until just stiff. Add the sugar 1 tablespoon at a time. Beat, increasing to a moderate speed, until the meringue is thick, glossy, and forms firm peaks when the beaters are lifted.

With a rubber spatula spread a thin layer of the meringue on top of the graham cracker crust. Use the spatula to make a thicker, fluffy meringue band around the sides, pulling some peaks above the cracker crust edge. The meringue peaks should come well above the rim of the pie pan. Bake at 325°F for 8 minutes. Turn the oven down to 200°F and, with the door ajar, bake the crust for another

45 minutes. The meringue should feel firm and dry when touched gently. Remove it from the oven and let it cool to room temperature.

FILLING

> 3 cups pitted Bing cherries
> 1/3 cup kirsch
> 2 tablespoons cornstarch
> 2 tablespoons water
> 1 tablespoon lemon juice
> 1/3 cup corn syrup
> 1 tablespoon butter
> 1/2 teaspoon cinnamon

Place the cherries in a shallow dish, pour the kirsch over them, and set them aside to marinate for an hour or so. In a heavy saucepan combine the cornstarch, water, and lemon juice. Stir until there are no lumps of cornstarch. Over very low heat stir until the mixture just begins to thicken, then add the corn syrup. Continue to stir over low heat for 5 to 7 minutes, until the custard is quite thick. Add the butter and cinnamon. Blend the ingredients thoroughly and then remove the saucepan from the heat.

Drain the cherries and add them to the custard while it is still warm. Stir the mixture until the cherries are well-coated. Set the saucepan aside on a trivet for about 30 minutes to let the filling cool to room temperature. Spoon it into the cooled double crust. Keep the pie in a cool, dry place until time to serve.

Yield: 6–8 servings

Latticed Apple-Walnut Pie

> 3 cups peeled, cored, chopped apples (I like Jonathans or
>   Cortlands)
> About 3 tablespoons lemon juice
> 1/4 cup sweet butter, softened
> 1/3 cup brown sugar, packed
> 1 egg, lightly beaten
> 1 egg yolk
> 2 tablespoons molasses
> 1/4 cup flour

½ *teaspoon cinnamon*
¼ *teaspoon freshly grated nutmeg*
1 *cup chopped walnuts*
1 *9-inch Basic Pie Crust, unbaked (page 219)*

Place the oven rack about a third up from the bottom. Preheat the oven to 350°F.

Brush the chopped apples with the lemon juice so that they don't discolor. Set them aside.

In a large mixing bowl cream the softened butter and brown sugar. In a small mixing bowl beat together the egg, egg yolk, and molasses. Combine the flour, cinnamon, and grated nutmeg and add these dry ingredients to the butter mixture alternately with the egg mixture. Blend well, and stir in the apples and chopped walnuts. Turn the batter into the unbaked pie crust.

Bake the pie at 350°F for about 35 minutes, until it is firm. Remove the pie from the oven and place it on a wire rack to cool. Reset the oven to 425°F.

MERINGUE LATTICE TOPPING

1 *egg white*
Pinch cream of tartar
3 *tablespoons sugar*

In a small or medium, grease-free mixing bowl beat the egg white at a slow steady speed. When it is foamy add the cream of tartar. Gradually add the sugar and continue to beat for another 3 to 5 minutes, until the meringue will form firm peaks when the beaters are lifted.

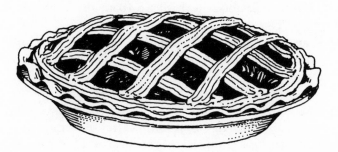

Use a rubber spatula to scoop the meringue into a pastry bag fitted with a small (number 1) star tip. Hold the bag firmly with both hands, keeping it closed and taut with the top hand. Pipe a 2-inch stripe of meringue across the top of the cooled pie, as close to the edge of the pie as possible. Continue to pipe parallel stripes about an inch apart.

When the pie is striped with meringue in one direction, start from the end of the first stripe and press out a line of meringue at a 90-degree angle. Cover the top of the pie with meringue stripes, an inch apart, parallel to this line. Overlap the ends of the meringue stripes at the crust whenever possible. Pipe a thin meringue band around the pie, where the filling meets the crust.

Bake the pie at 425°F for 6 to 8 minutes, until the meringue is brown. Serve warm or at room temperature.

Yield: about 8 servings

Ribboned Cherry-Apricot Pie

3 tablespoons flour
¼ teaspoon cinnamon
¼ teaspoon allspice
¼ cup light brown sugar
3 tablespoons butter or margarine
2 cups pitted fresh tart cherries (or use one 16-ounce can of cherries, packed in water)
4 small firm apricots, halved and pitted (or one 8¾-ounce can apricot halves, drained)
1 9-inch Basic Pie Crust, partially baked (page 219)

Place the oven rack about a third up from the bottom. Preheat the oven to 350°F.

In a medium mixing bowl sift together the flour, cinnamon, and allspice and blend with the brown sugar. Using two knives or pastry blender, cut the butter (or margarine) into the dry ingredients until the mixture forms coarse lumps of about even size.

Arrange the cherries in the bottom of the partially baked crust. Cover the cherries with the butter mixture. Arrange the apricot halves, rounded (outside) up, in the crust around the edge.

Bake the pie at 350°F for 35–45 minutes, until the top is firm, even, and brown. Remove the pie from the oven and place it on a wire rack to cool. Reset the oven to 425°F.

RIBBON MERINGUE TOPPING

2 egg whites
¼ teaspoon cream of tartar
3 tablespoons sugar

In a medium, grease-free mixing bowl beat the egg whites at a slow steady speed. When they are foamy add the cream of tartar. Gradually add the sugar and, when the meringue will form soft peaks, increase to a moderate beating speed. Beat for about another 5 minutes, until the meringue is thick, glossy, and forms firm peaks when the beaters are lifted.

Fit a small pastry bag with a flat tip number 114. Using a rubber spatula, fill the bag with meringue. Hold the bag firmly with both hands, keeping it taut and closed with the top hand. With the tip just over the pie, between any 2 apricot halves, press out a ribbon of meringue across the diameter of the pie. Loop the meringue back over itself, as a loose ribbon, several times. Break the meringue cleanly at the opposite edge of the crust between 2 apricots. Press out another ribbon of meringue perpendicular to the first, beginning and ending between apricot halves. Fill in with meringue ribbons between the other apricots, starting from the crust and breaking the meringue at the center as it meets the longer meringue ribbons.

Brown the pie at 425°F for 5–8 minutes, until the meringue is golden. Serve it warm or at room temperature.

Yield: about 8 servings

Cranberry-Orange Pie

The filling of this pie is quite tart—therefore the meringue is made with more sugar than is usually required for a Chantilly topping.

> ¼ cup butter or margarine, softened
> ½ cup sugar
> 2 egg yolks, lightly beaten
> 2 tablespoons flour
> 1 cup coarsely chopped fresh cranberries (wash and dry them first)
> 1 cup peeled, seeded orange pieces (about 2 oranges, I prefer navel oranges for this recipe)
> ¼ teaspoon cinnamon
> ⅛ teaspoon cloves
> 1 9-inch Basic Pie Crust, partially baked (page 219)

Place the oven rack about a third up from the bottom. Preheat the oven to 350°F.

In a large mixing bowl combine the butter (or margarine) and sugar. Gradually beat in the egg yolks. Stir in the flour, 1 tablespoon at a time. When the mixture is well-blended, fold in the chopped cranberries.

Place the orange pieces in a small bowl. Sprinkle the cinnamon and cloves evenly over them. Toss gently to distribute the spices and then stir the oranges into the filling mixture. Spoon the filling into the partially baked pie crust.

Bake the pie at 350°F for about 35 minutes, until it is firm and slightly brown. Remove the pie from the oven and place it on a wire rack to cool. Leave the oven set at 350°F.

MERINGUE TOPPING AND GARNISH

> 1 teaspoon sugar
> 2 teaspoons orange juice, lukewarm
> 1 tablespoon grated orange rind
> 2 egg whites
> ¼ teaspoon cream of tartar
> ¼ cup sugar
> 1 orange, including rind, thinly sliced

In a small bowl dissolve the teaspoon of sugar in the orange juice. Place the orange rind in this mixture and set it aside to soften.

In a medium, grease-free mixing bowl, beat the egg whites at a slow steady speed. When they are foamy add the cream of tartar. Gradually add the ¼ cup sugar and continue to beat for another few minutes, until the meringue will form soft peaks. Quickly drain the orange juice from the rind and use a rubber spatula to fold the rind into the meringue.

With the spatula, pile the meringue onto the center of the cooled pie, leaving about an inch border of uncovered filling. Arrange the orange slices, overlapping, around this border.

Return the pie to the oven. Brown it at 350°F for 5 to 8 minutes, until the meringue peaks are golden. Serve the pie warm from the oven or at room temperature.

Yield: about 8 servings

Double Meringue Pecan Pie

I like contrasting textures and subtle complementary flavors, so I have made a double meringue topping for this pie. You can also omit Meringue 1 and use just the Chantilly (Meringue 2).

MERINGUE 1

> 1 egg white
> Pinch cream of tartar
> 1 tablespoon sugar
> 3 tablespoons Praline Powder (page 223)

Place the rack in the center of the oven. Preheat the oven to 200°F. Line a small baking sheet with parchment paper and trace a circle 8 inches in diameter onto the parchment.

In a medium, grease-free mixing bowl beat the egg white at a slow steady speed. When it is foamy add the cream of tartar. Gradually add the sugar and then the praline powder. Beat for another 3 to 5 minutes, until the meringue is thick, glossy, and forms firm peaks.

Secure the parchment paper to the baking sheet with a few pinches of meringue. With a rubber spatula spread the meringue on the parchment inside the traced circle. It should be ½ inch to ¾ inch thick.

Bake the meringue at 200°F for about 1 to 2 hours, until it feels firm and dry when pressed gently in the center. Remove the meringue from the oven and peel away the parchment. This meringue circle can be stored in an airtight container for several weeks. Or move the oven rack to a third up from the bottom, reset the oven to 350°F and finish making the pie.

FILLING

⅓ cup light brown sugar, packed
¾ cup dark corn syrup
1 tablespoon molasses
2 tablespoons sweet butter, melted
2 egg yolks
1 egg
1 teaspoon vanilla extract
2 cups pecan halves
1 9-inch Basic Pie Crust, partially baked (page 219)

In a large mixing bowl beat the brown sugar with the corn syrup and molasses. Blend in the melted butter. Beat in the egg yolks, 1 at a time, and then beat in the egg. Add the vanilla extract. When the mixture is thoroughly blended, stir in about 1½ cups of the pecan halves, reserving the other ½ cup for garnish.

Spoon the pie filling into the partially baked crust. Bake the pie at 350°F for about 30 minutes. The pie should be an even light brown and almost firm when tilted gently from side to side. Remove the pie from the oven and place it on a wire rack to cool. Reset the oven to 400°F.

MERINGUE 2

3 egg whites
½ teaspoon cream of tartar
3 teaspoons sugar
½ teaspoon vanilla extract

In a large, grease-free mixing bowl beat the egg whites at a slow steady speed. When they are foamy add the cream of tartar. Gradually add the sugar and continue to beat for a few minutes, until the meringue will form soft peaks. Beat in the vanilla extract.

ASSEMBLING
Place the meringue circle (Meringue 1) on top of the cooled pie. Use a rubber spatula to cover the pie with Meringue 2, making sure that this topping meets the crust edge.

Brown the pie 4 to 6 minutes at 400°F, until the meringue peaks are golden. Garnish with the reserved pecan halves around the edge and serve at once.

Yield: about 8 servings

Walnut Spice Pie

6 ounces cream cheese, softened
2 egg yolks
¼ cup sugar
¼ teaspoon allspice
¼ teaspoon ground cloves
½ cup chopped walnuts
1 Vanilla Meringue Crust, partially baked (page 112)
1–1½ cups walnut halves

Place the oven rack about a third up from the bottom. Preheat the oven to 325°F.

In a medium mixing bowl whip the cream cheese with a large spoon or electric mixer on a slow speed. Beat in the egg yolks, 1 at a time. Sift together the sugar, allspice, and cloves and beat these dry ingredients into the cream cheese mixture. Fold in the chopped walnuts.

Spoon this filling into the partially baked pie crust, spreading it evenly with a rubber spatula. Starting from the crust edge, cover the pie filling with walnut halves placed close together in concentric circles. Bake the pie at 325°F for 3 to 5 minutes. (Do not let the crust color.) Turn the oven down to 200°F and leave the door open for 30 minutes or so. Bake the pie at 200°F for about an hour, until it appears firm when tilted gently from side to side. Remove from the oven and place it on a rack to cool. Keep the pie in a cool, dry place until time to serve.

Yield: about 8 servings

Applesauce and Almond Pie

This pie resembles an upside-down pudding. The meringue crust is made over heat and transferred to a warm pan before baking. And since the filling is added when the crust is only partially done, the meringue has a soft texture.

CRUST

> 4 egg whites
> ½ teaspoon cream of tartar
> 6 tablespoons sugar
> ½ teaspoon vanilla extract

Place the oven rack about a third up from the bottom. Preheat the oven to 200°F. Lightly butter a 9-inch shiny metal pie pan and place it in a pan of tepid water.

Make a double boiler using a large, grease-free, metal mixing bowl that fits snugly over a pot of hot water. Beat the egg whites in the mixing bowl at a slow steady speed. When they are foamy add the cream of tartar. Gradually add the sugar and, when the meringue will form soft peaks, increase to a moderate beating speed. Beat for another 5 to 8 minutes, until the meringue is thick, glossy, and forms firm peaks when the beaters are lifted. Quickly, while the meringue is still warm, add the vanilla extract and blend well.

With a rubber spatula spread the meringue into the warm prepared pan. Make a nest, pushing the meringue higher and thicker around the edge. Make sure that the crust bottom is smooth and even. Bake the crust at 200°F for 2 hours. Remove it from the oven and put it aside to cool. Leave the oven set at 200°F.

FILLING

> 1 egg yolk
> ⅔ cup Applesauce (page 225)
> 1 teaspoon lemon juice
> 2 tablespoons sugar
> ⅛ teaspoon cinnamon
> 1 tablespoon ground almonds
> 1 tablespoon flour
> 1 tablespoon butter or margarine
> ¼ cup sliced almonds
> 1 tablespoon sugar

In a small mixing bowl beat the egg yolk into the applesauce. Blend in the lemon juice. In another small bowl sift together the 2 tablespoons of sugar, the cinnamon, ground almonds, and flour. Use two knives or a pastry cutter to cut the butter into this dry mixture until it resembles coarse meal. Distribute the sliced almonds evenly in the bottom of the cooled partially baked crust. Gently spread the applesauce mixture evenly into the crust and sprinkle the butter mixture on top. Sift the 1 tablespoon of sugar over the pie, including the crust. Bake at 200°F for about 1½ hours, until the filling is firm. Let the pie cool before slicing.

Yield: 6–8 servings

Sweet Potato Pie

I've used texture and subtle spices here to complement the natural flavor of sweet potato. It's not a traditional style—a recipe to select when you want something not too sweet.

DOUBLE CRUST

> 1 9-inch Graham Cracker Crust, unbaked (page 220)
> 2 cups marshmallow pieces (cut marshmallows into quarters or use miniatures)
> 2 tablespoons water
> 2 egg whites
> ¼ teaspoon cream of tartar
> ½ teaspoon vanilla extract

Place the oven rack about a third up from the bottom. Preheat the oven to 375°F.

Line the unbaked graham cracker crust with foil and bake it at 375°F for 3 minutes. Remove it from the oven, lift out the foil, and place the pie pan on a wire rack to cool the crust. Reset the oven to 200°F.

In a small heavy saucepan or in the top of a double boiler over low heat, melt the marshmallow pieces with the water until the mixture is the consistency of thick syrup. Remove the pan from the heat but keep it warm. In a medium, grease-free mixing bowl beat the egg whites at a slow steady speed. When they are foamy add the cream of tartar. Pour the marshmallow syrup into the stiffened egg whites in a slow stream as you continue to beat. When the meringue will form soft peaks, increase to a moderate beating speed. Beat the meringue about another 5 minutes, until it is thick, glossy, and almost forms firm peaks when the beaters are lifted. Beat in the vanilla extract.

Use a rubber spatula to spread an even layer of the marshmallow meringue over the cooled graham cracker crust, leaving a ¼-inch edge of graham cracker crust. Bake the crust at 200°F for 2 hours, until the meringue feels dry in the center. Remove the crust from the oven and place it on a wire rack to cool.

FILLING

> 1 cup cooked mashed sweet potato (bake or boil 1 or 2 sweet
>   potatoes, peel them, and mash the pulp with a fork)
> 2 tablespoons butter, softened
> ¼ cup brown sugar
> 1 tablespoon unflavored gelatin
> ½ teaspoon freshly grated nutmeg
> 1 cup milk
> 3 tablespoons butter
> 2 egg yolks, lightly beaten
> 2 egg whites

Use a blender or electric mixer to combine the mashed sweet potato with the 2 tablespoons butter. Blend until smooth and set the mixture aside.

In a medium saucepan mix together the brown sugar, gelatin, and nutmeg. Place the pan over medium heat and stir in the milk. Cook the mixture for 5–10 minutes, still stirring, until the sugar and gelatin have dissolved. Gradually stir in the beaten egg yolks. Blend in the sweet potato mixture, in four additions. Add the 3 tablespoons butter, 1 at a time, and stir gently for another 5 minutes. The mixture should be smooth and thoroughly blended. Remove the saucepan from the heat and set it aside on a trivet to cool.

When the sweet potato custard has reached room temperature, whip the egg whites in a medium, grease-free mixing bowl at a slow steady speed. When they are quite stiff, fold the egg whites into the sweet potato custard. Spoon this filling into the cooled double crust and refrigerate the pie for an hour or more until it is firm.

Yield: about 8 servings

Pumpkin Spice Pie

I first made this dessert for children who requested a spicy pumpkin pie to warm a snowy winter evening in upstate New York. It's dense but not heavy.

> *2 egg yolks, lightly beaten*
> *⅓ cup brown sugar, packed*
> *⅓ cup milk*
> *2 tablespoons sweet butter, melted*
> *½ teaspoon cinnamon*
> *2 cups cooked, mashed pumpkin (I find it convenient to use a 16-ounce can of pumpkin. Read the label carefully—it must be 100 percent pumpkin, not pie filling.)*
> *1 9-inch Basic Pie Crust without fluted edge, partially baked (page 219)*

Place the oven rack about a third up from the bottom. Preheat the oven to 350°F.

In a large mixing bowl, combine the egg yolks and brown sugar. Stir in the milk and melted butter. When the mixture is smooth, add the cinnamon. Stir in the pumpkin, in three or four additions, and beat lightly for about a minute.

Pour this pie filling into the partially baked pie crust and bake at 350°F for about 30 minutes, until the pie appears firm when tilted gently from side to side. Remove the pie from the oven and place it on a wire rack to cool. Leave the oven set at 350°F.

MERINGUE SPICE TOPPING

> *¼ teaspoon cinnamon*
> *¼ teaspoon allspice*
> *¼ teaspoon freshly grated nutmeg*
> *2 tablespoons sugar*
> *2 egg whites*
> *¼ teaspoon cream of tartar*
> *Fresh nutmeg for grating*

In a small bowl or on wax paper, sift together the cinnamon, allspice, nutmeg, and sugar.

In a medium, grease-free mixing bowl beat the egg whites at a slow steady speed. When they are foamy add the cream of tartar.

Gradually add the sugar mixture and continue to beat for a few more minutes, until the meringue will form soft peaks.

Using a rubber spatula, spoon the meringue in a ring just covering the border of the pie. The crust edge should not show, and the center of the pie should be left exposed. Grate nutmeg generously over the meringue ring and pie center.

Return the pie to the oven and bake at 350°F for 8–10 minutes, until the meringue peaks are golden. This pie is best served immediately.

Yield: about 8 servings

Spicy Banana Pie

DOUBLE CRUST

> 1¼ cups sifted flour
> Pinch salt
> Pinch baking soda
> 2 tablespoons brown sugar
> ¼ teaspoon ground ginger
> 3 tablespoons butter or margarine
> 2 tablespoons molasses
> About 1 tablespoon milk
> 2 egg whites
> ¼ teaspoon cream of tartar
> 3 tablespoons sugar
> ¼ teaspoon vanilla extract

Place the oven rack about a third up from the bottom. Preheat the oven to 225°F. Lightly grease a 9-inch pie pan.

Sift together the flour, salt, baking soda, brown sugar, and ginger in a large mixing bowl. Use two knives or a pastry blender to cut in the butter. When the mixture is coarse, moist lumps, pour the molasses over and cut it in. Add the milk, a few drops at a time, and only as much as necessary to gather the dough into a ball. Place the dough on a pastry cloth or lightly floured board and use a rolling pin or heel of your hand to press it out to a diameter of 11–12 inches. Turn the dough into the prepared pie pan. Use your fingers to fit the crust around the side, and trim away the rough edges with a knife. Flute around the edge by lifting the crust with one thumb against the other thumb and forefinger. Set this gingerbread crust aside in the refrigerator.

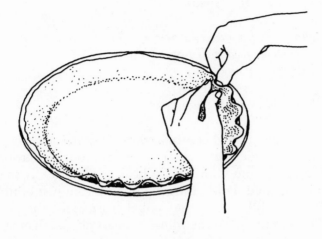

In a medium, grease-free mixing bowl beat the egg whites at a slow steady speed. When they are foamy add the cream of tartar. Gradually add the sugar and, when the meringue will form soft peaks, add the vanilla extract and increase to a moderate beating speed. Beat for another 5–8 minutes, until the meringue is thick, glossy, and forms firm peaks. Use a rubber spatula to spread the meringue on top of the chilled gingerbread crust. Shape a shallow nest, with about 1/2 inch of the gingerbread crust showing above it. Bake this double crust at 225°F for about 30 minutes, until the meringue edges are dry. Remove it from the oven and put it aside to cool. Reset the oven to 350°F.

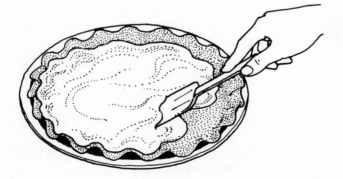

FILLING

2 egg yolks, lightly beaten
1/4 cup sugar
1 cup puréed banana (2 or 3 bananas; slice them and use a
    blender or food mill to purée)
1 tablespoon flour
1/2 teaspoon ground ginger
1/4 cup heavy cream, whipped

In a large mixing bowl combine the egg yolks and sugar. Gradually beat in the puréed banana. Sprinkle the flour and ground ginger over the mixture and continue to beat until batter is smooth and thoroughly blended. Fold in the whipped cream just until no white shows. Pour the filling into the cooled crust. Bake the pie at 350°F for 15–20 minutes, until the filling appears almost firm when tilted gently from side to side. Remove it from the oven and place it on a wire rack to cool. Reset the oven to 375°F.

MERINGUE TOPPING

3 egg whites
1/2 teaspoon cream of tartar
3 tablespoons sugar
1/2 teaspoon vanilla extract

In a large, grease-free mixing bowl beat the egg whites at a slow steady speed. When they are foamy add the cream of tartar. Gradually add the sugar and continue to beat a few minutes until the meringue will form soft peaks. Beat in the vanilla extract.

With a rubber spatula spread the meringue over the cooled pie. Cover any edges of the meringue crust but not the fluted gingerbread border. Return the pie to the oven and bake at 375°F for 5–8 minutes, until the meringue peaks are golden. This pie is excellent hot or cold.

Yield: about 8 servings

Banana Cream Pie

2 egg whites
¼ teaspoon cream of tartar
2 tablespoons sugar
1 cup half-and-half
1 inch vanilla bean, split
About ¼ cup heavy cream
3 egg yolks, lightly beaten
1 tablespoon unflavored gelatin
2 tablespoons sugar
2 tablespoons sweet butter
1 medium banana, split lengthwise
1 9-inch Vanilla Wafer Crumb Crust, baked (page 220)
¼ teaspoon cinnamon
1 medium banana for garnish

In a medium, grease-free mixing bowl beat the egg whites at a slow steady speed. When they are foamy add the cream of tartar. Gradually add 2 tablespoons of sugar and continue to beat for a few minutes until the meringue will form soft peaks.

In a medium saucepan over low heat, warm the half-and-half with the vanilla bean to just before scalding. Drop a heaping tablespoon of the meringue into the saucepan and poach the meringue 1 to 2 minutes on each side, turning it gently with two forks or a shallow strainer. Remove the meringue carefully and place it on a cloth to drain. Repeat the poaching process five or six times until all the meringue has been used. Turn the meringues once or twice on the cloth to be sure they are well-drained. Set them aside at room temperature.

Strain the half-and-half and measure. Add heavy cream to equal 1 cup liquid and pour it, still with the vanilla bean, into the saucepan over low heat. Gradually add the beaten egg yolks. Stir in the gelatin and 2 tablespoons sugar and continue to stir over low heat until these ingredients have dissolved. Add the butter, still stirring gently, and leave the mixture over heat only until it has melted. Take out the vanilla bean and remove the saucepan from the heat.

Slice the split banana into 2-inch sections so that you have 6 to 8 pieces of banana. Arrange the banana pieces like spokes in the bottom of the baked pie crust. You may have to trim the ends at the center so the banana pieces will fit flat. Sprinkle the cinnamon over the bananas evenly and spoon in the cream mixture to cover them completely. Refrigerate the pie for at least 2 hours, until it is firm.

When the pie is set, pile the meringues onto the center of it leaving about a ¾-inch border. Chill the pie in the refrigerator for at least an hour.

Just before serving, slice the other banana and garnish the pie border with overlapping banana slices.

Yield: 6–8 servings

Coconut Cream Pie

4 egg yolks, lightly beaten
¼ cup sugar
¾ cup half-and-half
4 ounces cream cheese, softened
2 tablespoons sweet butter, softened
½ teaspoon vanilla extract
½ teaspoon coconut extract
⅓ cup shredded unsweetened coconut
1 9-inch Basic Pie Crust, partially baked (page 219)

Place the oven rack about a third up from the bottom. Preheat the oven to 350°F.

In a heavy saucepan over low heat or in the top of a double boiler over water, beat the egg yolks together with the sugar. Gradually stir in the half-and-half. Continue to stir the custard gently over low heat for 8–10 minutes, until it begins to thicken. Add the softened cream cheese and butter and cook, stirring occasionally, until the mixture is thoroughly blended, about another 10 minutes. When the custard is smooth, add the vanilla and coconut extracts and re-move the pan from the heat. Stir in the shredded coconut.

Pour the pie filling into the partially baked crust and bake at 350°F for 15–20 minutes, until the pie feels firm when touched lightly in the center. Remove the pie from the oven and place it on a wire rack to cool. Reset the oven to 400°F.

COCONUT MERINGUE TOPPING

4 egg whites
1/2 teaspoon cream of tartar
3 tablespoons sugar
1/4 teaspoon coconut extract
2 tablespoons shredded unsweetened coconut

In a large, grease-free mixing bowl beat the egg whites at a slow steady speed. When they are foamy add the cream of tartar. Gradu-ally add the sugar and continue to beat for a few more minutes, until the meringue will form soft peaks. Beat in the coconut extract. Use a rubber spatula to fold in 1 tablespoon of the shredded coconut.

With the spatula spread the meringue over the cooled pie, piling it higher in the center and making sure the topping meets the crust edge. Pull up some meringue peaks using the spatula. Sprinkle the remaining tablespoon of coconut over the meringue.

Bake the pie at 400°F for about 8 minutes, until the meringue peaks are golden.

Yield: 6–8 servings

Pineapple-Cheese Pie

This pie has the taste of cheese cake but a lighter texture.

8 ounces cream cheese, softened
3 tablespoons sugar
3 egg yolks, lightly beaten
1/2 cup sour cream

1 teaspoon lemon juice
1 cup pineapple chunks
1 9-inch Graham Cracker Crust, partially baked (page 220)

Place the oven rack about a third up from the bottom. Preheat the oven to 350°F.

In a medium mixing bowl whip the cream cheese until smooth and creamy. Blend in the sugar and gradually beat in the egg yolks. Beat in the sour cream, about ¼ cup at a time, and continue to beat for several minutes, until the mixture is very smooth. Stir in the lemon juice.

Place the pineapple chunks evenly in the partially baked pie crust and pour the filling mixture over, making sure the pineapple is well covered.

Bake the pie at 350°F for 25 minutes, until it is firm when tilted gently from side to side. Remove the pie from the oven and place it on a wire rack to cool. Reset the oven to 375°F.

CREAM CHEESE MERINGUE TOPPING

2 ounces cream cheese, softened
1 teaspoon lemon juice
2 egg whites
¼ teaspoon cream of tartar
3 tablespoons sugar

In a small mixing bowl whip the cream cheese with the lemon juice until very light and creamy. Set the mixture aside.

In a medium, grease-free mixing bowl beat the egg whites at a slow steady speed. When they are foamy add the cream of tartar. Gradually add the sugar and continue to beat for a few minutes, until the meringue will form soft peaks. Quickly, using a rubber spatula, fold in the whipped cream cheese.

Use the spatula to pile the meringue over the cooled pie, making it quite high in the center and covering thinly toward the edge. Bake the pie at 375°F for about 8 minutes, until the meringue peaks are golden.

This pie is even better the day after it is baked. Keep it refrigerated until an hour or so before serving it. Serve it at room temperature.

Yield: 8–10 servings

Mocha-Raisin Pie

3 tablespoons sweet butter, softened
1/4 cup brown sugar, packed
2 egg yolks, lightly beaten
1/3 cup strong, freshly brewed coffee (cooled to room
    temperature)
1/2 teaspoon cinnamon
1/4 teaspoon nutmeg
1 tablespoon flour
1 cup raisins
1/2 cup heavy cream
1 9-inch Basic Pie Crust, partially baked (page 219)

Place the oven rack about a third up from the bottom. Preheat the oven to 350°F.

In a large mixing bowl combine the softened butter with the brown sugar. Beat in the egg yolks. Gradually stir in the coffee. Beat until thoroughly mixed. In a small bowl or on a sheet of wax paper, sift together the cinnamon, nutmeg, and flour. Dredge the raisins in these dry ingredients and stir into the butter mixture.

In a medium chilled bowl with chilled beaters, whip the heavy cream. When the cream is stiff, use a rubber spatula to fold it into the main batter. Spoon this filling into the partially baked pie crust.

Bake the pie at 350°F for about 20 minutes, until it is just firm. (Test by tilting it gently from side to side.) Remove the pie from the oven and place it on a wire rack to cool. Leave the oven set at 350°F.

MOCHA MERINGUE TOPPING

2 tablespoons strong, freshly brewed coffee
2/3 cup brown sugar, loosely packed
1 egg white
1/4 teaspoon cream of tartar
Fresh nutmeg for grating

In a saucepan combine the coffee and brown sugar over medium heat. Stir occasionally and bring the mixture to a boil. Let it boil for about 2 minutes, until it is the consistency of syrup. Remove the saucepan to very low heat. In a medium, grease-free mixing bowl whip the egg white at a slow steady speed. When it is foamy add the cream of tartar. Continue to beat and pour in the heated syrup in a slow continuous stream. Beat the meringue for another 3 to 4 minutes, until it is quite thick, glossy, and cool.

Using a rubber spatula, spread the meringue over the cooled pie. Garnish with a light grating of nutmeg. Bake the pie at 350°F for about 8 minutes, until the meringue is lightly brown. Serve warm.

Yield: about 8 servings

Butterscotch Pie

CRUST

> 4 egg whites
> ½ teaspoon cream of tartar
> 6 tablespoons sugar
> 1 teaspoon butterscotch flavor

Place the oven rack about a third up from the bottom. Preheat the oven to 200°F.

In a large, grease-free mixing bowl beat the egg whites at a slow steady speed. When they are foamy add the cream of tartar. Gradually add the sugar and, when the meringue will form soft peaks, add the butterscotch flavor and increase to a moderate beating speed. Beat for another 5 to 8 minutes, until the meringue is thick, glossy, and forms firm peaks when the beaters are lifted.

Use a rubber spatula to scoop the meringue into a 9-inch pie pan. Shape it into a nest, making sure the center is smooth and even and piling the meringue high around the edge. Bake the crust at 200°F for 1½ hours. Watch that it does not color. Remove the partially baked crust from the oven and put it aside to cool. Reset the oven to 325°F.

FILLING

> ⅔ cup brown sugar
> 3 tablespoons sweet butter, softened
> 2 egg yolks, lightly beaten
> 3 tablespoons flour
> ½ teaspoon vanilla extract
> 1 teaspoon butterscotch flavor
> ½ cup chopped walnuts or pecans

In a medium mixing bowl combine the brown sugar and butter. When thoroughly blended, beat in the egg yolks. Stir in the flour, 1 tablespoon at a time, and add the vanilla extract and butterscotch flavor. Sprinkle 2 or 3 tablespoons of the chopped nuts evenly into the cooled pie crust. Fold the remaining nuts into the filling batter and spread the filling into the crust in a thin even layer. Bake at 325°F for 3 to 5 minutes. (Again, do not let the crust color.) Turn the oven down to 200°F, leave the oven door open for about 30 minutes, and let the pie bake for about 2 hours, until it appears almost firm when tilted gently from side to side. Remove the pie from the oven and put it aside to cool. Store the pie in a cool, dry place. This pie is best the day after you make it.

Yield: about 8 servings

Buttered Rum Pie

The texture of this pie resembles a rich pudding.

> ½ cup sweet butter, softened
> ¼ cup brown sugar, packed
> 3 egg yolks, lightly beaten
> 2 tablespoons flour
> ½ cup dark rum
> 1 teaspoon vanilla extract
> ¼ cup heavy cream
> 2 tablespoons sugar
> 1 9-inch Chocolate Wafer Crumb Crust (page 221) or
>   Vanilla Wafer Crumb Crust (page 220), partially baked

Place the oven rack about a third up from the bottom. Preheat the oven to 350°F.

In a medium mixing bowl combine the softened butter with the brown sugar. Blend well and gradually add the beaten egg yolks. Stir in the flour, 1 tablespoon at a time. Pour in the rum, in three or four additions, beating well after each addition. Blend in the vanilla extract. Set this mixture aside.

In a chilled bowl with chilled beaters, whip the heavy cream, adding the 2 tablespoons of sugar gradually. When the cream is stiff, fold it into the rum mixture in two additions. Spoon this filling into the partially baked pie crust.

Bake the pie at 350°F for 45–50 minutes, until it is firm and the top is brown. Remove the pie from the oven and place it on a wire rack to cool. Reset the oven to 375°F.

VANILLA MERINGUE TOPPING

> *4 egg whites*
> *½ teaspoon cream of tartar*
> *¼ cup sugar*
> *2 teaspoons vanilla extract*

In a large, grease-free mixing bowl beat the egg whites at a slow steady speed. When they are foamy add the cream of tartar. Gradually add the sugar and continue to beat for a few minutes until the meringue will form soft peaks. Beat in the vanilla extract, ½ teaspoon at a time.

Use a rubber spatula to pile the meringue over the cooled pie. Be sure that it covers the edge so that no filling or crust shows. Bake the pie at 375°F for 8–10 minutes, until the meringue peaks are brown. This pie is best served warm from the oven.

Yield: 6–8 servings

Mocha Cream Pie

> *3 egg yolks*
> *¾ cup heavy cream*
> *¼ cup sugar*
> *1 tablespoon cornstarch*
> *⅔ cup strong freshly brewed coffee, cooled to lukewarm*
> *1 teaspoon vanilla extract*
> *1 Vanilla Meringue Crust, baked (page 112)*

In a medium mixing bowl with a wire whisk beat the egg yolks, 1 at a time, into the heavy cream. Beat the mixture until it is frothy and then set it aside.

Sift together the sugar and cornstarch in a heavy saucepan or top of a double boiler. Over low heat gradually stir in the coffee. Cook, stirring the mixture to blend it, for about 5 minutes. Add the egg yolk mixture in a slow steady stream, continuing to stir gently.

Let the custard cook for another 30 minutes, until it is bubbling slightly. From time to time while it is cooking, stir it with vigor to prevent lumping. Scrape the sides and bottom of the pan occasionally so that the custard thickens evenly. Stir in the vanilla extract and remove the pan from the heat.

Place the pan on a trivet and cover the custard with a round of wax paper or plastic wrap to prevent a skin from forming. After 15–20 minutes place the pan in the refrigerator to chill for another 30–45 minutes. Spoon the chilled custard into the meringue crust and serve the pie cold.

Yield: 6–8 servings

Sunflower

This delicate confection is a buttery almond cream pie. Prepare it with patience and care.

¼ cup sweet butter, softened
⅓ cup sugar
2 egg yolks
1 teaspoon almond extract
¼ teaspoon vanilla extract
2 tablespoons flour
¼ cup ground blanched almonds
3 egg whites
½ teaspoon cream of tartar
⅔ cup sugar
½ teaspoon almond extract

Place the oven rack about a third up from the bottom. Preheat the oven to 325°F.

In a medium mixing bowl combine the butter and the ⅓ cup sugar. Beat the mixture until the texture is quite light, then beat in the egg yolks 1 at a time. Add the 1 teaspoon almond extract and the vanilla extract. Stir in the flour and the ground almonds, 1 tablespoon at a time. Set this filling aside.

In a large, grease-free mixing bowl beat the egg whites at a slow steady speed. When they are foamy add the cream of tartar. Gradually add the ⅔ cup sugar and, when the meringue will form soft peaks, add the ½ teaspoon almond extract and increase to a moderate beating speed. Beat for another 5 to 8 minutes, until the meringue will form firm peaks when the beaters are lifted.

With a rubber spatula scoop the meringue into an unlined 9-inch metal pie pan. Shape it into a nest, making sure the center is smooth and even and piling the meringue higher around the edge. Very gently spoon the filling into the pie crust. With as little pressure as possible, smooth it into a thin even layer.

Bake the pie at 325°F for 3 to 5 minutes. Watch that the crust edge does not color. Turn the oven down to 200°F, leave the oven door open for about 30 minutes, and let the pie bake for 3 to 4 hours, until it appears almost firm when tilted gently from side to side. Remove the pie from the oven and set it aside to cool. This pie is best the day after you make it. Keep it covered and at room temperature or cooler.

Yield: 6–8 servings

Vanilla Cream Pie

You may also like to try this delicate, creamy pie filling in a Vanilla Meringue Crust (page 112). Either way, I suggest serving it with a pot of espresso.

DOUBLE CRUST

> *3 egg whites*
> *½ teaspoon cream of tartar*
> *¼ cup vanilla sugar*
> *1 9-inch Vanilla Wafer Crumb Crust, partially baked and cooled (page 220)*

Place the oven rack about a third up from the bottom. Preheat the oven to 200°F.

In a medium, grease-free mixing bowl beat the egg whites at a slow steady speed. When they are foamy add the cream of tartar. Gradually add the sugar and, when the meringue will form soft peaks, increase beating speed to moderate. Continue to beat for about another 5 minutes, until the meringue is thick, glossy, and forms firm peaks when the beaters are lifted.

Use a rubber spatula or large spoon to scoop the meringue into the partially baked crust. Pile it higher on the edges, pull up some meringue peaks with the spatula, and make sure the bottom is evenly covered. Bake the crust at 200°F for 3–4 hours, until it feels firm and dry when pressed gently in the center. (Watch that it doesn't color; this crust should be snow white when finished. Leave the oven door open if necessary.) Remove the crust from the oven and let it cool.

FILLING

> 1/3 cup sugar
> 1 tablespoon arrowroot
> 2 egg yolks
> 1 1/2 cups half-and-half (or milk)
> 2 inches vanilla bean, split
> 2/3 cup heavy cream

Sift the sugar and arrowroot together into a heavy saucepan. In a mixing bowl beat the egg yolks, 1 at a time, into the half-and-half (or milk). Place the saucepan over medium heat and stir in the egg yolk mixture, pouring it in a slow steady stream. Add the vanilla bean. Continue to stir, occasionally scraping the sides and bottom of the pan to eliminate any lumps. In about 8–10 minutes the mixture will begin to thicken. Stir a little more vigorously and, as the custard starts to bubble, remove the pan from the heat. Discard the vanilla bean pieces and set the saucepan aside on a trivet to cool. When the custard is lukewarm, pour it into a medium mixing bowl and place it in the refrigerator to chill for about an hour.

In a chilled bowl with chilled beaters whip the heavy cream until it is stiff. Fold the whipped cream into the chilled vanilla custard. Spoon this filling into the prepared pie crust. Keep the pie cool.

Yield: about 8 servings

Cookies and Bars

Meringue Madeleines

. . . With thanks to Marcel Proust, Leslie, and Sally for their respective contributions to this recipe.

> *3 egg whites*
> *Pinch salt*
> *⅓ cup sugar*
> *½ teaspoon vanilla extract*
> *¾ cup sifted cake flour*
> *½ cup sweet butter, melted*

Place the oven rack on the lowest rung. Preheat the oven to 400°F. Butter and lightly flour a dozen large madeleine shells (or muffin tins).

In a large, grease-free mixing bowl (not one of copper this time) beat the egg whites with the pinch of salt at a slow steady speed. When they begin to stiffen, gradually add the sugar. Beat in the vanilla extract. Continue to beat for a few minutes, until the meringue will form soft peaks.

With a rubber spatula fold in the flour, in six additions. Fold in the melted butter quickly, but only about a teaspoon at a time. Use a large spoon to fill the prepared madeleine shells. (This batter must be used at once or the butter will separate.)

Bake the madeleines at 400°F for about 15 minutes, until they are browned and the tops spring back when touched lightly. Remove the tray of shells from the oven. Turn the madeleines onto a wire rack, or directly onto a serving platter or into a basket. They should fall right from the tins (use a knife to loosen them if necessary) and are best eaten right away while they are warm from the oven.

Yield: 12 madeleines

Brownie-Chip Bars

½ recipe Chocolate Butter Cream (page 207)
1 recipe Brownies (page 210), baked in an 8-inch square pan, cooled in the pan, and not sliced
1 Chocolate Chip Vacherin layer (½ recipe, page 89), made in an 8-inch square

Spread the butter cream over the brownies still in the baking pan. Add the chocolate chip meringue layer on top. Use a serrated knife to slice it into bars. Lift the bars out of the pan with a spatula. The edges may need to be trimmed with the knife. Put the bars in the refrigerator for 30–45 minutes, just until the butter cream is firm. Serve them cool.

Yield: about 20 bars

Praline Squares

These confections will melt in your mouth.

3 egg whites
¼ teaspoon cream of tartar
⅓ cup sugar
½ teaspoon vanilla extract
¾ cup Praline Powder (page 223)
¼ cup chopped pecans
½ recipe Praline Butter Cream (page 208)
About 24 pecan halves

Place the oven rack about a third up from the bottom. Preheat the oven to 250°F. Line an 12 × 16-inch baking sheet with parchment paper.

In a large, grease-free mixing bowl beat the egg whites at a slow steady speed. When they are foamy add the cream of tartar. Gradually add the sugar and, when the meringue will form soft peaks, add the vanilla extract and increase to a moderate beating speed. Beat for another 5 to 8 minutes, until the meringue is thick, glossy, and forms firm peaks when the beaters are lifted. Use a rubber spatula to fold in the praline powder, in three additions, and the chopped pecans. Spread the praline meringue evenly on the prepared baking sheet.

Bake at 250°F for at least an hour, until the meringue feels firm and dry when pressed lightly. Remove it from the oven and use a sharp knife to slice the meringue sheet in half. Peel away the paper from both halves. When they are cool, spread one of the meringue pieces with the praline butter cream, reserving about a tablespoon of it. Place the other meringue piece on top and cut into 2-inch squares. Use a pinch of the reserved praline butter cream to secure a pecan half on each square.

Yield: about 24 squares

Raspberry Bars

1 cup sugar
2 cups sifted flour
1 cup butter or margarine, softened
3 egg yolks, lightly beaten
1 teaspoon vanilla extract
¾ cup raspberry preserves (or jam)
3 egg whites
¼ teaspoon cream of tartar
⅓ cup sugar
¾ cup chopped walnuts

Place the oven rack about a third up from the bottom. Preheat the oven to 350°F. Grease the bottom of a 9 × 13-inch pan.

Sift together the cup of sugar and flour and set this dry mixture aside. In a large mixing bowl cream the softened butter. (Use a large spoon; you don't need an electric mixer.) Blend in the dry mixture, in three additions. Combine the beaten egg yolks with the vanilla extract and stir this mixture into the main batter. Use your fingertips, if necessary, to blend thoroughly. Press the dough evenly into the prepared pan. Prick it with a fork. Bake this base at 350°F for 15–20 minutes, until the edges are lightly browned. Remove this cake base from the oven and spread the raspberry preserves over it.

In a large, grease-free mixing bowl beat the egg whites at a slow steady speed. When they are foamy add the cream of tartar. Gradually add the ⅓ cup sugar and continue to beat for a few more minutes, until the meringue will form soft peaks. Use a rubber spatula to fold in the chopped walnuts. Spread the meringue over the preserves with the spatula, making sure it is completely covered and sealed.

Return the cake to the oven, still set at 350°F, and bake it for another 15–20 minutes, until the meringue is lightly browned. Remove the pan from the oven and place it on a wire rack to cool for just a few minutes. While the cake is still warm slice it into bars and remove them from the pan with a spatula. These bars are good warm or at room temperature. They will keep, stored in a cool dry place, for a few days.

Yield: about 18 bars

S'mores

Here's a grown-up version of Girl Scout campfire treats.

> *1 cup light brown sugar*
> *2 cups graham cracker crumbs*
> *1 teaspoon vanilla extract*
> *¾ cup butter (or margarine) melted*
> *½ cup chopped walnuts*
> *½ cup semisweet chocolate pieces*
> *3 cups marshmallow pieces (cut marshmallows into quarters or*
> *   use miniatures)*
> *⅓ cup water*
> *3 egg whites*

Place the oven rack about a third up from the bottom. Preheat the oven to 375°F. Grease a 9 × 13-inch pan.

Combine the sugar and graham cracker crumbs in a large mixing bowl. Stir the vanilla extract into the melted butter and then pour it over the dry ingredients. Stir with a large spoon until the mixture is evenly moistened. Fold in the chopped walnuts. Turn the mixture into the prepared pan and use your fingertips to distribute it evenly and pack it firmly. Bake this base for 5 minutes at 375°F. Remove the pan from the oven, scatter the chocolate pieces over the base, and set it aside. Leave the oven set at 375°F.

In a medium saucepan over low heat, combine the marshmallows and water. Heat until the marshmallows have melted. Immediately start to beat the egg whites in a large, grease-free mixing bowl at a slow steady speed. When they are foamy add the marshmallow syrup in a slow steady stream. Continue to beat for a few minutes, until the meringue will form very soft peaks. With a rubber spatula spread the meringue evenly over the chocolate-covered base and return it to the oven. Bake at 375°F for another 8–10 minutes, until the meringue peaks are golden. Remove the s'mores from the oven, let them cool for 10 minutes, slice into bars, and remove from the pan with a spatula.

Yield: about 18 bars

Walnut-Cheese Bars

2 tablespoons cocoa
6 tablespoons sugar
4 egg whites
1/2 teaspoon cream of tartar
1/4 cup sugar
3 egg yolks, lightly beaten
1/4 cup heavy cream
1 pound cream cheese, softened
1/2 cup chopped walnuts

Place the oven rack about a third up from the bottom. Preheat the oven to 225°F. Line a 12 × 16-inch shallow pan or baking sheet with parchment paper.

Sift together the cocoa and 6 tablespoons sugar. In a large, grease-free mixing bowl beat the egg whites at a slow steady speed. When they are foamy add the cream of tartar. Gradually beat in the sugar/cocoa mixture and, when the meringue will form soft peaks, increase to a moderate beating speed. Beat for another 5–8 minutes, until the meringue is thick, glossy, and forms firm peaks when the beaters are lifted.

Glue the parchment paper to the pan with a few pinches of meringue. Use a large rubber spatula to spread the meringue evenly into the prepared pan. Smooth away any peaks and press it lightly so that the thickness is uniform. Bake the meringue at 225°F for 45–60 minutes, until it feels firm and dry when touched gently in the center. Remove the meringue from the oven and let it cool just a minute or so. With a small sharp knife slice the meringue lengthwise into two pieces each measuring 6 × 16 inches. Peel the paper away from the meringue pieces but leave them in the pan while you prepare the filling.

In a heavy saucepan or in top of a double boiler beat the ¼ cup sugar into the egg yolks. Over very low heat gradually stir in the heavy cream. After 5–8 minutes, when the mixture starts to thicken, blend in the cream cheese 1 tablespoon at a time. Beat the mixture with a little more vigor as you add the cream cheese so that it becomes velvety smooth. Let it cook, still beating, for another 5 minutes or so, until the texture is quite thick but even. Remove the saucepan from the heat and fold in the chopped walnuts. Set the pan aside on a trivet and let the filling cool to lukewarm.

With a small rubber spatula spread the filling on one of the meringue pieces still in the baking pan. Place the other meringue piece on top. Again, with a very sharp knife (or serrated knife), slice the filled meringue lengthwise. Then slice each length into eight bars. Use a spatula to remove the bars from the pan. Wrap them loosely in foil and store them in the refrigerator.

Yield: 16 bars

Lemon-Walnut Slices

Contrary to the rules, this dessert has a sticky meringue topping and is best when prepared a few days ahead.

> ½ cup sweet butter
> ¾ cup sugar
> 2 eggs, beaten
> 3 egg yolks, beaten
> 1 tablespoon grated lemon rind
> ¾ cup flour
> 1¼ teaspoons baking powder
> 2 tablespoons cognac
> 2 tablespoons milk

Place the oven rack about a third up from the bottom. Preheat the oven to 350°F. Grease and lightly flour a 9 × 13-inch pan.

In a large mixing bowl blend the butter and sugar. Beat in the eggs and then the egg yolks. Blend well and stir in the lemon rind. Sift the flour and baking powder together. In a small bowl combine the cognac and milk. Add the dry ingredients to the egg mixture, about 2 tablespoons at a time, alternately with the cognac/milk mixture. Stir until blended and then beat well after each addition. Spread the batter into the prepared pan.

Bake the cake at 350°F for about 15 minutes, until the top springs back when touched lightly in the center. Remove the cake from the oven and cool it, still in the pan, on a wire rack. Turn the oven down to 300°F.

MERINGUE

> 3 egg whites
> ⅓ cup sugar
> 1 tablespoon lemon juice
> 1½ cups chopped walnuts

In a medium, grease-free mixing bowl beat the egg whites at a slow steady speed until foamy. Gradually add the sugar and beat at a moderate speed until it has dissolved and the meringue forms soft peaks. Beat in the lemon juice. Use a rubber spatula to fold in the chopped walnuts. Spread this meringue evenly over the cooled cake. Bake at 300°F for 15 minutes, until the meringue is lightly browned. Remove it from the oven. Let the cake, still in the baking pan, cool slightly.

TOPPING

> ½ cup water
> ¼ cup sugar

Combine the water and sugar in a small saucepan over medium heat. Stirring occasionally, let the mixture boil for about 10 minutes. When it has the consistency of a light syrup, remove from the heat and pour over the cake immediately. Still leaving it in the baking pan, slice the cake into individual servings. Cover loosely with aluminum foil and store at room temperature for a few days. Freeze leftovers wrapped in foil and warm them in a moderate oven before serving.

Yield: 12–18 slices

Cupcakes

1 cup sugar
6 tablespoons sweet butter, melted
2 egg yolks
1 egg
¾ cup ground blanched almonds
1 teaspoon baking powder
2 teaspoons vanilla extract

Place the oven rack in the center. Preheat the oven to 350°F. Line about 18 muffin cups with buttered paper liners.

In a large mixing bowl combine the sugar and melted butter. Beat in the egg yolks 1 at a time. Add the egg and beat until blended. Stir together the ground almonds and baking powder. Blend this dry mixture, in at least three additions, into the batter. Beat in the vanilla extract.

Spoon a heaping tablespoon of batter into each prepared muffin tin. Bake the cupcakes at 350°F for about 20 minutes, until the centers have fallen and the edges are brown. Remove the cupcakes from the oven and place them, still in the muffin tins, on a wire rack to cool slightly. Reset the oven to 400°F.

JELLY MERINGUE

About 2 tablespoons cream cheese (optional)
2 egg whites
½ teaspoon cream of tartar
1 cup raspberry or red currant jelly, melted

If you are using cream cheese, spread a thin layer over each cupcake. In a large, grease-free mixing bowl beat the egg whites at a slow steady speed. When they are foamy add the cream of tartar. Beat in the melted jelly 1 tablespoon at a time and continue to beat for about 5 minutes, until the meringue is thoroughly blended and smooth. (This meringue will have a softer consistency than a sugar meringue at soft-peak stage.)

Spoon the meringue in mounds over each of the cupcakes. The meringue should peak well above the rims of the muffin tins. Bake the cupcakes at 400°F for about 5 minutes, just until the meringue feels dry. Do not let the meringue brown; it should remain a pink or rosy color.

The cupcakes are best served warm. They can be stored in an airtight container for a day or two.

Yield: about 18 cupcakes

Cheese Tortelets

2 tablespoons sweet butter, melted
⅓ cup chocolate wafer crumbs
1 tablespoon finely chopped nuts (optional)
8 ounces cream cheese, softened
¼ cup sour cream
¼ cup sugar
4 egg yolks, lightly beaten
½ cup sugar
2 tablespoons water
1 egg white
½ teaspoon vanilla extract
¾ cup sour cream

Place the oven rack about a third up from the bottom. Preheat the oven to 350°F. Line muffin cups with lightly greased paper liners.

In a small or medium mixing bowl pour the melted butter over the chocolate wafer crumbs and chopped nuts and stir or toss until the crumbs are evenly moistened. Set the mixture aside.

In a large mixing bowl whip the softened cream cheese. Use an electric mixer, if necessary, to obtain a smooth light texture. Whip in the ¼ cup sour cream. In a separate bowl beat the sugar into the egg yolks. Gradually whip this mixture into the cream cheese. Set this mixture aside.

In a small saucepan combine the ½ cup sugar and water over medium heat. Stir occasionally until the sugar syrup reaches 234°F (soft-ball stage). Remove the pan from the heat. Quickly, in a medium mixing bowl beat the egg white at a slow steady speed. When it begins to stiffen, pour in the sugar syrup in a slow steady stream. Continue to beat for 3 to 5 minutes, until the meringue has cooled and is quite thick and smooth. Beat in the vanilla extract. Use a rubber spatula to fold in the ¾ cup of sour cream, about ¼ cup at a time.

With your fingertips press the cracker crumb mixture into the prepared muffin tins, about a tablespoon in each. Then fill the tins about two-thirds full with the cream cheese mixture, and top them with the sour cream meringue. Bake the tortelets at 350°F for 20–25 minutes, just until the tops are firm. Remove from the oven and let them cool on a rack. These tortelets freeze nicely. Let them thaw at room temperature and peel off the papers before serving.

Yield: 12–15 tortelets

Nest Cookies

These cookies are decorative and fun—a great easy dessert for a children's party.

>1 cup sweet butter, softened
>1⅓ cups sugar
>2 egg yolks, lightly beaten
>1 teaspoon vanilla extract
>1 teaspoon coconut extract
>¼ teaspoon baking powder
>2 heaping cups sifted flour
>2 egg whites
>¼ teaspoon cream of tartar
>3 tablespoons sugar
>½ teaspoon coconut extract
>⅓ cup shredded coconut
>About 1 cup jelly beans

Place the oven rack about a third up from the bottom. Preheat the oven to 350°F. Butter one very large cookie sheet (or two smaller sheets).

In a large mixing bowl cream the butter. Gradually blend in the sugar. Stir in the egg yolks and the teaspoons of vanilla and coconut extracts. Beat the mixture to blend it thoroughly. Add the baking powder to the flour and stir this dry mixture, about ½ cup at a time, into the batter. Use your fingertips if necessary to make the dough smooth and even.

Divide the dough into six equal parts and roll each into a ball. Place the balls, at least 6 inches apart, on the prepared cookie sheet. Bake the cookies at 350°F for 10–12 minutes, until they are almost dry but not yet brown around the edges. Remove the cookie sheet from the oven. Reset the oven to 375°F.

While the cookies are baking, make the meringue. In a medium, grease-free mixing bowl beat the egg whites at a slow steady speed.

When they are foamy add the cream of tartar. Gradually add the 3 tablespoons sugar and continue to beat for a few more minutes, until the meringue will form soft peaks. Beat in the ½ teaspoon coconut extract.

Use a rubber spatula to pile meringue around the edge of each cookie, leaving about a half-inch border. Pull up some peaks of meringue with the spatula and spread a thin layer of meringue inside each "nest." Sprinkle shredded coconut over the meringue nests. Return the cookies to the oven at 375°F for about 8 minutes, until the meringue peaks are golden. Remove the cookie sheet from the oven. With a spatula loosen the cookies and place them on a wire rack to cool.

When the cookies are lukewarm fill each one with jelly beans.

Yield: 6 very large cookies

VARIATION

Add another teaspoon of vanilla extract to the cookie dough and omit the coconut extract and the meringue. Fold 1 cup of semisweet chocolate chips into the dough before shaping it into balls. Bake these large chocolate chip cookies at 350°F for about 15 minutes, until the edges are light brown.

Pignoli Cookies

2 egg whites
Pinch salt
⅔ cup vanilla sugar
¼ teaspoon coconut extract
⅓ cup grated or shredded coconut (fresh is best; if you use
    sweetened coconut, reduce vanilla sugar to a scant ½ cup)
1 cup pignoli

Place the oven rack in the center. Preheat the oven to 350°F. Line a large cookie sheet with parchment paper.

In a large, grease-free mixing bowl beat the egg whites with the salt at a slow steady speed. Gradually add the vanilla sugar and, when the meringue will form soft peaks, beat in the coconut extract and increase to a moderate beating speed. Beat for about another 5 minutes, until the meringue will form firm peaks when the beaters are lifted. Use a rubber spatula to fold in the grated coconut in three additions, and then add the pignoli about 2 tablespoons at a time.

Drop scant tablespoonfuls of the batter onto the prepared cookie sheet. Bake the cookies at 350°F for about 15 minutes, until they feel dry and the edges are brown. (The cookies should be chewy in the center.) Remove the cookie sheet from the oven and loosen the cookies from the parchment with a spatula. Let them cool for a few minutes.

Yield: about 40 cookies

Butterscotch Cookies

1 cup sugar
¼ cup water
2 egg whites
2 teaspoons butterscotch flavor
2 tablespoons flour
About ¾ cup pecan halves

Place the rack in the center of the oven. Preheat the oven to 325°F. Line a cookie sheet with parchment paper.

In a saucepan combine the sugar and water over medium heat and stir until the mixture comes to a boil. Let it boil for a few minutes to 234°F (soft-ball stage). Remove the saucepan from the heat but keep it warm. Quickly, in a large, grease-free mixing bowl beat the egg whites at a slow steady speed. When they begin to stiffen, pour in the warm sugar syrup in a thin stream and continue to beat for a few more minutes until the meringue is thick, glossy, and cool. Beat in the butterscotch and use a rubber spatula to fold in the flour.

Arrange the pecan halves at 1½-inch intervals on the prepared cookie sheet. Drop shallow tablespoonfuls of meringue over them. Bake the cookies at 325°F for about 20 minutes, until they feel dry. Remove them from the cookie sheet with a spatula.

Yield: 3–4 dozen cookies

Chocolate Macaroons

1 cup sugar
¼ cup water
2 egg whites
¼ teaspoon cream of tartar

¼ *cup cocoa*
1⅓ *cups shredded or grated coconut (If you use sweetened*
   coconut, reduce sugar to ¾ cup and water to 3 tablespoons.)

Place the oven rack about a third up from the bottom. Preheat the oven to 325°F. Generously grease a baking sheet.

In a saucepan combine the sugar and water and bring the syrup to a boil. Let it boil over medium heat for 2 to 3 minutes until it reaches 234°F (soft-ball stage). Remove the saucepan from the heat. Quickly, in a large, grease-free mixing bowl beat the egg whites at a slow steady speed. When they are foamy add the cream of tartar. When the egg whites are stiff, gradually beat in the boiled syrup, pouring it in a continuous stream. As soon as the meringue is blended and will form soft peaks, add the cocoa, sifting it in 1 tablespoon at a time. Continue to beat for a few minutes until the meringue is thick, glossy, and cool. With a rubber spatula fold in the shredded or grated coconut in four additions.

Spoon rounded tablespoonfuls of the meringue onto the prepared baking sheet about ½ inch apart. Bake the macaroons at 325°F for about 20 minutes, until they feel firm and dry when pressed gently. (Do not let them brown. Turn the oven down or leave the door ajar if necessary.) Remove the baking sheet from the oven and use a spatula to transfer the macaroons to a wire rack. Let them cool for about 15 minutes.

Yield: about 2 dozen macaroons

Chocolate Meringue Kisses

These cookies have the taste and chewy texture of brownies but are lighter and easier to make.

2 *egg whites*
⅔ *cup confectioners' sugar*
4 *ounces bittersweet chocolate, melted*
2–3 *tablespoons finely chopped pecans*

Place the oven rack about a third up from the bottom. Preheat the oven to 350°F. Line a baking sheet with parchment paper.

In a medium or large, grease-free mixing bowl beat the egg whites at a slow steady speed until stiff. Gradually add the confectioners' sugar and increase to a moderate beating speed. Beat the meringue for 3–5 minutes, until it is glossy and will form soft peaks. Add the melted chocolate, pouring it in gradually, and beat the mixture a few minutes to blend thoroughly. Use a rubber spatula to fold in the chopped pecans.

Glue the parchment paper to the baking sheet with a few pinches of meringue. Drop teaspoonfuls of the meringue onto the prepared baking sheet about 2 inches apart. Bake at 350°F for 10–15 minutes, until just crisp. Remove the baking sheet from the oven and use a spatula or knife to lift the kisses from the parchment. Let them cool for about 15 minutes. They will keep nicely for up to two weeks in a cookie tin or other airtight container.

Yield: about 36 kisses

Nut Kisses

The story has been told that when Queen Elizabeth I first tasted meringues, she kissed the napkin on which they had been served and named these charming delicacies kisses.

> *1 egg white*
> *1 cup brown sugar, loosely packed*
> *¾ cup chopped pecans (or walnuts)*

Place the oven rack about a third up from the bottom. Preheat the oven to 350°F. Line a baking sheet with parchment paper.

In a medium, grease-free mixing bowl beat the egg white at a slow steady speed until it is stiff but not dry. Add the brown sugar gradually, sifting it through your fingertips to break up any lumps, and increase to a moderate beating speed. Beat the meringue for about 5 minutes, until it is thick, glossy, and almost forms firm peaks. With a spoon or rubber spatula fold in the chopped nuts.

Glue the parchment paper to the baking sheet with a few pinches of meringue. Drop rounded teaspoonfuls of the meringue onto the prepared baking sheet about 2 inches apart. Bake at 350°F for 15 minutes, until crisp and slightly browned. (The edges are quick to burn, so watch carefully.) You may need a spatula to loosen the kisses from the parchment. Let them cool for about 15 minutes. They'll keep in an airtight container for up to two weeks.

Yield: about 24 kisses

Granola Cookies

3 egg whites
¼ teaspoon cream of tartar
3 tablespoons brown sugar
1 teaspoon vanilla or almond extract
3 cups granola cereal (I prefer the kind with nuts or nuts and
    raisins)
Maraschino cherries for garnish (optional)

Place the oven rack about a third up from the bottom. Preheat the oven to 350°F. Line a cookie sheet with parchment paper and lightly grease it.

In a large, grease-free bowl beat the egg whites at a slow steady speed. When they are foamy add the cream of tartar. Gradually add the brown sugar, sifting it in through your fingertips to be sure it is free of lumps. Beat in the vanilla or almond extract and continue to beat until the meringue forms soft peaks. Use a rubber spatula to fold in the granola, about ½ cup at a time. When the batter is evenly blended, drop it by rounded tablespoonfuls onto the prepared cookie sheet.

Bake the cookies at 350°F for about 20 minutes, until they are brown. Press a maraschino cherry into the center of each if you wish to garnish them, and remove the cookies from the cookie sheet with a spatula while they are still warm.

Yield: about 3 dozen cookies

Puddings, Alaskas, Fruits, Vegetables, and Even Some Cheese

Rum Alaska

I served this dessert to a friend who is not terribly fond of meringue. He asked for second and third helpings. It is quite simple to prepare—the base can be made ahead and frozen for up to a week. Then allow yourself about 15 minutes to make the meringue and put on the finishing touches before serving this spectacular flaming Alaska.

> *1 recipe Rum Brownies, baked in an 8-inch round pan*
> *(page 226)*
> *1 tablespoon rum (optional)*
> *1 quart rum raisin (or vanilla) ice cream, softened*

Put the baked rum brownie base on an ovenproof serving platter. If the base is dry or if you like a strong rum taste, sprinkle the base with the optional tablespoon of rum. Shape the ice cream into a mound on the cake base, leaving a 1-inch border around its perimeter. Cover the prepared base with plastic wrap and freeze it for several hours. (This prepared base can also be frozen for a week or two.)

MERINGUE TOPPING

> 5 egg whites
> ½ teaspoon cream of tartar
> ½ cup sugar
> 1 teaspoon vanilla extract
> ⅓ cup rum

Place the oven rack in the center and preheat the oven to 500°F. Spread ice cubes evenly in the bottom of a shallow ovenproof dish that is at least 9 inches in diameter.

In a large, grease-free mixing bowl beat the egg whites at a slow steady speed. When they are foamy add the cream of tartar. Gradually add the sugar and continue to beat for a few minutes until the meringue will form soft peaks. Beat in the vanilla extract.

Remove the prepared Alaska base from the freezer and place it in the ice-filled dish. Using a rubber spatula, quickly cover the base with the meringue. Bring the meringue slightly over the base border to seal in the ice cream. Place the Alaska, still in the ice-filled dish, in a 500°F oven for 3 to 5 minutes, just until the meringue is browned. While the meringue is browning, heat the rum in a small lipped saucepan. Remove the Alaska from the oven and lift the platter from the ice-filled dish. Ignite the heated rum and pour it over the meringue. Take the flaming Alaska to the table and serve immediately.

Yield: 6–8 servings

Butterscotch Alaska

One Fourth of July I made this Alaska recipe for a friend who is fond of butterscotch. It was a hot and rainy evening but we rushed it from the oven to the table with such haste that the ice cream had not a chance to melt nor did the meringue wilt.

> 1 recipe Butterscotch Brownies (page 211), baked in a 9-inch round cake pan

1 quart butter pecan ice cream, softened
6 egg whites
1 teaspoon cream of tartar
¼ cup sugar
1½ teaspoons butterscotch flavor
About ½ cup pecan halves

Put the brownie base on an ovenproof platter. Shape the ice cream into a mound on the base, leaving about a 1-inch border. Cover this prepared base with plastic wrap and freeze it for several hours. (It can be kept in the freezer for up to two weeks.)

Place the oven rack in the center and preheat the oven to 500°F. Spread ice cubes evenly in the bottom of a shallow ovenproof dish that is at least 10 inches in diameter.

In a large, grease-free mixing bowl beat the egg whites at a slow steady speed. When they are foamy add the cream of tartar. Gradually add the sugar and then the butterscotch flavor. Continue to beat for a few minutes, until the meringue will form soft peaks.

Remove the prepared Alaska base from the freezer and place it in the ice-filled pan. Quickly, using a rubber spatula, pile the meringue over the ice cream and cover the brownie border with meringue so that the ice cream is sealed in. Garnish with a ring of pecan halves around the border. Bake the Alaska in the ice-filled pan at 500°F for 3 to 5 minutes, until the meringue peaks are golden. Remove it from the oven, lift the platter from the ice-filled tray, and serve immediately.

Yield: 6–8 servings

Mint Alaska

1 recipe Brownies, baked in a 9-inch round pan (page 210; if you like lots of mint flavor add ½ teaspoon mint extract to the batter before baking)
1 quart mint chocolate chip ice cream, softened
¼ cup cocoa
⅔ cup sugar
6 egg whites
½ teaspoon cream of tartar
½ teaspoon mint extract
1–2 tablespoons bittersweet chocolate shavings or chips for garnish (optional)

Put the baked brownie base on an ovenproof platter. Shape the ice cream in a mound on the base, leaving about a ¾-inch border. Cover this prepared base with plastic wrap and freeze it for several hours. (It can be kept in the freezer for up to two weeks.)

Place the rack in the center of the oven and preheat the oven to 500°F. Spread ice cubes evenly in the bottom of a shallow ovenproof dish that is at least 10 inches in diameter.

Sift together the cocoa and sugar. In a large, grease-free mixing bowl whip the egg whites at a slow steady speed. When they are foamy add the cream of tartar. Gradually add the cocoa/sugar mixture and continue to beat until the meringue will form soft peaks. Add the mint extract and increase to a moderate beating speed. Beat for another 5 to 8 minutes, until the meringue is thick, glossy, and forms firm peaks when the beaters are lifted.

Use a rubber spatula to scoop the meringue into a pastry bag fitted with a medium star tip (I like number 7A, which is a swirl/star shape). Remove the prepared Alaska base from the freezer and place it in the ice-filled pan. Hold the pastry bag firmly with both hands, using the top one to keep it closed and taut. Press out two circles of meringue on the brownie base border. Continue to spiral the meringue around the mound of ice cream, making sure that the ice cream is completely sealed in. Bake the Alaska, in the ice-filled pan, at 500°F for about 3 minutes, just until the meringue feels dry when touched lightly. Remove it from the oven and, if desired, garnish with chocolate shavings or chips. Lift the platter from the ice-filled pan and serve the Alaska immediately.

Yield: about 6 servings

Meringue and Ice Cream

Here are a few more ideas for combining meringue with ice cream; the list could go on endlessly.

1. Make individual Alaskas. Freeze a scoop of ice cream on a slice of Yolk Cake (page 212). Preheat the oven to 500°F and prepare a shallow ovenproof tray of ice cubes. Allow 2 servings per egg white. Beat the egg whites with sugar (2 tablespons per white) and ½–1 teaspoon extract or flavor to a meringue that forms soft peaks when the beaters are lifted. Place the frozen cake slices on an ovenproof platter. Set the platter on the tray of ice cubes. Heap meringue over the ice cream, sealing it well. Bake the individual Alaskas at 500°F for about 3 minutes, until the meringue peaks are golden. Serve immediately.

2. Line ovenproof bowls with a thick layer of coarse vanilla wafer crumbs or graham cracker crumbs. Scoop a mound of vanilla ice cream into each dish. Place the dishes in an ice-lined ovenproof tray in the freezer. Make a butterscotch meringue. Allow 3 servings per every 2 egg whites. Beat the whites with 3 tablespoons sugar per 2 whites and ½ teaspoon butterscotch flavor into a meringue that forms soft peaks when the beaters are lifted. Remove the ice-filled tray from the freezer and pile meringue into the dishes, covering the ice cream thoroughly. Bake these Alaska dishes, still on ice, at 500°F for 3 minutes.

3. Make an Alaska cake. Spread a pint of softened ice cream between two layers of Génoise (page 227). Freeze for about an hour. Make a meringue Chantilly with 4 egg whites, ⅓ cup sugar, and 1 teaspoon vanilla extract. Beat the meringue until it forms soft peaks when the beaters are lifted. Fold ½ cup chopped nuts into the meringue. Spread the meringue over the frozen cake. Bake the cake, on an ice-lined ovenproof tray, at 500°F for 3 to 5 minutes, until the meringue peaks are golden.

Applesauce Pudding

2 egg yolks
2 ounces cream cheese, softened
3 tablespoons sugar
1 teaspoon vanilla extract
1 tablespoon flour
¼ teaspoon allspice
¼ teaspoon cinnamon
½ cup raisins
1 recipe Applesauce (page 225)
2 egg whites
¼ teaspoon cream of tartar
3 tablespoons sugar
Cinnamon and allspice for garnish

Place the rack in the center of the oven. Preheat the oven to 325°F. Butter a shallow 1½- or 2-quart casserole.

In a medium mixing bowl beat the egg yolks until they are light and thick. Beat in the cream cheese, about a tablespoon at a time (I suggest using an electric mixer at a medium speed). When the mixture is smooth and creamy, add the sugar, 1 tablespoon at a time, and the vanilla extract. Set the mixture aside.

Sift together the flour, allspice, and cinnamon. Dredge the raisins in these dry ingredients and fold the raisin mixture into the whipped cream cheese. Add the applesauce, folding it in about ½ cup at a time. Stir just until the pudding is blended. Spoon the pudding into the prepared casserole.

Bake the pudding at 325°F for 45–60 minutes, until the edges are faintly brown. (The pudding will not be firm.) Remove it from the oven and let it cool while you make the meringue. Reset the oven to 375°F.

In a medium, grease-free mixing bowl beat the egg whites at a slow steady speed. When they are foamy add the cream of tartar. Gradually add the sugar and continue to beat for a few more minutes until the meringue will form soft peaks. With a rubber spatula spread the meringue over the pudding. Dust it lightly with cinnamon and allspice.

Return the pudding to the oven and bake it at 375°F for about 8 minutes, until the meringue is golden. Remove the pudding from the oven and place it on a trivet to cool for about 30 minutes. Serve it lukewarm.

Yield: about 6 servings

Michael's Rice Pudding

Named for the concierge at the Plaza Hotel because it is one of his favorite desserts and he suggested this lovely way of layering the pudding with poached meringue. You can also omit the poaching process, make the pudding and, when it's almost done, top it with the meringue and a generous grating of nutmeg and bake until the meringue peaks are golden.

3–4 cups milk
4 egg whites
½ teaspoon cream of tartar
⅓ cup vanilla sugar
1 inch vanilla bean, split
½ cup uncooked rice
2 tablespoons sweet butter
4 egg yolks
2 eggs
⅓ cup sugar
1 cup heavy cream
½ teaspoon freshly grated nutmeg
*1 cup raisins (marinated in 1 tablespoon of cognac or bourbon
   if desired)*

Place the rack in the center of the oven. Preheat the oven to 350°F. Butter a 2- to 3-quart casserole.

Put about 3 cups of the milk, reserving the other cup, into a saucepan over low heat. While it is heating (do not let it scald) beat the egg whites at a slow steady speed in a large, grease-free bowl. When they are foamy add the cream of tartar. Gradually add the vanilla sugar and continue to beat for another few minutes, until the meringue will form soft peaks. By now the milk should be sufficiently hot. Drop the meringue by heaping tablespoonfuls into the milk and poach the meringue 1–2 minutes on each side, turning it gently with a fork or shallow strainer. Remove each meringue to a cloth or paper towel to drain, turning them once or twice. Repeat the poaching process until all the meringue has been used. Set the meringues aside in a cool place.

Remove the milk from the heat, strain and measure it, and add enough of the reserved milk to again equal 3 cups. Return the milk to the saucepan over low heat and stir in the rice. Add the vanilla bean and butter. Stir a few times until the butter has melted, then cover the pan and let the mixture cook for 20–25 minutes, until the rice is fluffy but not quite all the milk has been absorbed. Discard the vanilla bean. Remove the saucepan from the heat, still covered, and set it aside.

In a large mixing bowl beat the egg yolks and eggs with a whisk or electric mixer at a high speed, until the mixture is a light color. Gradually beat in the sugar and then the cream. When the mixture is frothy, add the nutmeg. Use a spoon or spatula to fold in heaping tablespoonfuls of the rice alternately with the raisins. Spoon the pudding into the prepared casserole. Place the casserole in a shallower pan of hot water. Bake the pudding at 350°F for about 30 minutes, until the edges are beginning to brown and the center stays separated slightly after a knife has been inserted. Remove the pudding from the oven and let it cool just a few minutes.

Spoon a layer of warm rice pudding into a tall, clear parfait glass. Add a layer of poached meringue (fit in as many meringue pieces as necessary to make an even layer) and then another pudding layer. Top the glass with poached meringue and a generous grating of nutmeg. There should be enough pudding and meringue to fill at least six glasses, but fill as many as you need and refrigerate the remaining pudding and meringue. The pudding is also excellent cold.

Yield: 6 servings

Blueberry Fog

One of my favorite places in late summer is the coast of Maine. And not the least of the pleasures there is the bountifulness of fresh blueberries. This recipe recalls some special memories.

> 2 egg whites
> ¼ teaspoon cream of tartar
> 2 tablespoons sugar
> ¼ teaspoon vanilla extract
> 2–2½ cups milk
> 4 egg yolks, lightly beaten

3 tablespoons sugar
3 tablespoons flour
¼ teaspoon salt
1 teaspoon vanilla extract
2 tablespoons sweet butter
2 cups fresh blueberries, washed and dried

In a medium, grease-free mixing bowl beat the egg whites at a slow steady speed. When they are foamy add the cream of tartar. Gradually add the 2 tablespoons sugar and continue to beat for a few more minutes, until the meringue will form soft peaks. Beat in the ¼ teaspoon vanilla extract.

In a large saucepan over low heat, warm 2 cups of milk to just before scalding. Drop a heaping tablespoon of the meringue into the saucepan and poach the meringue a minute or so on each side, turning it gently with a fork or shallow strainer. Remove the cooked meringue carefully and place it on a cloth or paper towel to drain. Repeat the poaching process five or six times (I like to make an extra meringue, in case one breaks) using all the meringue. Turn the meringues once or twice on the cloth to be sure they are well drained. Set them aside at room temperature.

Strain the milk and measure. Add milk to again equal 2 cups and scald it in the saucepan over low heat. Put the egg yolks into another large saucepan and beat in the 3 tablespoons sugar and flour, 1 tablespoon at a time. Add the salt and the 1 teaspoon vanilla extract. Place this mixture over low heat and gradually stir in the scalded milk. Cook, stirring gently, for 30–45 minutes. The custard should be quite thick. Beat in the butter and remove from the heat. Fold in the blueberries.

Spoon the pudding into six parfait glasses or bowls. Top each with a meringue. Chill thoroughly before serving.

Yield: 6 servings

Peach Pudding

3 tablespoons flour
⅓ cup brown sugar, packed
¼ teaspoon ground cloves
6 tablespoons sweet butter
4 large (or 5 medium) peaches, peeled and sliced
½ cup pecan halves

3 egg whites
¼ teaspoon cream of tartar
¼ cup sugar
½ teaspoon vanilla extract
Ground cloves for garnish

Place the oven rack about a third up from the bottom. Preheat the oven to 350°F. Butter a 1- or 1½-quart casserole.

In a medium mixing bowl sift together the flour, brown sugar, and cloves. With two knives or a pastry blender cut the butter into the dry mixture just until it is coarse but even-sized grains. Pile the peach slices into the prepared casserole. Fold the pecan halves into the peaches and sprinkle the butter mixture evenly over the top. Use a spatula or large spoon to pack it gently.

Bake the pudding at 350°F for about 30 minutes, until the butter topping is firm and dry. Remove the pudding from the oven and place it on a trivet to cool for 5–10 minutes while you make the meringue. Reset the oven to 375°F.

In a large, grease-free mixing bowl beat the egg whites at a slow steady speed. When they are foamy add the cream of tartar. Gradually add the sugar and continue to beat for a few more minutes until the meringue will form soft peaks. Beat in the vanilla extract.

Use a rubber spatula to spread the meringue evenly over the pudding. Be sure that the sides are sealed. Pull up a few meringue peaks with the spatula and dust the top lightly with ground cloves. Return the pudding to the oven at 375°F and bake it for 5–8 minutes, until the meringue peaks are golden. Serve the pudding warm from the oven.

Yield: 6–8 servings

American Floating Islands

2 egg whites
¼ teaspoon cream of tartar
¼ cup sugar
½ teaspoon vanilla extract
2 cups milk
¼–½ cup heavy cream
4 egg yolks, lightly beaten
¼ cup sugar
2 teaspoons vanilla extract
½ teaspoon freshly grated nutmeg

In a medium, grease-free mixing bowl beat the egg whites at a slow steady speed. When they are foamy add the cream of tartar. Gradually add the ¼ cup sugar and continue to beat for a few minutes, until the meringue will form soft peaks. Beat in the ½ teaspoon vanilla extract.

Heat the milk in a large saucepan to just before scalding. Using a tablespoon drop 6 to 8 heaping spoonfuls of meringue into the heated milk. Poach the meringues for a minute or so. Turn them, with two forks or a shallow strainer, and poach them on the other side briefly. Remove the saucepan from the heat. Gently lift the meringues from the milk with the strainer or forks and set them aside on a towel to drain. Turn them once or twice to be sure they are well drained. Set them aside on the towel at room temperature.

Strain the milk into a 2-cup measure. Add enough heavy cream to the strained milk to equal 2 cups of liquid. In a saucepan over low heat combine this mixture with the beaten egg yolks. Gradually stir in the other ¼ cup sugar. Continue to stir gently for about 30 minutes, until the custard thickens. Blend in the 2 teaspoons vanilla extract. Pour this custard into a shallow serving dish and sprinkle it with the freshly grated nutmeg. Arrange the meringue islands on top and chill for about 2 hours in the refrigerator before serving.

Yield: 6–8 servings

Figlets

The tiny almond tart shells in this recipe can be made a day or two ahead (just keep them cool and dry).

> 16 fresh or dried figs
> 1 recipe Almond Pie Crust dough (page 222)
> ½ recipe Honey Meringue (page 52)

Place the rack in the center of the oven. Preheat the oven to 375°F. Line a baking sheet with foil.

If you are using fresh figs, wash and peel them. Set them aside. If you use dried figs you might like to marinate them in about ¼ cup medium-dry sherry while you prepare the shells.

Divide the pie crust dough into sixteen pieces and press each piece of dough out in a 2-inch pastry mold. Trim around the edges with a knife. Place the pastry molds on an unlined baking sheet and bake the tart shells at 375°F for about 5 minutes, until they are lightly browned. Remove the baking sheet from the oven, place it on a wire rack, and loosen the tart shells from the molds while they are cooling. When the shells are room temperature, remove them from the molds. Reset the oven to 325°F.

Place the tart shells on the prepared baking sheet. Drain the figs if they've been marinating and place a fig in each shell. Scoop about a tablespoon of honey meringue into each shell, covering the figs. Bake the figlets at 325°F for about 5 minutes just until the top of the meringue feels dry.

Remove the baking sheet from the oven and put the figlets on a serving platter. They are best eaten warm from the oven.

Yield: 16 figlets; allow 3–4 per serving

Apples Meringue

This dessert is quite effective yet simple to prepare, an ideal recipe to put together in a last-minute rush.

> 4 large, tart apples (Cortland, Winesap, etc.)
> 2–3 tablespoons lemon juice
> 2 egg whites
> ¾ cup confectioners' sugar
> ½ teaspoon vanilla extract
> About ½ cup red currant jelly

Place the oven rack about a third up from the bottom. Preheat the oven to 375°F. Butter the bottom and sides of a medium casserole.

Peel and core the apples. Brush them with lemon juice so that they won't discolor. In a saucepan with water to cover, boil the apples for 8 to 10 minutes, until just tender. Remove the apples to the prepared casserole and set it aside.

In a medium, grease-free mixing bowl beat the egg whites at a slow steady speed until foamy. Gradually add the confectioners' sugar while increasing to a moderate beating speed. Add the vanilla extract and continue to beat for 5 to 8 minutes, until the meringue is thick, glossy, and forms firm peaks.

Stuff the cores of the apples with the currant jelly and use a rubber spatula to cover the apples with the meringue. Brown the dessert at 375°F for 10 to 15 minutes, until the meringue feels firm and dry. Serve warm.

Yield: 4 servings

Oranges Meringue

6 large navel (or other thick-skinned) oranges
1 6-ounce can orange juice concentrate, thawed
¼ cup water
2 teaspoons lime juice
½ cup sugar
2 teaspoons unflavored gelatin
½ cup heavy cream

Slice off the tops of the oranges about a quarter of the way down. Grate enough rind from the tops to equal 1 tablespoon, reserve it, and discard the rest. Scoop out the fruit using a grapefruit knife or spoon. Squeeze and strain enough of the fruit to equal ½ cup of juice. Reserve the juice and save the rest of the fruit for another use. With a pair of scissors snip a zigzag pattern around the tops of the orange shells and then set the shells aside.

In a saucepan combine the reserved orange juice and rind, orange juice concentrate, water, lime juice, sugar, and gelatin. Stir over low heat until the sugar and gelatin have dissolved. Set the mixture aside to cool.

In a chilled bowl with chilled beaters whip the cream until it will hold a soft shape. Use a rubber spatula or large spoon to fold the cooled orange custard into the whipped cream, about ¼ cup at a time. Fold just until the color is uniform. Spoon the filling into the prepared orange shells to just below the zigzag, and put them in the refrigerator for at least an hour. (You can keep them refrigerated for a day or two, covered loosely with plastic wrap.)

LIME MERINGUE TOPPING

> *3 egg whites*
> *¼ teaspoon cream of tartar*
> *⅓ cup sugar*
> *1 teaspoon lime extract*
> *6 twists of lime rind for garnish*

Place the oven rack about a third up from the bottom. Preheat the oven to 500°F. Put the prepared orange shells into a shallow ovenproof dish filled with ice.

In a large, grease-free mixing bowl beat the egg whites at a slow steady speed. When they are foamy add the cream of tartar. Gradually add the sugar and continue to beat until the meringue will form soft peaks. Add the lime extract and increase to a moderate beating speed. Beat for another 5 to 8 minutes, until the meringue is thick, glossy, and forms firm peaks when the beaters are lifted.

Use a rubber spatula to scoop the meringue into a pastry bag fitted with a small or medium (I use a number 3B) star tip. Hold the bag firmly with both hands, keeping it closed and taut with the top one. Press out a spiral of meringue over each orange shell, starting just inside the zigzag top. The meringue spirals should be about 1½ inches high and closed at the top.

Bake the orange shells at 500°F for 3 minutes, just until the meringue begins to brown. Remove from the oven and garnish each shell with a lime twist pushed gently into the top of the meringue spiral. Transfer the oranges to a serving platter or individual dishes. Like baked Alaskas, Oranges Meringue must be consumed at once.

Yield: 6 servings

Pineapples Meringue

Serve these for a light dessert or on a bed of lettuce as a salad course. The cream cheese mix can be made well ahead of time, so they're quick to prepare.

4 ounces cream cheese, softened
⅓ cup chopped pecans, walnuts, or almonds
⅓ cup grated coconut
8½-inch-thick pineapple slices
8 maraschino cherries
3 egg whites
½ teaspoon cream of tartar
½ cup sugar

Place the oven rack about a third up from the bottom. Preheat the oven to 375°F. Butter a shallow casserole.

In a small mixing bowl combine the softened cream cheese, chopped nuts, and grated coconut. Place the pineapple slices in the prepared casserole and put a maraschino cherry into the center of each. With your fingers shape mounds of the cream cheese mixture and place them over the cherries, leaving most of the pineapple bare. Set the casserole aside.

In a large, grease-free mixing bowl beat the egg whites at a slow steady speed. When they are foamy add the cream of tartar. Gradually add the sugar and, when the meringue will form soft peaks, increase to a moderate beating speed. Beat for another 5–8 minutes, until the meringue is thick, glossy, and forms firm peaks when the beaters are lifted.

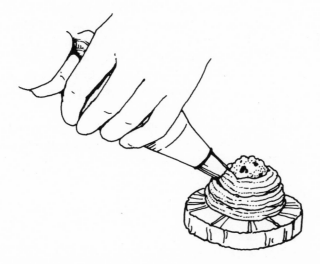

With a rubber spatula scoop the meringue into a pastry bag fitted with a medium (number 5 or 6) star tip. Hold the bag firmly with both hands, keeping it closed and taut with the top hand. Starting on the pineapple base, press out a spiral of meringue around each cream cheese mound. Bake them at 375°F for 10–15 minutes, until the meringue is golden. Serve immediately.

Yield: 8 servings

Sweet Potatoes Meringue

One Thanksgiving I made a double recipe of these sweet potatoes and asked my guests to select the meringue topping they preferred. The consensus was that both were wonderful, so I give you a choice here.

> 4 cups mashed sweet potatoes (bake or boil about 3 pounds, peel them and mash the pulp)
> 1 cup half-and-half
> 2 egg yolks, lightly beaten
> Nutmeg for grating
> 2 tablespoons sweet butter

Place the oven rack about a third up from the bottom. Preheat the oven to 350°F. Butter a large shallow casserole.

In a large mixing bowl whip the sweet potatoes with an electric mixer at a slow speed. Gradually whip in the half-and-half and then the egg yolks. When the mixture is thoroughly blended and a light, fluffy texture, spread it into the prepared casserole. Grate about a teaspoon of nutmeg over the sweet potato mixture and then dot it with butter. Bake the casserole at 350°F for about 15 minutes, just until it is heated through. Remove from the oven and let it cool for about 10 minutes, while you prepare the meringue topping of your choice. Reset the oven to 375°F.

MERINGUE 1 (SWEET)

> 4 egg whites
> 3 tablespoons sugar
> 1/2 cup chopped walnuts (or pecans)
> 1/2 cup raisins
> 2 tablespoons maple syrup
> 1 teaspoon water

In a large, grease-free mixing bowl beat the egg whites at a slow steady speed. Gradually add the sugar and beat until the meringue will form soft peaks. Use a rubber spatula to fold in the nuts and raisins and then spread the meringue evenly over the warm sweet potato casserole. Return the casserole to the oven at 375°F.

Meanwhile, in a small saucepan heat the maple syrup and water until just boiling. As soon as you've prepared the syrup, remove the sweet potatoes from the oven just long enough to drizzle it over the meringue. Let it bake about another 5 minutes, until the meringue peaks are brown. Remove from the oven and serve.

MERINGUE 2 (SALTY)

> *6 egg whites*
> *¼ teaspoon salt*
> *1 cup chopped walnuts (or pecans)*

In a large, grease-free mixing bowl beat the egg whites at a slow steady speed, gradually sprinkling in the salt. Beat until the meringue is quite stiff. Use a rubber spatula to fold in the chopped nuts and then spread the meringue evenly over the warm sweet potato casserole. Return the casserole to the oven at 375°F and bake for 10–15 minutes, until the meringue peaks are brown. Remove from the oven and serve.

Yield (either meringue topping): about 10 servings

A Musical Sandwich

. . . So named by two composers who were served it at a breakfast meeting in my kitchen. This is my favorite nonsweet meringue and makes an excellent light meal any time of the day or a first course for dinner.

> *8 English muffin halves*
> *½ pound muenster cheese, sliced*
> *8 thin onion slices (about 1 medium onion)*
> *8 thick tomato slices (about 2 firm tomatoes)*
> *8 egg yolks, unbroken*
> *4 egg whites*
> *¼ teaspoon salt*

1 teaspoon paprika
½ cup grated Parmesan cheese
Dijon mustard

Place the oven rack about a third up from the bottom. Preheat the oven to 375°F. Line a baking sheet with foil.

Place the muffin halves on the baking sheet. Top with the sliced muenster cheese and onion slices. Use a paring knife to carve a small hollow in the center of each tomato slice, and add the tomatoes to the sandwich stack. Carefully spoon an egg yolk into the hollow of each tomato slice.

In a large, grease-free mixing bowl beat the egg whites at a slow steady speed. When they are foamy add the salt and paprika. Continue to beat until the egg whites are quite stiff. Use a rubber spatula to fold in the grated Parmesan cheese, in three additions. Spread this meringue over the tomato slices—leaving the yolks exposed— and the sides of the sandwiches. Bake at 375°F for 15–20 minutes, until the cheese slices have melted and the meringue is dry and golden. Serve immediately and pass the Dijon mustard.

Yield: 8 open-face sandwiches

Queen's Pudding

Meringue is the traditional topping for this bread pudding. It is also called Hanover Pudding.

3 cups fresh or dried bread cubes, trimmed of crust
¼ cup sweet butter
1 tablespoon sugar
1 teaspoon cinnamon
4 egg yolks
2 eggs
¼ cup sugar
1 quart milk
1 teaspoon vanilla extract
½ cup red or black currant jelly
4 egg whites
¼ teaspoon cream of tartar
¼ cup sugar
½ teaspoon vanilla extract

Place the oven rack about a third up from the bottom. Preheat the oven to 400°F. Line a baking sheet with foil. Butter a 3-quart casserole.

Place the bread cubes in a large bowl. Pour the melted butter over the cubes and toss them until they are evenly coated. Spread the buttered cubes on the prepared baking sheet. Sift together the 1 tablespoon of sugar and the cinnamon and sprinkle the mixture over the bread cubes. Bake the cubes at 400°F for about 10 minutes, until they are toasted. Remove the baking sheet from the oven and turn the toasted bread cubes into the prepared casserole. Set it aside. Reset the oven to 350°F and move the rack to the center.

In another large mixing bowl use a wire whisk to beat together the egg yolks and eggs until they are frothy. Add the ¼ cup sugar. Gradually beat in the milk and then the 1 teaspoon vanilla extract. Pour this mixture over the bread cubes in the casserole. Place the casserole in a shallower pan of hot water. Bake the pudding at 350°F for about an hour, until it is almost firm and the edges are light brown. Remove the casserole, still in the pan of hot water, from the oven. Spread the currant jelly over the top of the pudding and then set it aside while you make the meringue. Reset the oven to 375°F.

In a large, grease-free mixing bowl beat the egg whites at a slow steady speed. When they are foamy add the cream of tartar. Gradually beat in the ¼ cup sugar and continue to beat for another few minutes until the meringue will form soft peaks. Beat in the ½ teaspoon vanilla extract.

With a rubber spatula spread the meringue over the pudding. Use the spatula to pull up some peaks of meringue. Return the pudding, in the pan of hot water, to the oven. Bake it at 375°F for 8 to 10 minutes, until the meringue peaks are golden. Remove the pudding from the oven and lift the casserole from the pan of hot water. The pudding is best served warm from the oven.

Yield: about 8 servings

Recipes for Leftover Yolks

Basic Custard

This custard is so easy to make, and it's an ingredient for all kinds of desserts. Below I suggest just a few ways to use it. After a day's refrigeration I think the custard is even better than fresh. If you want to serve it warm, reheat it in a saucepan over a very low heat for about 10 minutes.

> 4 egg yolks
> ¼ cup sugar
> 1 cup milk
> 1 teaspoon vanilla extract

Beat the egg yolks in a small heavy saucepan (or in top of a double boiler). Gradually beat in the sugar. Then stir in ¼ cup of the milk. Place the pan over low heat and slowly stir in the remaining ¾ cup milk. Continue to stir gently, for about 20 minutes, until the custard starts to coat the spoon. Add the vanilla extract.

Remove the pan from the heat and place it on a trivet to cool slightly. When the custard is lukewarm strain it. Transfer the custard to a small covered container and store it in the refrigerator for up to three days.

Yield: about 1¼ cups custard

SERVING SUGGESTIONS

1. Line a shallow casserole with alternating but overlapping rows of sliced bananas (2 or 3 bananas) and vanilla wafers (about 2 cups). Pour one recipe of basic custard over and you have an instant banana pudding.

2. Fold pieces of leftover Angel Cake (page 64–66) and pineapple chunks (8¼-ounce can, drained) into one recipe of basic custard. Spoon into individual serving dishes and top each with a heaping tablespoon of whipped cream.

3. Pour custard generously over chunks of Bittersweet Chocolate Cake (page 214) or Rich Chocolate Layers (page 213).

4. Top slices of 1-2-3-4 Cake (page 228) or other plain cake with teaspoonfuls of Rich Nut Mix (page 224) and pour custard over each serving.

VARIATIONS

Substitute 1 teaspoon almond, coconut, rum, etc., extract for the vanilla extract.

Chocolate Custard

Serve this custard solo, or pour it over a bed of chocolate wafers, ice cream, or warm cake slices.

> *4 egg yolks*
> *½ cup sugar*
> *1 cup milk*
> *2 ounces bittersweet chocolate, broken into pieces*

Beat the egg yolks in a small heavy saucepan (or in the top of a double boiler) over very low heat. Gradually beat in the sugar. When it is well blended stir in ¼ cup of the milk. Place the pan over low heat and slowly stir in the remaining ¾ cup milk. Continue to stir gently for about 10 minutes, until the custard just begins to thicken. Add the chocolate pieces and, still stirring, cook the custard for another 8–10 minutes.

When the custard will coat the spoon, remove the pan from the heat and place it on a trivet to cool slightly. When the custard is lukewarm, strain it. Store the custard in a small covered container in the refrigerator for up to three days.

Yield: about 1¼ cups custard

Lemon Custard

Pour this custard over fresh fruit, cake, or ice cream. This is also good on its own.

> *4 egg yolks*
> *½ cup sugar*
> *¾ cup milk*
> *¼ cup lemon juice*
> *½ teaspoon lime juice*
> *¼ cup heavy cream*

Beat the egg yolks in a small heavy saucepan (or in top of a double boiler) over very low heat. Gradually beat in the sugar. When the mixture is well blended stir in the milk gradually. Add the lemon juice and continue to stir gently for about 20 minutes. When the custard starts to thicken, add the lime juice and then the heavy cream, 1 tablespoon at a time. Cook, still stirring, for another 5 minutes or so, until the custard will coat the spoon.

Remove the pan from the heat and place it on a trivet to cool slightly. When it is lukewarm, strain the custard. Store it in a small covered container in the refrigerator for up to three days.

Yield: about 1¼ cups custard

Yolk Parfait

The nice thing about this parfait (and most of the parfaits in this book) is that they keep well in the freezer and you can just keep dipping in for a variety of desserts and garnishes. Also try changing the flavor by using other dessert liqueurs.

> *⅔ cup sugar*
> *¼ cup water*
> *6 egg yolks*
> *¼ cup curaçao or Amaretto*
> *2 cups heavy cream*

In a saucepan over medium heat combine the sugar and water. Bring the mixture to a boil and let it boil to 234°F (soft-ball stage). Remove this sugar syrup from the heat but keep it warm. In a large mixing bowl beat the egg yolks with an electric mixer at high speed for 2–3 minutes, until they are thick and a light color. Pour in the sugar syrup in a slow steady stream, still beating at a high speed. Continue to beat for 5–10 minutes, until the mixture is cool, quite thick, and light in color. Beat in the liqueur. Chill this custard in the refrigerator for at least 45 minutes.

In a large chilled mixing bowl with chilled beaters, whip the heavy cream. When it is stiff use a rubber spatula to fold it into the chilled yolk mixture, about ½ cup at a time. Fold with broad strokes just until the texture and color are uniform.

Spoon the parfait into a shallow tray or into individual serving dishes. Freeze it for at least 2 hours. It will keep in the freezer for about a week.

Yield: about 3½ cups

SERVING SUGGESTIONS

1. I know someone whose idea of "the perfect dessert" is this parfait piled over very cold slices of fresh mango. Another friend prefers it folded into a bowl of fresh raspberries.

2. Fold in about ½ cup slivered almonds before freezing the parfait and spoon it into tall clear parfait glasses.

3. Line the bottoms of brandy snifters with a few walnut halves and candied cherries. Spoon the parfait into the snifters and freeze.

4. Scoop mounds of frozen parfait into nutted Dessert Shells (page 32). Serve immediately.

Chocolate Parfait

This parfait has a rich, thick texture, suitable for shaping from a pastry bag. You can serve it in small cups on its own or use it as a garnish or filling.

> 1 cup sugar
> ⅓ cup water

    8 egg yolks
    4 ounces unsweetened chocolate, melted
    2 cups heavy cream

In a saucepan over medium heat combine the sugar and water. Bring the mixture to a boil and let it boil to 234°F (soft-ball stage). Remove this sugar syrup from the heat but keep it warm. In a large mixing bowl beat the egg yolks with an electric mixer at a high speed for 4–5 minutes, until they are thick and a light color. Pour in the sugar syrup in a slow steady stream, still beating at a high speed. Gradually beat in the melted chocolate. Continue to beat for 5–10 minutes, until the mixture is cool and quite thick. Chill this custard in the refrigerator for about 45 minutes.

In a large chilled mixing bowl with chilled beaters, whip the heavy cream. When it is stiff use a rubber spatula to fold it into the chilled yolk custard, about ½ cup at a time. Spoon the parfait into a shallow tray (you may need two trays) and freeze it for at least 2 hours. It will keep in the freezer for about a week. Soften the parfait at room temperature for about 15 minutes before serving.

    Yield: about 4 cups

Chestnut Pudding

I am particularly proud of this recipe. It wasn't the easiest for me to create and it will take a little extra time and effort for you to make, but the results are such a reward.

    ¾ pound chestnuts
    1½ cups milk
    2 inches vanilla bean, split
    6 egg yolks, lightly beaten
    ⅓ cup sugar
    1½ teaspoons unflavored gelatin
    6 tablespoons sweet butter, cut into tablespoons
    1½ cups heavy cream

Use a sharp knife to slash crosses into the flat sides of the chestnuts. In a large saucepan cover the chestnuts with boiling water (at least 2 quarts) and let them boil for about 30 minutes, until the shells and inner skins are soft enough to be peeled away. Add water if necessary to keep them covered. Remove the saucepan from the heat, but I suggest leaving the chestnuts in the hot water as you peel them one by one. Force the warm peeled chestnut pieces through a strainer or food mill.

In a saucepan combine the strained chestnuts with the milk and split vanilla bean. Place it over low heat to simmer, stirring or swirling the pan occasionally, for about 15 minutes, until most of the milk has been absorbed. Gradually beat in the egg yolks. Sift together the sugar and gelatin, stir in these dry ingredients, and continue to stir for a few minutes, until they have dissolved. Add the tablespoons of butter and stir gently until the butter has melted and the custard is thoroughly blended.

Remove the saucepan from the heat and discard the vanilla bean. Whirl the chestnut custard, about ½ cup at a time, in a blender at the highest speed for about 10 seconds. Whirl again, if necessary, until the custard is free of any chestnut grains. (Test by rubbing a sample between your fingertips.) After all the custard is smooth and blended, put it aside in a bowl to cool.

In a large chilled bowl with chilled beaters whip the heavy cream. When it will hold a soft shape, use a rubber spatula to fold in the cooled chestnut custard, ¼ cup at a time. Fold only until the color is uniform. Chill the pudding in individual serving dishes or a large bowl. It is ready to serve after about an hour in the refrigerator.

Yield: about 6 servings

Whole Lemon Custard

This tart, flavorful garnish is quite rich and should be used sparingly as a topping for plain cakes, ice creams, and parfaits.

> ½ *cup water*
> 3 *whole medium lemons, chopped very fine*
> 1⅓ *cups sugar*
> *Pinch of salt*
> 3 *tablespoons sweet butter, melted*

3 egg yolks, beaten
1 egg, beaten
½ teaspoon cloves

Place the oven rack about a third up from the bottom. Preheat the oven to 350°F. Lightly butter a shallow glass baking dish.

Combine the ½ cup water with enough of the chopped lemon (about 1 lemon) to equal ¾ cup liquid mixture. Spread the rest of the chopped lemon in the prepared baking dish and set it aside.

In a medium mixing bowl combine the sugar, salt, and melted butter. Gradually add the beaten egg yolks and egg. Add the water/lemon mixture and beat well. Stir in the cloves. Pour this batter over the lemons in the baking dish. Bake at 350°F for 30–40 minutes, until the edges are slightly browned. (The custard will not be firm.) Remove it from the oven and place the baking dish on a trivet to cool to lukewarm. Unless you are using it right away, transfer the custard to a small covered container and keep it in the refrigerator.

Yield: about 1½ cups custard

Chocolate Sauce

3 egg yolks
¾ cup milk
3 tablespoons sugar
3 ounces bittersweet chocolate, melted

In a saucepan beat the egg yolks and gradually beat in the milk. When the mixture is thoroughly blended place the pan over low heat. Stir in the sugar, 1 tablespoon at a time, and continue to stir for 10–15 minutes. When the mixture begins to coat the spoon, gently beat in the melted chocolate. Let the sauce cook, still stirring, for another minute, until it thickens slightly.

Remove the pan from the heat and place it on a trivet to cool for about 10 minutes. It will thicken a little more. Use this sauce immediately or keep it in a covered container in the refrigerator and reheat it in the top of a double boiler over hot water just before serving.

Yield: about 1 cup sauce

Butterscotch Sauce

4 egg yolks, lightly beaten
⅓ cup milk
½ cup sweet butter, melted
½ cup brown sugar, loosely packed
¼ teaspoon butterscotch flavor

In a saucepan over low heat combine the egg yolks with the milk. When the mixture is thoroughly blended, gradually stir in the melted butter and then the brown sugar. Cook this mixture, still stirring gently over low heat, for 15–20 minutes.

When the sauce has thickened enough to coat the spoon, remove the pan from the heat and stir in the butterscotch flavor. Place the pan on a trivet to cool for a few minutes. The sauce will thicken slightly as it cools. It can be used immediately or refrigerated for up to a week in a small covered container. This sauce is excellent warm or cool.

Yield: about 1 cup sauce

Rum Sauce

6 egg yolks
⅓ cup sugar
1 cup milk
2 tablespoons sweet butter
3 tablespoons dark rum
½ cup heavy cream (optional)

In a saucepan or in top of a double boiler over low heat beat the egg yolks together with the sugar. Gradually stir in the milk. After 15–20 minutes, when the mixture starts to thicken, add the butter and stir gently until it melts. Remove the pan from the heat. Stir in the rum and place the pan on a trivet to cool for about 10 minutes. Strain the sauce, if necessary, so that it is smooth. This sauce is excellent as is, served warm.

Or chill it in the refrigerator for at least an hour. In a chilled bowl with chilled beaters whip the heavy cream until it will hold soft shapes. Fold the whipped cream, in three or four additions, into the chilled rum sauce. Keep the sauce in a small covered container in the refrigerator until you are ready to use it.

Yield: about 1⅓ cups warm sauce, about 1¾ cups cold sauce

Grand Marnier Sauce

> 1 cup milk
> ½ cup heavy cream
> 1 inch vanilla bean, split
> 6 egg yolks
> ¼ cup sugar
> 3 tablespoons Grand Marnier
> 1 cup heavy cream, whipped

In the top of a double boiler over hot water combine the milk and the ½ cup heavy cream. Add the vanilla bean pieces and let the liquid heat to just before scalding. Meanwhile, in a medium mixing bowl whisk the egg yolks, gradually adding the sugar, until the mixture is quite frothy. Stir the egg yolk mixture, pouring it in a slow stream, into the heated liquid. Continue to stir this custard, letting it cook for about 10 minutes, until it thickens enough to coat the spoon.

Remove the pan from the heat and strain the custard. Stir in the Grand Marnier and chill the custard in the refrigerator for about an hour.

Fold the 1 cup whipped cream, a heaping tablespoon at a time, into the chilled custard. Keep the sauce in a covered container in the refrigerator for up to 4 days.

Yield: about 2½ cups sauce

Vanilla Butter Cream

The flavor of this basic butter cream—a rich filling or icing—can be varied by substituting a teaspoon of another extract for the vanilla.

> 2 egg yolks, lightly beaten
> 3 tablespoons sugar
> 3 tablespoons milk
> 1 teaspoon vanilla extract
> ½ cup sweet butter, cut into tablespoons

In the top of a double boiler over hot water, beat together the egg yolks and sugar. Beat in the milk and continue to beat or stir vigorously for 5 to 10 minutes, until the custard thickens. (If necessary use an electric mixer at a low speed to keep the egg yolks from curdling.) Beat in the vanilla extract. Remove the top of the double boiler and place it over a bowl filled with ice. Use an electric mixer to beat in the butter, 1 tablespoon at a time. Continue to beat at a moderate speed until the butter cream is evenly blended and fluffy in texture. Use at once or refrigerate (it keeps for several weeks) and then let it soften at room temperature for about 30 minutes before using.

Yield: about 1¼ cups butter cream

Chocolate Butter Cream

1 recipe Vanilla Butter Cream (page 206)
4 ounces bittersweet chocolate, melted

Let the butter cream soften at room temperature for a few minutes. In a medium mixing bowl over a larger bowl filled with ice, gradually beat the chocolate into the butter cream using an electric mixer at a slow speed. Use at once or refrigerate and then let it soften for about 30 minutes before using.

Yield: about 1½ cups butter cream

Lemon Butter Cream

2 egg yolks, lightly beaten
2 tablespoons sugar
3 tablespoons lemon juice
½ cup sweet butter, cut into tablespoons

In the top of a double boiler over hot water, beat together the egg yolks and sugar. Beat in the lemon juice and continue to beat or stir vigorously for 5 to 10 minutes, until the custard thickens. (If necessary use an electric mixer at a low speed to keep the egg yolks from curdling.) Remove the top of the double boiler and place it over a bowl filled with ice. Use an electric mixer to beat in the butter, 1 tablespoon at a time. Continue to beat at a moderate speed until the butter cream is evenly blended and fluffy in texture. Use at once or refrigerate (it keeps for several weeks) and then let it soften at room temperature for about 30 minues before using.

Yield: about 1¼ cups butter cream

Praline Butter Cream

1 recipe Vanilla Butter Cream (page 206)
⅓ cup Praline Powder (page 223)

Let the butter cream soften at room temperature for a few minutes. In a medium mixing bowl gradually beat the praline powder into the butter cream using an electric mixer at a slow speed. Use at once or refrigerate and then let it soften at room temperature for about 30 minutes before using.

Yield: about 1¼ cups butter cream

Rum Butter Cream

For Kirsch Butter Cream, substitute 3 tablespoons kirsch for the rum.

2 egg yolks, lightly beaten
2 tablespoons sugar
2 tablespoons rum
½ teaspoon vanilla extract
½ cup butter, cut into tablespoons

In the top of a double boiler over hot water, beat together the egg yolks and sugar. Beat in the rum and continue to beat or stir vigorously for 5 to 10 minutes, until the custard thickens. (If necessary use an electric mixer at a low speed to keep the egg yolks from curdling.) Beat in the vanilla extract. Remove the top of the double boiler and place it over a bowl filled with ice. Use an electric mixer to beat in the butter, 1 tablespoon at a time. Continue to beat at a moderate speed until the butter cream is evenly blended and fluffy in texture. Use at once or refrigerate (it keeps for several weeks) and then let it soften at room temperature for about 30 minutes before using.

Yield: about 1¼ cups butter cream

Yolk Cookies

This is a simple recipe that can be dressed up in a variety of ways. I offer some suggestions that have been particularly popular at location lunches I have catered for hungry film crews.

1 cup sweet butter, softened
1 cup sugar
2 egg yolks, lightly beaten
2 teaspoons vanilla extract (see Variations below)
1¾ cups sifted flour

Place the rack in the center of the oven. Preheat the oven to 350°F. Lightly grease a cookie sheet.

In a medium mixing bowl cream the butter and sugar. Beat in the egg yolks. Add the vanilla extract and blend well. Stir in the flour. Shape the dough into balls about 1 inch in diameter and place them on the prepared cookie sheet about 1½ inches apart. Bake at 350°F for 12–15 minutes, until the edges are browned. Remove the cookies from the oven and use a spatula to lift them from the cookie sheet. Let the cookies cool on a wire rack before serving or storing.

This dough freezes well and will keep for several weeks. Just roll it into 8-inch sections, an inch in diameter, and wrap tightly. The frozen sections can be sliced with a sharp knife and placed on a cookie sheet to bake.

VARIATIONS
1. Press a pecan or walnut half into each cookie before baking.

2. Substitute 1 teaspoon almond extract for 1 of the teaspoons vanilla and fold ½ cup sliced or slivered almonds into the dough before shaping.

3. Use only ½ teaspoon vanilla extract and add 2 teaspoons cherry juice. Press half a maraschino or candied cherry into each cookie before baking.

4. Combine 1 tablespoon cocoa with 3 tablespoons sugar. Roll the dough balls in the mixture. Place them on the cookie sheet and press an M & M into each cookie.

5. Fold ½ cup miniature chocolate chips (or shavings) into the dough before shaping.

6. Sift 1 teaspoon cinnamon and ½ teaspoon ground cloves into the flour before stirring it into the batter. Fold ½ cup raisins into the dough before shaping.

Yield (any variation): 3–4 dozen cookies

Brownies

For years I have been changing this brownie recipe—varying texture, sweetness, richness. . . . The version here seems to be most versatile. It's an excellent cake layer, Alaska base, and just right sliced warm from the oven.

> *4 tablespoons sweet butter, softened*
> *⅔ cup sugar*
> *4 egg yolks*
> *3 ounces bittersweet chocolate, melted*
> *⅓ cup flour*
> *1 teaspoon vanilla extract*
> *1 tablespoon water*
> *½ cup chocolate chips, chopped walnuts, or pecans (optional)*

Place the oven rack about a third up from the bottom. Preheat the oven to 350°F. Lightly grease an 8-inch square pan, line the bottom with greased paper, and dust it with flour.

In a medium mixing bowl blend the softened butter with the sugar. Beat in the egg yolks, 1 at a time, and then the melted chocolate. Stir in the flour, in three additions. When the batter is a smooth, even consistency, beat in the vanilla extract and water. If you are using chocolate chips or chopped nuts, fold them in. Spread the batter evenly into the prepared pan.

Bake the brownies at 350°F for 20–30 minutes, until a toothpick inserted in the center comes out clean. Remove the brownies from the oven and loosen them from the sides of the pan with a knife. Invert the pan over a rack, lift the pan away, and peel off the wax paper. Let the brownies cool slightly before slicing them.

Yield: about 20 brownies

Butterscotch Brownies

6 tablespoons sweet butter or margarine, melted
1 cup brown sugar
3 egg yolks
2 tablespoons dark corn syrup
1 cup flour
1 teaspoon baking powder
¼ teaspoon salt
1 teaspoon vanilla extract
⅓ cup pecan pieces

Place the oven rack about a third up from the bottom. Preheat the oven to 350°F. Lightly grease a 9-inch square pan. Line the bottom of the pan with wax paper and grease it lightly.

In a medium mixing bowl combine the melted butter and brown sugar. Beat in the egg yolks, 1 at a time. Add the corn syrup and beat well. Sift together the flour, baking powder, and salt. Stir in this dry mixture, in three additions, beating well after each. Beat in the vanilla extract. Fold in the pecan pieces and spoon the batter into the prepared pan.

Bake the brownies at 350°F for about 40 minutes, until the edges are evenly browned and the top springs back when pressed lightly in the center. Remove the brownies from the oven and loosen them from the sides of the pan using a knife. Let them cool for about 15 minutes in the pan. Then slice the brownies and remove them with a spatula.

Yield: 16–20 brownies

Almond Loaf Cake

This deceptively plain-looking loaf has the moistness of a pudding cake and richness of a pound cake.

¾ cup sweet butter, softened
1 cup sugar
5 egg yolks, lightly beaten
Pinch salt
Pinch baking soda
¾ cup sifted flour

½ cup buttermilk
½ teaspoon vanilla extract
1 teaspoon almond extract
¾ cup ground blanched almonds

Place the oven rack about a third up from the bottom. Preheat the oven to 350°F. Lightly grease a loaf pan. Line the bottom with wax paper and grease it. Dust the pan with flour.

In a large mixing bowl cream the softened butter and gradually add the sugar. Beat in the egg yolks. Stir the salt and baking soda into the flour and add half of this dry mixture to the main batter. Gradually beat in the buttermilk alternately with the remaining flour mixture. Blend the batter thoroughly and add the vanilla and almond extracts. Fold in the ground almonds, a third at a time. Pour the batter into the prepared pan.

Bake the cake at 350°F for about an hour, until the center springs back when pressed lightly. Remove the cake from the oven and use a knife to loosen it from the pan. Invert the pan over a wire rack and lift it away. Peel off the paper and leave the cake on the rack to cool.

This cake is full of almond flavor. I suggest serving thin slices without any icing or sauce.

Yield: 10–12 slices

Yolk Cake

This cake is a plain, dense, single layer. It is an excellent base for baked Alaskas, other ice cream desserts, and with fruit toppings. Several recipes in this book call for it.

6 egg yolks
½ cup sugar
1 teaspoon vanilla extract
¼ teaspoon baking powder
¾ cup sifted flour
3 tablespoons milk
5 tablespoons sweet butter, melted

Place the oven rack about a third up from the bottom. Preheat the oven to 350°F. Line the bottom of a 9-inch cake pan with wax paper that has been lightly buttered.

In a large mixing bowl beat the egg yolks with an electric mixer at high speed. When they are light in color, gradually add the sugar and the vanilla extract. Continue to beat for 5–10 minutes, until the mixture is thick and light. Stir or sift the baking powder into the flour and use a large spoon or rubber spatula to fold this dry mixture into the batter in three additions alternately with the milk. Fold in the melted butter, 1 tablespoon at a time.

Pour the batter into the prepared pan. Bake the cake at 350°F for 20–30 minutes, until the top springs back when touched lightly in the center. Remove the cake from the oven and use a knife to loosen the sides from the pan. Invert the pan over a wire rack and lift it away. Peel off the paper and leave the cake on the rack to cool for 20–30 minutes.

Yield: 4–8 servings (varies with use or topping)

Rich Chocolate Layers

2½ cups flour
1 teaspoon baking soda
1 teaspoon baking powder
¾ cup sweet butter or margarine, softened
2½ cups sugar
1 egg
5 egg yolks
¾ cup strong freshly brewed coffee
1 cup buttermilk
2 teaspoons vanilla extract
5 ounces unsweetened chocolate, melted

Place the rack in the center of the oven. Preheat the oven to 350°F. Grease three 9-inch round cake pans and line them with wax paper. Grease the paper and dust the pans lightly with flour.

Sift together the flour, baking soda, and baking powder and set this mixture aside. In a large mixing bowl cream the butter. Add the sugar and blend until smooth. Beat in the egg and then the yolks, 1 at a time. Add the coffee, stirring it in ¼ cup at a time. Blend in the flour mixture in five additions, alternately with the buttermilk. Beat in the vanilla and, still beating, gradually pour in the melted chocolate. Pour the batter, in three equal parts, into the prepared pans.

Bake the layers at 350°F for about 30 minutes, until the centers spring back when touched lightly. (Test each layer for doneness.) Remove from the oven and use a knife to loosen the layers from the sides of the pans. Invert the pans on a wire rack, lift them away, and peel off the paper. Let the layers cool to room temperature.

SERVING SUGGESTIONS
1. This layer cake is excellent iced with Quick Icing (page 52). Try making the icing with coconut (or almond) extract and fold in grated coconut (or slivered almonds).

2. These layers are rich enough to be served in single sheets. Use a rich garnish such as Meringue Parfait (page 43). Or slice the layers and generously cover each piece with warm dessert sauce (Rum Sauce, Grand Marnier Sauce, etc., see pages 205–206 for recipes) and top with a tablespoonful of whipped cream.
    Yield: about a dozen slices as a layer cake; about 30 slices of single layers

Bittersweet Chocolate Cake

This chocolate pound cake should be iced or garnished (see suggestions below). It's also excellent served warm from the oven with your favorite ice cream.

> *2 cups flour*
> *½ teaspoon baking soda*
> *½ pound butter, softened*
> *1¾ cups sugar*
> *4 egg yolks, lightly beaten*
> *2 eggs*
> *¾ cup buttermilk*
> *1 teaspoon vanilla extract*
> *¼ cup strong freshly brewed coffee*
> *3 ounces unsweetened chocolate, melted*
> *3 ounces bittersweet chocolate, melted*

Place the oven rack about a third up from the bottom. Preheat the oven to 350°F. Lightly butter a 9-inch tube pan. Line the bottom with wax paper, butter the paper, and dust it lightly with flour.

Sift together the flour and baking soda and set the mixture aside. In a large mixing bowl cream the butter. Gradually beat in the sugar. When the mixture is smoothly blended, add the egg yolks and then beat in the eggs, 1 at a time. Stir in the flour, in three additions, alternately with the buttermilk. Beat in the vanilla extract. Use a rubber spatula to fold the coffee into the melted chocolates. Beat this chocolate mixture into the main batter, pouring in a few table-spoons at a time and then beating to blend well.

Spoon or pour the batter into the prepared tube pan. Cut around the pan through the center of the batter with a rubber spatula to release any air pockets. Bang the pan on a counter or tabletop two or three times to level the batter. Bake the cake at 350°F for about 60–90 minutes, until a toothpick or cake tester comes out almost clean and the top springs back when pressed lightly.

Remove the cake from the oven and loosen the sides from the pan with a knife. Place it upside down on a wire rack and lift the pan away. Peel off the waxed paper and leave the cake to cool on the rack for about 30 minutes.

SERVING SUGGESTIONS

1. This cake is quite rich but not terribly sweet, so I suggest covering it with a thick coat of Quick Icing (page 52).

2. For an elegant-looking dessert, put about 2 cups Meringue Parfait (page 43) into a pastry bag fitted with a medium (number 5 or 6) star tip and press out a crisscross design around the top of the cake. After it's sliced add a heaping tablespoon of the parfait to each piece.

Yield: 12–15 slices

Bittersweet Marble Cake

2 cups sifted flour
1 teaspoon baking soda
Pinch salt
½ cup butter (or margarine), softened
1 cup sugar
3 egg yolks, lightly beaten
1 egg, lightly beaten
1 cup buttermilk

4 ounces unsweetened chocolate, melted
¼ cup strong freshly brewed coffee
3 tablespoons vegetable shortening
¼ cup vanilla sugar
1 egg white
¼ cup buttermilk

Place the oven rack about a third up from the bottom. Preheat the oven to 350°F. Lightly grease and flour a 9-inch tube pan.

Sift together the flour, baking soda, and salt several times so that it is thoroughly blended. Measure ⅓ cup of this dry mixture, reserve it, and set both portions aside.

In a large mixing bowl cream the butter, gradually blending in the sugar. Beat in the egg yolks and then the egg and beat until the batter is thoroughly blended. Add the larger portion of dry ingredients in four additions, alternately with ¼-cup portions of the cup of buttermilk. Stir in the melted chocolate and then the coffee. When all the ingredients are blended, beat the mixture for about a minute. Set this chocolate batter aside.

In a smaller mixing bowl combine the vegetable shortening with the vanilla sugar. Add the egg white and beat until the mixture is blended. Stir in the reserved ⅓ cup dry ingredients, in two additions, alternately with the ¼ cup buttermilk. Beat this vanilla batter for about a minute.

Pour about two-thirds of the chocolate batter into the prepared pan. Spoon the vanilla batter around the center and fold or cut it into the chocolate with a rubber spatula just until there are veins of the vanilla. Spoon the remaining chocolate into the pan and smooth the top of the batter with the spatula.

Bake the cake at 350°F for about 45 minutes, until the top springs back when touched lightly. Remove the cake from the oven and loosen it from the sides and center of the pan with a knife. Invert the pan over a wire rack and lift it away. Leave the cake on the rack to cool to room temperature.

Quick Icing (page 52) is a good garnish for this cake. Fold ½ ounce melted unsweetened chocolate into ⅓ cup of the icing and reserve it. Split the cake into two layers with a large serrated knife. Ice the bottom layer, stack the layers, and cover the cake with the remaining icing. Use a small rubber spatula to swirl the reserved chocolate icing around the sides and top.

Yield: 12–15 slices

Dessert Salads

Sometimes instead of serving a sweet dessert course I like to end a meal with a salad of the freshest, most beautiful fruits or vegetables in season. Here are two dressing recipes with a few produce suggestions.

1. MAYONNAISE

This version is better than what you can buy already prepared, and it takes about 5 minutes to make if you use a blender or food processor.

> 3 egg yolks, beaten
> 2 teaspoons Dijon mustard (or other strong mustard)
> 2 tablespoons vinegar (or lemon juice)
> 1/2 teaspoon salt
> 1/4 teaspoon paprika
> 1/3 cup vegetable oil
> 2/3 cup olive oil

Put the beaten yolks, mustard, vinegar, salt, paprika, and vegetable oil into a blender or food processor and blend the mixture at the highest speed for 10 seconds. With the machine at medium speed add the olive oil in a steady stream. Blend just until the mayonnaise is smooth.

If you use a wire whisk, combine the beaten yolks gradually with the mustard, vinegar, salt, and paprika in a medium mixing bowl. Whisk the mixture with a steady brisk motion and add the vegetable oil in drops. The mixture should thicken gradually. Still whisking, add the olive oil in a slow steady stream. Whisk until the mayonnaise is thick and thoroughly blended.

Store the mayonnaise in a covered container in the refrigerator. It will keep for up to a month.

Yield: about 1 1/3 cups mayonnaise

2. LEMON CREAM DRESSING

> 1/2 cup sour cream
> 1 recipe Lemon Custard (page 200)

Both ingredients should be chilled. In a mixing bowl fold the sour cream, in three additions, into the lemon custard.

Store the dressing in a small covered container in the refrigerator. It will keep for up to 4 days.

Yield: about 1½ cups dressing

SUGGESTED USES

1. Place peach or pear halves, sliced lengthwise, on individual beds of lettuce. Top each with either dressing.

2. Top individual cups of mandarin oranges with 2 tablespoons of either dressing.

3. Carve out a half melon (honeydew, cantaloupe) with a grapefruit knife. Chop the fruit and combine it with ½ cup sliced strawberries or seedless grapes. Spoon the fruit into the melon shell and chill it in the refrigerator for about an hour. Drizzle a little of the lemon cream over the chilled salad. Serve and pass the rest of the dressing. Or omit the lemon cream and fold about ½ cup of mayonnaise into the fruit mixture before chilling it. Yields about 4 servings.

4. Core and chop 2 apples; peel, section, and seed 3 tangerines. Combine the fruit with ½ cup raisins. Fold in 1 cup mayonnaise or drizzle over 1 cup lemon cream. Garnish the salad with ¼ cup chopped walnuts. Yields about 6 servings.

5. Combine 2 cups grated carrots with ½ cup raisins and ¼ cup pecan halves. Fold in ½ cup mayonnaise or ⅓ cup lemon cream. Yields about 6 servings.

Basic Dessert Recipes

Basic Pie Crust

This pie crust recipe is useful far beyond the scope of this book. I usually have several unbaked crusts in my freezer for quiches, tarts, and pies since they keep nicely for a month or so.

1 heaping cup flour
¼ teaspoon salt
3 tablespoons margarine
3 tablespoons vegetable shortening
2–3 tablespoons cold water

Sift the flour and salt together in a medium mixing bowl. Use two knives or a pastry blender to cut the margarine and shortening into the dry ingredients. When the mixture is still quite coarse but evenly blended, mix in only enough water to hold the dough together.

Place the dough on a lightly floured board or pastry cloth and press it out with the heel of your hand to a diameter of 11–12 inches. (I prefer this method to using a rolling pin because the resulting slight unevenness produces a flakier crust.)

Turn the dough into a 9-inch pan. Use your fingers to fit the crust around the side, and trim away the rough edges with a knife. Flute around the edge by lifting the crust with one thumb against the other thumb and forefinger. Prick the bottom with a fork, cover the crust loosely with foil, and refrigerate for at least 30 minutes. (If there's time, I prefer to freeze the pie crust, then fit the foil snugly against the fluting and let the crust thaw at room temperature for only a few minutes before baking. This method seems to insure against shrinkage and collapse of the fluting.)

To partially bake, place the oven rack in the center and preheat the oven to 400°F. Bake the chilled crust, still lined with foil, for 7 minutes. Remove it from the oven and lift away the foil. The crust should be dry but not browned. Place it on a wire rack to cool for about 20 minutes before filling it.

If a recipe calls for a baked crust, do not cool it, but prick the bottom with a fork after removing the foil. Return the crust to the oven for about 5 minutes, until the edges are evenly browned.

Vanilla Wafer Crumb Crust

¼ *cup sweet butter*
½ *teaspoon vanilla extract*
1 *cup vanilla wafer crumbs*

In a small saucepan over low heat, melt the butter. Remove from the heat and stir in the vanilla extract. In a medium mixing bowl stir the melted butter mixture into the vanilla wafer crumbs until they are evenly moistened. Turn the mixture into a 9-inch pie pan and spread it evenly with your fingertips. Press another pan of the same size firmly on top. Remove the empty pan and trim the edges of the crust with a knife. Chill in the refrigerator for about an hour.

To partially bake, place the oven rack in the center and preheat the oven to 375°F. Cover the chilled crust with foil. Bake it for 5 minutes. Remove it from the oven, lift the foil away, and let it cool before filling. If a recipe calls for a completely baked crust, return it to the oven for another 8 minutes after removing the foil.

Graham Cracker Crust

3 *tablespoons sweet butter*
¾ *cup graham cracker crumbs*
½ *teaspon cinnamon*
2 *tablespoons confectioners' sugar*

Lightly butter a 9-inch pie pan and set it aside.

In a small saucepan over low heat, melt the butter. In a medium mixing bowl combine the graham cracker crumbs with the cinnamon and confectioners' sugar. Pour the melted butter over the dry ingredients and stir or toss until the crumbs are evenly moistened. Turn the mixture into the prepared pan and spread it evenly with your fingertips. Press another pan of the same size firmly on top. Remove the empty pan and use a knife to trim the edges of the crust. Chill it in the refrigerator for about an hour.

To partially bake, place the oven rack in the center and preheat the oven to 300°F. Cover the chilled crust with foil. Bake it for 5 minutes. Remove it from the oven, lift the foil away, and let it cool before filling. If a recipe calls for a completely baked crust, return it to the oven for another 3 minutes after removing the foil.

Chocolate Wafer Crumb Crust

¼ cup sweet butter
½ ounce bittersweet chocolate
1 cup chocolate wafer crumbs
1 tablespoon confectioners' sugar

In a double boiler over hot water or in a heavy saucepan over low heat, melt the butter and chocolate and stir them together. In a medium mixing bowl blend the chocolate wafer crumbs with the confectioners' sugar. Pour the melted mixture in and stir or toss until the crumbs are evenly moistened. Turn the mixture into a 9-inch pie pan and spread it evenly with your fingertips. Press another pan of the same size firmly on top. Remove the empty pan and trim the edges of the crust with a knife. Chill in the refrigerator for about an hour.

To partially bake, place the oven rack in the center and preheat the oven to 375°F. Cover the chilled crust with foil. Bake it for 5 minutes. Remove it from the oven, lift the foil away, and let it cool before filling. If a recipe calls for a completely baked crust, return it to the oven for another 8 minutes after removing the foil.

Sweet Pie Crust

1 cup flour
2 tablespoons sugar
¼ cup butter
¼ cup heavy cream

In a large mixing bowl sift together the flour and sugar. Use two knives or a pastry blender to cut in the butter. When the mixture is still quite coarse but even, stir in the cream, a few drops at a time. Shape the dough into a ball, using your fingers if necessary. Place the ball of dough on a lightly floured board or pastry cloth and press it out, using the heel of your hand or a rolling pin, to a diameter of 11–12 inches. Turn the dough into a 9-inch pie pan. Use your fingers to fit the crust around the side and trim away the rough edges with a knife. Flute around the edge by lifting the crust with one thumb against the other thumb and forefinger. Prick the bottom with a fork and cover the crust with foil. Chill it in the refrigerator for at least an hour. It can also be frozen, wrapped in plastic or foil, if you wish to keep it unbaked for several weeks.

To partially bake the crust, place the oven rack in the center and preheat the oven to 400°F. Bake the chilled crust, lined with foil, for 8 minutes. To completely bake the crust, remove the foil, prick the bottom of the crust, and return it to the oven at 400°F for another 5 to 8 minutes, until the edges begin to brown.

Almond Pie Crust

1½ cups blanched ground almonds
3 tablespoons sugar
1 tablespoon butter, melted

Place the rack in the center of the oven. Preheat the oven to 375°F.

In a medium mixing bowl combine the ground almonds and sugar. Pour in the melted butter and use your fingertips to blend the crust mixture. Gather the dough into a ball and turn it into a shiny metal pie pan. Firmly press the dough out evenly in the pan. Trim the top edge with a knife. Line the crust snugly with foil.

Bake the crust at 375°F for 5 minutes. Remove the foil and bake the crust for about another 3 minutes, until it is lightly browned. Remove it from the oven and let the crust cool on a wire rack.

TART SHELL

Place the ball of dough on a baking sheet inside a 9- or 10-inch tart ring. Press the dough out and fit it against the sides of the ring, making it slightly thicker around the bottom edge. Trim the top edge with a knife. Bake the tart shell at 375°F for 8–10 minutes, until it is lightly browned. Remove the baking sheet from the oven, place it on a wire rack, and let the tart shell cool for a few minutes. Loosen the shell from the ring with a knife but do not remove the ring until the shell has cooled to room temperature.

Praline Powder

Here is one of the most useful recipes in this book. It can be a garnish for ice cream, cake icings, cookies, and fruit as well as an essential ingredient in other dessert recipes. I keep a jar of it in my freezer always.

> *⅔ cup sugar*
> *¼ cup water*
> *1 cup pecan (or walnut) pieces*

Lightly butter a cookie sheet and set it aside.

Combine the sugar and water in a saucepan and bring to a boil over high heat. When the sugar has dissolved and the mixture is clear, cover the pan and boil for about 2 minutes. Uncover the pan when the liquid has thickened to a syrup. Continue to boil, swirling the pan above the heat occasionally, just until the syrup is a caramel color (5 to 7 minutes). Remove the saucepan from the heat and quickly stir in the pecan pieces.

Spread the mixture on the prepared cookie sheet and set it aside at room temperature for about 30 minutes. When the mass has hardened, break it into pieces and use a blender or food processor to grind them into fine powder. Store praline powder in an airtight container. It will keep in the freezer for several months.

Yield: about 2 cups praline powder

Rich Nut Mix

This filling should be used sparingly. It's just right for very small tart shells or as a garnish for a plain-looking dessert.

> 1 cup brown sugar
> ¼ cup water
> 1 teaspoon vanilla extract
> ¾ cup ground hazelnuts (or almonds)
> ¼ cup heavy cream
> 1 cup chopped walnuts (or pecans)
> ¾ cup pignoli

Combine the brown sugar and water in a saucepan and bring the mixture to a boil over medium heat. Stir the sugar syrup a few times and let it boil until it reaches 234°F (soft-ball stage). Remove the saucepan from the heat and place it on a trivet. Beat in the vanilla extract and ground hazelnuts, 1 tablespoon at a time. Gradually stir in the heavy cream. Fold in the chopped walnuts and then the pignoli. Stir the mixture for several minutes to coat all the nuts evenly and blend well.

The nut mix is best while it is warm. You can store it in the refrigerator in a small covered container. To reheat, spread it in a shallow pan and place that pan in a slightly larger pan of hot water. Replace the hot water as necessary until the nut mix is warm.

Yield: 2 cups nut mix

Lemon Curd

Lemon curd is a British condiment. Its tartness is a wonderful change from jams and preserves. I use it often to ice cakes and breads. Try it on Meringue Madeleines (page 164) with a pot of your favorite tea.

> ¼ cup sweet butter
> ½ cup sugar
> 6 tablespoons lemon juice (juice of about 2 lemons)
> 2 eggs, beaten

Melt the butter in a double boiler over hot water. Stir in the sugar and, when blended, the lemon juice. Cook, stirring gently, for 2 or

3 minutes, until the sugar has dissolved. Pour the beaten eggs into the heated mixture in a slow steady stream, stirring constantly with a fast circular motion. Continue to cook and stir for about another 15 minutes, until the mixture thickens enough to coat the spoon.

Remove the saucepan from the heat and let the curd cool. It should be even thicker when it reaches room temperature. Keep lemon curd in a covered container in the refrigerator.

Yield: about 1 cup lemon curd

Raspberry Sauce

This sauce is not thick but it is tart and flavorful. Fresh berries make all the difference.

> ¼ *cup sugar*
> ½ *teaspoon arrowroot*
> ½ *cup water*
> 1 *teaspoon lemon juice*
> 1 *cup fresh raspberries, washed and dried*

Sift together the sugar and arrowroot. Mix the water and lemon juice in a small saucepan and place it over medium heat. When the liquid is quite hot stir in the sugar mixture. Continue to stir for about 2 minutes, until the sugar has dissolved and the syrup is just before boiling.

Add the raspberries and reduce the heat to very low. Stir gently for about 15 minutes, until the raspberries are falling apart. Remove the pan from the heat and strain the sauce to remove the seeds. Stir just to mix it well after straining and chill the sauce, in a small covered container, in the refrigerator before using.

Yield: about ¾ cup sauce

Applesauce

It's so easy to make, why bother with "store bought?"

> 6 *tart apples, pared, cored, and chopped (about 6 cups)*
> About 1 *cup water*
> 3 *tablespoons lemon juice*
> 2 *tablespoons sugar*
> ¼ *teaspoon cinnamon*

In a saucepan cover the apples with the water and lemon juice. Place the pan over medium heat and bring the mixture to a boil. Stir in the sugar. Stir occasionally while letting the mixture boil for another 10–15 minutes. Add a little water if necessary to keep the apples just covered. When the apples have softened enough that they can be mashed easily with a fork, stir in the cinnamon and remove the pan from the heat.

Purée the apples in a blender, force them through a food mill, or, for a coarser sauce, mash them with a fork or vegetable masher. This applesauce is excellent hot or cold. Store it in the refrigerator in a covered container. It will keep for up to 10 days.

Yield: about 2½ cups sauce

Rum Brownies

5 tablespoons sweet butter, softened
1 cup sugar
6 tablespoons cocoa
2 eggs, lightly beaten
¼ teaspoon salt
½ teaspoon baking powder
½ cup flour
2 tablespoons water
1 tablespoon rum (or 1 teaspoon rum extract)

Place the rack in the center of the oven. Preheat the oven to 350°F. Grease and flour an 8-inch pan.

In a medium mixing bowl cream the butter and sugar. Add the cocoa, 1 tablespoon at a time, and blend well. Beat in the eggs. Sift together the salt, baking powder, and flour and add these dry ingredients, half at a time, alternately with the water. Beat the mixture and stir in the rum. Spread the batter into the prepared pan.

Bake the brownies at 350°F for about 20 minutes, until an inserted toothpick comes out clean. Remove the cake from the oven, loosen the sides from the baking pan with a knife, and place it on a wire rack to cool. Slice the brownies in the pan and remove them with a spatula.

Yield: 14–18 brownies

Génoise

This cake is one of the most delightful and versatile desserts I know. It has a light, airy texture and so is a perfect complement to meringue. I call for génoise layers in several recipes in this book and give a few other preparation suggestions below.

> *6 eggs, at room temperature*
> *1 cup sugar*
> *1 teaspoon vanilla extract*
> *1 cup sifted cake flour*
> *⅓ cup sweet butter, melted*

Place the oven rack about a third up from the bottom. Preheat the oven to 350°F. Butter two 9-inch cake pans that are 2 inches deep. (Or use three 7-inch pans.) Line them with wax paper and lightly grease the paper.

Beat the eggs with an electric mixer at a high speed in a large mixing bowl which has been fitted snugly over a bowl or pan of hot water. (Ideally this bowl or pan should be copper since it retains heat well.) When the eggs are a light color, add the sugar by sifting it in steadily as you beat. Continue to beat at a high speed for 15–20 minutes, until the batter is a very light color and thick enough in texture to form soft shapes. Beat in the vanilla extract.

Add the flour in four additions by sprinkling it over the batter and folding it in with a rubber spatula or large flat spoon. Spoon the melted butter over the batter and fold it in, 1 teaspoon at a time. Fill each prepared pan with the batter and bake the génoise layers at 350°F for 20–30 minutes, until the centers spring back when touched lightly. Remove the génoise layers from the oven and loosen the sides from the pans. Lift the cakes from the pans, peel the wax paper away, and place them on a wire rack to cool. Génoise can be frozen for a week or two.

SERVING SUGGESTIONS
1. Make three layers of génoise and ice them with Chocolate Meringue Icing (page 54) for a layer cake.

2. These layers are light enough to be iced with well-chilled Rum Sauce (page 205) or Grand Marnier Sauce (page 206). Make a double recipe of either sauce. Spread it generously on two layers of

génoise. Stack them and apply a thick coat of sauce to the sides. Garnish with a dusting of Praline Powder (page 223). Keep the cake in the refrigerator until you are ready to serve it.

3. Make petit fours by cutting génoise into 2-inch squares and circles. Ice the various shapes with any flavor butter cream (see pages 206–208) and top each with a pecan half, almond sliver, or a cluster of candied cherries.

Yield: 8–10 slices as a layer cake; about 36 petit fours

1-2-3-4 Cake

This was the first cake I ever baked and, in fact, was my entire dessert repertory for a number of years. The recipe is ubiquitous, with slight variations. Here is the version given to me by my mother.

> 1 cup butter or margarine, softened (or, for a lighter cake, use
> ½ cup butter and ½ cup vegetable shortening)
> 2 cups sugar
> 3 cups sifted self-rising flour
> 4 eggs, well-beaten
> 1 cup milk, water, or fruit juice

Place the oven rack in the center. Preheat the oven to 350°F. Lightly grease three 9-inch pans. Line them with wax paper and grease it lightly. Dust the lined pans with flour.

In a large mixing bowl gradually combine the softened butter with the sugar. Beat until it is thoroughly blended. Stir in about a cup of the flour in two additions alternately with the beaten eggs. Stir in the remaining flour, in four additions, alternately with the liquid. Beat the batter for about a minute. Pour it, in equal parts, into the prepared pans.

Bake the cake layers at 350°F for 25–30 minutes, until the tops spring back when touched lightly in the center. (Test each layer for doneness.) Remove them from the oven and use a knife to loosen them from the sides of the pan. Turn the cake layers onto a wire rack, lift the pans away, and peel off the paper. Let the layers cool for about 45 minutes.

ASSEMBLING SUGGESTIONS

1. Ice the layers with Quick Icing (page 52) or Quicker Icing (page 53). Vary the liquid in the cake layers and the flavor of the icing (for example, use orange juice in the cake batter and lemon or lime extract in the icing).

2. If you make the cake with milk, ice it as a layer cake with Chocolate Meringue Icing (page 54).

3. Cut the individual layers into generous squares. Pour a warm dessert sauce (Chocolate, Butterscotch, Rum, pages 204–205) over each piece. Top the slices with Meringue Dust (page 51).

Yield: 10–12 slices as a layer cake; about 24 slices of single layers

Spice Cake

This single-layer cake is excellent covered with Quicker Icing (page 53) or slice it and top each piece with Honey Meringue (page 52).

> 2 cups sifted flour
> 1 teaspoon baking powder
> 1 teaspoon baking soda
> Pinch salt
> 1 teaspoon freshly grated nutmeg
> ½ teaspoon cinnamon
> ¼ teaspoon allspice
> ½ cup butter (or margarine), softened
> 1½ cups sugar
> 3 eggs, lightly beaten
> 1 cup plain yogurt
> 1 teaspoon vanilla exract

Place the rack in the center of the oven. Preheat the oven to 325°F. Lightly grease a 9 × 13-inch baking pan and dust it with flour.

Sift together the flour, baking powder, baking soda, salt, nutmeg, cinnamon, and allspice. Set these dry ingredients aside.

In a large mixing bowl blend the butter with the sugar. Beat the mixture and then beat in the eggs. Stir in the dry ingredients in four additions, alternately with the yogurt. Beat in the vanilla extract.

Pour the batter into the prepared pan. Bake the cake at 325°F for 30–40 minutes, until the top springs back when pressed lightly in the center. Remove the cake from the oven and place it, still in the baking pan, on a wire rack to cool. Before you ice it, loosen the sides of the cake from the pan with a knife. Slice it in the pan and lift out the pieces with a spatula.

Yield: about 20 slices

Honey Cake

½ cup light brown sugar
½ cup sweet butter, melted
3 eggs
1 cup honey
2 cups sifted flour
1 teaspoon baking soda
1 teaspoon baking powder
¼ teaspoon cinnamon
Pinch allspice
¾ cup milk
2 tablespoons honey

Place the oven rack about a third up from the bottom. Preheat the oven to 350°F. Butter a 9 × 13-inch pan and line it with buttered wax paper.

In a large mixing bowl beat together the light brown sugar and melted butter. Beat in the eggs 1 at a time and then gradually beat in the cup of honey. Sift together the flour, baking soda, baking powder, cinnamon, and allspice. Add this dry mixture, a quarter at a time, alternately with the milk in three additions. When the batter is thoroughly blended, pour it into the prepared pan. Drizzle the 2 tablespoons honey over the top of the batter.

Bake the cake at 350°F for about 25 minutes, until the top springs back when touched lightly. Remove the cake from the oven and loosen the sides from the pan, using a knife if necessary. Invert the pan over a wire rack and lift it away. Peel off the wax paper and let the cake cool on the rack for 20–30 minutes.

I like this cake iced with a thin covering of whipped cream, sliced into squares, and served with a generous scoop of Honey Meringue (page 52) on each slice.

Yield: about 20 slices

Applesauce Cake

Ice this cake with a thin coat of Quick Icing (page 52) or Quicker Icing (page 53).

>*½ cup sweet butter, softened*
>*1 cup light brown sugar*
>*2 eggs, lightly beaten*
>*1¾ cups sifted flour*
>*½ teaspoon salt*
>*1 teaspoon baking soda*
>*½ teaspoon cinnamon*
>*½ teaspoon cloves*
>*2 tablespoons molasses*
>*1 cup Applesauce (page 225)*
>*1 cup raisins*
>*½ cup chopped walnuts*

Place the oven rack about a third up from the bottom. Preheat the oven to 350°F. Lightly butter and flour a 9 × 13-inch pan.

In a large mixing bowl combine the butter and sugar. Beat in the eggs. Sift together the flour, salt, baking soda, cinnamon, and cloves. Add these dry ingredients to the butter mixture and blend the batter thoroughly. Stir the molasses into the applesauce and add the mixture to the main batter. Beat for a minute. Fold in the raisins and walnuts.

Pour the batter into the prepared pan. Bake the cake at 350°F for 30–40 minutes, until the top springs back when lightly touched in the center. Remove it from the oven. Leave the cake in the pan and place it on a wire rack to cool. Ice it in the pan and cut it into serving slices.

Yield: 16–20 slices

Fluffy Banana Layer Cake

Try this cake iced with Quicker Icing (page 53).

>*2½ cups flour*
>*1⅔ cups sugar*
>*1¼ teaspoons baking powder*
>*1 teaspoon baking soda*

1 teaspoon salt
⅔ cup butter (or margarine), softened
1 cup puréed banana (2 or 3 bananas; slice them and use a
   blender or food mill to purée)
⅔ cup buttermilk
2 eggs, lightly beaten
1 egg yolk, lightly beaten
1 teaspoon vanilla extract

Place the oven rack about a third up from the bottom. Preheat the oven to 350°F. Line two 9-inch cake pans with wax paper.

In a large mixing bowl sift together the flour, sugar, baking powder, baking soda, and salt. Using a tablespoon, cut the butter into the dry mixture. Stir in the puréed bananas and ⅓ cup of the buttermilk. Beat for 2 minutes. Add the remaining buttermilk, the beaten eggs and egg yolk, and then the vanilla extract. Blend well and beat the mixture for 2 minutes. Pour the batter into the prepared pans.

Bake at 350°F for 30–35 minutes, until the centers spring back when touched lightly. (Test each layer for doneness.) Remove the cake layers from the oven and let them cool for a few minutes. Shake them loose from the pans, invert the pans over a wire rack, and lift them away. Peel off the wax paper and leave the cake layers on the rack to cool to room temperature before icing them.

Yield: 10–12 servings

Carrot Loaf Cake

2 cups brown sugar
1½ cups peanut oil
4 eggs
2 cups flour
1 teaspoon baking soda
½ teaspoon salt
½ teaspoon baking powder
2 teaspoons cinnamon
½ teaspoon allspice
3 cups grated carrots
½ recipe Quick Icing (page 52)
¼ cup Praline Powder (page 223)

Place the oven rack about a third up from the bottom. Preheat the oven to 350°F. Grease and flour two 9 × 5-inch loaf pans.

In a large mixing bowl beat the brown sugar and oil until thoroughly mixed. Beat in the eggs, 1 at a time. Sift together the flour, baking soda, salt, baking powder, cinnamon, and allspice. Gradually add these dry ingredients to the main batter, about ¼ cup at a time. Beat the mixture for 1 minute. Stir in the grated carrots.

Pour the batter into the prepared pans. Bake at 350°F for 50–55 minutes, until the tops spring back when touched lightly in the center. Remove the loaves from the oven, take them out of the baking pans, and place them on a wire rack to cool. Ice each loaf with the Quick Icing and sprinkle the tops with the Praline Powder.

Yield: 2 loaves, about 10 slices per loaf

Zucchini Bread

The original recipe for this bread was given to me by a friend. Over the years I have made subtle changes and refined it. Drizzle Honey Meringue (page 52) over the tops of the loaves or spoon some onto each slice.

> 2 cups sifted flour
> 2 teaspoons baking soda
> ¼ teaspoon baking powder
> 2 teaspoons cinnamon
> ¼ teaspoon allspice
> 3 eggs, lightly beaten
> 2 cups brown sugar, loosely packed
> 1 cup peanut or safflower oil
> 2 cups grated zucchini
> 1 cup chopped walnuts

Place the rack in the center of the oven. Preheat the oven to 350°F. Grease two 9 × 5-inch metal loaf pans and dust them lightly with flour.

Sift together the flour, baking soda, baking powder, cinnamon, and allspice and set these dry ingredients aside. In a large mixing bowl use a large spoon or spatula to beat the eggs together with the brown sugar. Gradually pour in the oil as you continue to beat. When the mixture is thoroughly blended stir in the dry ingredients, about ½ cup at a time. Fold in the zucchini, in four additions, and beat the batter for about a minute. Fold in the chopped walnuts.

Pour half of the batter into each of the prepared loaf pans.

Bake the bread at 350°F for about an hour, until the tops spring back when pressed lightly in the center. (Test each loaf for doneness.) Remove the bread from the oven and invert the pans over a wire rack. Turn the loaves right side up and leave them on the rack to cool for about 30 minutes before slicing.

Yield: 2 loaves, about 10 slices per loaf

Appendix

The following kitchenware dealers carry most of the equipment I've mentioned in this book. They welcome mail orders in the U.S.

Bazaar de la Cuisine, Inc., 1003 Second Avenue, New York, NY 10022. (212) 421-8028.

Bridge Company, 214 East 52nd Street, New York, NY 10022. (212) 688-4220.

The Professional Kitchen, 18 Cooper Square, New York, NY 10003. (212) 254-9000.

The Cook's Mart, 835 North Michigan Avenue, Chicago, IL 60610. (312) 280-0929.

Forrest Jones, 3274 Sacramento Street, San Francisco, CA 94115. (415) 567-2483.

The Kitchen, 57 Boylston Street, Cambridge MA 02138. (617) 492-7677.

M. & S. Bloom, 2405 Larkspur Landing Circle, Larkspur, CA 94939. (415) 461-1640.

Williams-Sonoma, Mail Order Department, P.O. Box 3792, San Francisco, CA 94119. (415) 652-1515 or 652-1555.

Index